FIGHTIN' WORDS
KENTUCKY VS. LOUISVILLE

BY JOE COX AND RYAN CLARK

Foreword by
Joe B. Hall and Denny Crum

SPORTS
PUBLISHING

Sports Publishing books may be purchased in bulk at special discounts for sales promotion, corporate gifts, fund-raising, or educational purposes. Special editions can also be created to specifications. For details, contact the Special Sales Department, Sports Publishing, 307 West 36th Street, 11th Floor, New York, NY 10018 or info@skyhorsepublishing.com.

Sports Publishing® is a registered trademark of Skyhorse Publishing, Inc.®, a Delaware corporation.

Visit our website at www.skyhorsepublishing.com.

10 9 8 7 6 5 4 3 2 1

Library of Congress Cataloging-in-Publication Data is available on file.

ISBN: 978-1-61321-641-5

Printed in the United States of America

DEDICATION

For my father, a UofL fan who would have enjoyed this run.
—RC

To my brother in Christ, Josh Estep, who not only believed in the idea for this book ten years ago, but told me then that I should write it.
—JC

TABLE OF CONTENTS

FOREWORD

by Joe B. Hall and Denny Crum

FORMER KENTUCKY COACH *Joe B. Hall and former Louisville coach Denny Crum were once adversaries, but now they share a popular daily radio sports talk show, which has aired across the state of Kentucky since 2004.*

Coach Joe B. Hall (Summer 2013):

I spoke over at Richmond one time, for a (group of) homebuilders, and the president of Eastern (Kentucky University) was in the audience, and he stood up and asked me why we wouldn't play Eastern. There was always that pressure of schools out in the state that wanted to play Kentucky. I inherited an unwritten policy not to play in-state schools. I inherited that policy from the University of Kentucky. I would've played anybody, in-state, out-of-state, or even in the universe, if they had teams.

I knew (when I became head coach at Kentucky) there would be high expectations. But what other kind of program would you want to be a part of? One that people didn't care [about]? There were expectations every year of the Kentucky program. On the other hand, you had the greatest of traditions. You were following a coach that had won more NCAA games than any other coach. You had a team that had won more NCAA games than any other team. You had great facilities, you had tradition and fan support; that was all that you could hope for. Sure, there was going to be pressure, but I wouldn't have wanted it any other way. It's a laboratory of life experiences to be involved with sports, and the lessons are never ending.

(Dream Game I) was a pressure game, to play an in-state rival like that. We had more to lose than to gain in a game like that. The pressure of playing that game was enormous, and I'm sure it was more pressure for us than it was for them because they were the better team. The implications were a lot more than just winning or losing to Louisville.

I've been a Louisville fan (for many years). I coached in high school in Bullitt County and I was a fan of Louisville, although I had played at Kentucky. I went to Louisville's practices when Peck Hickman and John Dromo were coaching. I picked up a lot of good coaching tips from the Louisville coaches. I've got a closeness to Louisville. I was a friend of John Dromo's. I went to his funeral. People wondered why I was there, but my association with Louisville, when I coached at Shepherdsville, was one that was a very friendly relationship, and I enjoyed those coaches.

My granddaughter (Amy Summers) went to school there to play softball. I was there at her softball games in her freshman year and I was impressed with their staff at every position. Their coaches were always warm and friendly and Tom Jurich was just one of the biggest people-persons that you'd ever meet, and you couldn't help but be a fan and a friend of the Louisville program during those years. My son-in-law (former UL football assistant coach Mike Summers) being there was certainly a joy, to have him back home and in the state.

There's no one that doesn't like Coach Crum, and that includes me. Denny and I have so much in common. We both work hard for our communities. We both love hunting and fishing, and whenever we would meet on the road recruiting or whenever we played or were at clinics together, we didn't talk basketball, we talked hunting and fishing. The idea [for the radio show] came across when I was doing the *Wimp and Sonny Show*. A friend of mine wrote on the napkin in the restaurant where we were doing the show "The Joe B and Denny Show?" And it just rang a bell, and I liked Denny. I knew we could get along, so it was what you call a no-brainer. I have enjoyed doing it with Denny and I never resent a moment for getting involved in it. I look forward to getting on the radio with him every day.

*****

Coach Denny Crum (Summer 2013)

I've always been in favor of doing what's best for basketball, and I always thought all the teams in the state needed to play each other. Yeah, there's going to be loyalty to one or the other, but the bottom line is it's good for creating interest in basketball.

There's always been a great interest in basketball in this state, but you don't want to lose it to some other sport. It isn't automatic.

I was probably the one person that was vocal about (Louisville playing Kentucky in basketball). I talked about it. I said we all ought to play each other, and we did—we played Western (Kentucky) and Eastern (Kentucky). It was good for college basketball in general and certainly good for the interest of the people who were going to be here and watch it.

For me, it wasn't about the winning and the losing, it was about playing the best competition you could play, and Kentucky was one of those. Whether you won or lost, it would create interest, it would be something that everybody would talk about.

(UK Coach Joe B. Hall) was trying very hard to keep the traditions that Adolph Rupp had established. Coach Rupp wouldn't play anyone in the state because he didn't want to give them the recognition. So (Hall) was trying very hard to maintain that, which he probably should have.

Joe and I always got along fine. I think we had an honest respect for each other. We had a lot of the same interests and stuff. We weren't best personal friends, only because he lived in Lexington and I lived (in Louisville). We didn't have much of a relationship—the only time I ever saw him was occasionally on the road recruiting or something or on TV. I had no bad or hard feelings about Joe—I had an honest respect for him. I thought he did a great job coaching his kids and they were always competitive.

We were competitors, and that's about all you could say about it. But I knew we had a lot in common. Now we talk sports (on the radio)—that's what we do. Joe and I have gotten a whole lot closer. We've had a world of fun. And to be honest, I think it's been great for relationships between Kentucky and Louisville, because it shows you can have different allegiances but still be friends.

I root for Kentucky when they're not playing Louisville. I don't root against them. Everybody's got their own likes and dislikes, but I respect their program.

It's history, boy. And history is always fun.

INTRODUCTION

MARCH 31, 2012—*Superdome, New Orleans, La.:*

Peyton Siva knew the score and the time remaining. Without fear, the Louisville point guard gave his defender a quick jab step. He got a sliver of space.

It was all he needed.

Siva, maligned by Cardinals coach Rick Pitino during the season for his faulty decision making, thought it was now or never. He cocked his arm and let the shot fly.

Louisville's Peyton Siva, whose three-pointer tied Dream Game 32 in the 2012 Final Four. Though Siva and Louisville lost that game, their moment would come a year later. *(Photo by Tim Sofranko)*

When it found the bottom of the net, the Cardinals found themselves in a place few expected them to be: tied at 49 with No. 1 Kentucky with nine minutes to go and a spot in the national championship game on the line.

✶✶✶✶✶

The 73,000 fans in the New Orleans Superdome were buzzing—not from so many Hurricane drinks, but from a game that was living up to its hype.

A look across the arena at the precise moment when Siva made his shot would reveal an array of emotions.

Pitino, forever known as a savior as well as a traitor to the UK fanbase, leaned in, guiding the shot from the Cardinal bench. As it went in, he pumped his fist excitedly. It was Pitino's twentieth appearance in the Kentucky/Louisville rivalry, and his Cardinals had positioned him to pull the monumental upset on the biggest of stages.

In the crowd, former UK and UofL coaches Joe B. Hall and Denny Crum sat together, both seeming to enjoy the competitiveness of the game. The two former rivals, now turned radio cohosts, had an interesting arrangement that typified their mutual respect. Hall had packed a red shirt and, if Louisville won, he would wear it Monday to the NCAA title game. Crum had similarly packed a blue shirt to support UK, should the Wildcats have won.

"We've tried to demonstrate that we're both Kentuckians, and if we lose to one another, we hope the other one goes on to great success," Hall told ESPN. "We're not into slashing tires or spray painting cars or getting into fights at dialysis clinics. That's not what an in-state rivalry should be about."

✶✶✶✶✶

Six rows up, another expert on the rivalry, former UK legend Jim Master, sat watching, his stomach in knots. Master had made a shot like Siva's long ago, back in 1983 when the NCAA Tournament matched up UK and UofL in a tilt known as The Dream Game. On the line was a spot in the Final Four.

Just ahead of the buzzer, Master capped what was arguably the biggest game of his career by hitting a fifteen-foot jump shot from the left baseline to tie the score and send the game into overtime. It is one of the most remembered shots in UK history—but it went for naught as Louisville ran away with the game in the extra period, winning 80-68.

Master wanted revenge—and the Wildcats had their chance against the Cardinals in the Superdome in the 2012 Final Four. But when Siva tied the game for the Cards, things looked uncertain for UK.

"Oh yeah, I was nervous," Master says. "On paper, it looked like Kentucky should win, of course. But you never know what can happen, especially when emotion gets involved. A rivalry game is different. When Siva hit that shot, you felt a little bit of doubt. Kentucky would have to respond."

✶✶✶✶✶

Louisville had followed the blueprint, which many had hoped to achieve but few had actually done in 2012—slow down Kentucky, bang bodies with them, make them gut out a tough game. Louisville was confident and assertive and Kentucky was, well, inexperienced.

Throughout the 2011–2012 season, critics had cautioned that John Calipari's youngest group of Wildcats would run into an NCAA Tournament matchup where their lack of experience might doom them. Many of the Kentucky fans in the crowd, stunned that the Cardinals had come back to tie the game, wondered if the critics were right.

Oh no, the Blue faithful thought. *Not here. Not now. Not to these guys.*

The Red-clad portion of the Superdome crowd smelled blood. The upset was theirs.

Kentucky was going to lose, and Louisville was going to beat them.

✶✶✶✶✶

But why did it matter so much? Why did friends, who were otherwise cordial to each other, become divided, as if this rivalry was more war than game? Why would a city and state become filled with such hatred once (and now twice) a basketball season?

To fans in the state of Kentucky, the reasons are clear. Louisville fans say UK cheats. Kentucky fans say UofL has an inferiority complex.

Louisville says UK was scared to play the Cards for decades. Kentucky says they had nothing to gain, referring to the program as their "Little Brother."

As they say, them's fightin' words.

And don't forget to add that possibly half the fans in the city of Louisville root for Kentucky, and that the coach for the Cards was at one time a national championship-winning coach for the Cats, and that the UofL coach's main rival currently holds the head spot at Kentucky.

You get the picture.

But there was one more thing that made this rivalry the most blood-thirsty in college basketball. It was something that even Duke and North Carolina had never done. In 2012, Kentucky and Louisville became the only pair of in-state programs to square off in a Final Four since Ohio State and Cincinnati played for the championship in 1962.

And Louisville, the unanimous underdog, had just tied the game on Peyton Siva's three-pointer.

*****

On the opposite sideline, John Calipari watched Siva hit the shot and the UK coach was not surprised. In fact, he'd told his team prior to the game that the Cardinals would play above their heads. The UK coaches felt this would still be a competitive game with just a few minutes remaining.

They were right.

The two teams traded punches over the next four minutes—Louisville dogged and experienced, Kentucky talented and intense. UK's youngest star, 18-year-old freshman Michael Kidd-Gilchrist, made a tough shot in the lane and followed a Louisville turnover with a hard-fought drive to the basket for a power dunk.

Siva answered with a pair of free throws. The two teams swapped possessions, driving to the basket and missing close shots, swinging the ball around the perimeter, but missing open looks. While Louisville could not capitalize and surge ahead, they held the Kentucky lead to only two to four points and remained within striking distance.

*****

As the tension ebbed and flowed in New Orleans, it did likewise in millions of family living rooms around the world. In Richardsville, Kentucky, two hours southwest of Louisville, Brent and Lauren Young sat in their living room watching the game unfold. The mood in the room had swung several times.

As with any UK/Louisville game, it was tense. Brent, a self-employed farmer, is a lifelong Cardinals fan. Lauren, a paralegal, is a diehard Wildcats backer. (Their son, Jon Asher, is stuck in the middle. Lauren identifies him as blue over red, while Brent says, "They've got him brainwashed.")

"It doesn't get that serious," Brent says of the familial hoops rivalry. "We've never had a marital problem over it." But, he admits, "It does get a little tense."

As the pair watched the 2012 Final Four game, it was hard not to think back to 1998, the last time UK had won a national championship. During that title run, Lauren and Brent were dating, and he was watching the NCAA semifinal at her house. Lauren accused Brent of cheering against UK.

"Shut up or get the hell out of my house," she told him.

"I was not rooting for Kentucky, I'll put it that way," Brent remembers.

Brent definitely wasn't rooting for Kentucky in the 2012 Final Four. Lauren had invited his brothers, as well as some other family friends, to join them and watch the game. The majority of those at the gathering were Wildcat backers and when Kentucky played well, there were large cheers.

But Brent, who expected a loss, had been rather quiet throughout the game, as had the handful of other Louisville fans in the room. However, when Siva's three tied it up, suddenly he noticed it was Lauren who had gotten very quiet.

"I was *aggravated*," she admits.

As the game seesawed back and forth, the Youngs' nerves did the same.

*****

Kentucky led 55-51 with just over five minutes to play when the game began to turn. UK freshman point guard Marquis Teague, one of Calipari's three freshman starters (each of whom would be an NBA first round draft pick in the ensuing months), drew the Louisville defense and swung the ball to the right shoulder. He passed to Kentucky's graybeard Darius Miller, a senior who had missed the NCAA Tournament altogether as a freshman under former head coach Billy Gillispie and who had watched Louisville's Edgar Sosa beat UK with a buzzer-beating three in that season.

Miller, who hailed from the basketball powerhouse of Mason County, Kentucky, was a veteran, a component part, a quiet, team-first leader who knew the meaning of the Kentucky/Louisville rivalry. Under Calipari, he had grown from an unassuming youngster whom Gillispie threw off the team bus to the tough-minded veteran who lived for these pressure-packed moments.

With just over five minutes to go in the game, Miller found himself open at the elbow and Teague passed him the ball in stride. The 6'7" Miller rose up, and with the confidence of a senior, drained the biggest shot in the biggest game of his life. The Kentucky lead ballooned to seven.

Across the court, Pitino's head dropped, and the Louisville coach called a quick timeout.

*****

It would not matter. Calipari bear-hugged Miller when the senior reached the Kentucky bench. Across the arena, UK fans began to feel like the victory was theirs. A chant of "Go Big Blue!" rang out through the arena. In the sixth row, Jim Master finally felt at ease.

"Darius's shot just made me so happy," Master says. "Happy for him. Happy for all of us. I just wanted to win so badly. I didn't want to lose to them."

As the game clock ticked down, Joe B. Hall and Denny Crum shook hands. So many times the pair had squared off as opposing coaches in big basketball games. Now the best of friends, it was nice to be off the battlefield, so to speak.

When the clock hit zero, John Calipari met Rick Pitino at half-court. "Congratulations," Pitino said, shaking his rival's hand. "I'll be pulling for you. Bring the trophy back home to Kentucky."

In Lexington, Kentucky, fraternity boys were celebrating on the streets of Euclid and Vine, burning couches and turning over cars.

Back in Richardsville, Lauren Young watched Miller's three-point dagger drop in. She jumped up from her seat and shouted, "IT'S MILLER TIME!"

The other side of the room, where her husband sat, was quiet. For her part, Lauren had been confident coming into the game. Several weeks before, she had even requested to take a vacation day on April 3, which was the day after the NCAA title game. She wanted to celebrate what she expected to be a UK victory.

"We didn't have the horses to play with Kentucky," her husband Brent says. "Nobody did." While he was excited by Louisville's early second-half run, he grudgingly conceded that Lauren "got to come back and enjoy her moment."

Brent says Louisville "played probably as well as we could play . . . but we were outmanned a little bit."

He smiles.

"I feel like we might be on the other side next year," he says.

*****

"Next year." It would become a Cardinal rallying cry. Going into the 2012–2013 season, both Kentucky and Louisville were ranked in the top five. The Cardinals were No. 2 but were acknowledged as a legitimate championship possibility. Kentucky, beginning the year at No. 3, was the defending national champion.

In the grand history of the rivalry, it is possible that both teams never held such high expectations at the same time.

All the pomp and pageantry led up to December 29, 2012, when the teams were scheduled to meet in Louisville's sparkling arena, the Yum! Center, located on the banks of the Ohio River. On their home court, with a talented and deep squad, Louisville looked to be a solid favorite over the rebuilding Wildcats. Pitino, who had not defeated the Wildcats in three years, would finally get his best shot at Calipari. UofL could break its streak of four losses and pave the way for their own March triumphs.

The annual game stood to be a magical environment, a way to celebrate nearly 30 years of amazing rivalry games. Though the matchup was born in 1913, it did not really become the cutthroat competition of today until 1983. Nevertheless, Kentucky and Louisville share a fascinating and tumultuous basketball history.

And whenever one team bests the other, the rallying cry is heard from Jefferson County to Jessamine County.

Wait 'til next year, the losing fans will say.

Wait 'til next year.

Prelude 1—1913–1959: The Pre-Rivalry

BEFORE LOOKING TOWARD the future, it is instructive to go back to last year—and the year before that, and the year before that. Let's begin at the beginning—not of UK/UofL, but of Kentucky.

The state of Kentucky has a long history of being torn between bitter rivals. Six years before Kentucky separated from Virginia and became the 15th state in 1792, battles in and around modern Kentucky constituted the first stirrings in the Northwest Indian War. Seventy-five years later, in the midst of the US Civil War, Kentucky had two capitals, but ultimately there was no clear allegiance in the battle between north and south.

Approximately fifty years later, another skirmish occurred. This war would cost few, if any, lives, but many hearts. With its golden anniversary now past (complete with starts and stops to rival any medieval European campaign), the basketball rivalry between the University of Kentucky and the University of Louisville is nothing less than a microcosm of the culture clash that defines the very roots of Kentucky's dark and bloody ground—and provides an attempt to forecast the next turn of history and society.

The history of that rivalry begins sometime around 1780, when the Virginia General Assembly approved the town charter establishing Louisville. Located on the Ohio River, Louisville's growth was initially slowed by Spain's ownership of the Southern waters of the Mississippi

River. With American Indian attacks a common occurrence and no downstream commerce available, Louisville's initial progress was stilted.

Lexington, devoid of major waterways, was established on the banks of what was then known as Elkhorn Creek, two years after its neighbor to the West. Lexington quickly became a community of affluence. Well-to-do settlers promptly noted that the calcium-rich soil produced unusually healthy and speedy horses. By 1809, the Lexington Jockey Club was established.

Meanwhile, Louisville flourished as the Spanish monopoly on the lower Mississippi River ended and the steamboat suddenly ensured more and larger river traffic. Still more significantly, the Louisville and Portland Canal, completed in 1830, allowed passage from Pittsburgh to New Orleans without navigating the difficult falls of the Ohio River. Two years prior, Louisville had become Kentucky's first city. The 1830s saw the institution of the first of many Louisville hotels to be named The Galt House, as well as a local horse race that drew more than 10,000 spectators. The 1850 census noted Louisville as the tenth most populous city in the United States.

Lexington would never catch Louisville in population, but its burgeoning sphere of influence was notable. The city was noted for its wealth and culture and was coined "The Athens of the West." Notable citizens included John Wesley Hunt, one of the first millionaires to live west of the Alleghany Mountains, and the father to a notable Civil War general and grandfather to a Nobel Prize winner. Lexingtonian Henry Clay was thrice defeated as a US presidential candidate, but is still one of the most notable US senators ever, particularly in light of his attempts to prevent the US Civil War. Mary Todd was also a well-healed Lexington beauty, who moved to Illinois and met and married Abraham Lincoln.

The Civil War deepened the rivalry between Kentucky's two most prominent cities. Lexington, being the more southern and wealthy of the two, while unallied officially, featured a great deal of prominent southern sympathizers, including, allegedly, the aforementioned Mary Todd Lincoln. Louisville, meanwhile, remained a stronghold for Union forces. Union Generals Sherman and Grant met at The Galt House to plan their spring 1864 campaign, which famously culminated with Sherman laying waste to Georgia. That said, no aspect of the Civil War in Kentucky is even open and closed, as a Confederate memorial has stood in downtown Louisville since 1895, when it was established on the edges of the University of Louisville's campus.

Following the end of the Civil War, in 1865 John Henry Bowman established the beginning of the University of Kentucky when he set up the Agricultural & Mechanical College of Kentucky, which was a department of Kentucky University. That university (rather confusingly) would later become Transylvania University. In 1878, A&M split off from KU and became the modern University of Kentucky—although it would not operate under that name until 1916.

Similarly, the beginnings of the University of Louisville are quite tangled. While the first University of Louisville was chartered in 1798, it closed in 1829. The modern University began in 1846, when Louisville Medical Institute, Louisville Collegiate Institute, and a law school were combined under the University's name. The University initially operated downtown, and the Belknap campus, which is where most of the modern, non-medical facilities are now located, was purchased in 1923 after an aborted attempt to purchase property in Louisville's Highlands.

Accordingly, in 1913, the State University of Lexington team and a University of Louisville squad played against one another for the first time. Of course, the schools were hardly the only thing that would be unrecognizable to modern die-hards.

Basketball was invented in 1891 by Dr. James Naismith as a trial game to keep his physical education students in shape when the weather prohibited outdoor games. Four years before the first UK/UofL matchup, players were first allowed to take more than one dribble, and a dribbling player then received the license to take shots. That said, the game was quite different—the center jump followed every basket, a traveling violation was a foul, and teams had designated free throw shooters. The jump shot was still several decades from its invention, and above the rim basketball would have been unimaginable.

It is against this auspicious background that the Kentucky rivalry began. While these games are difficult to judge against modern basketball standards, they form the historical beginning of the rivalry and illustrate the change and growth of basketball, in Kentucky and beyond.

*****

The University of Kentucky, although still operating as State University, began playing college basketball in 1903. The school had an all-time record of 41-50 at the time of the first UK/UofL game. The 1911–12 Kentucky team had finished 9-0, and this was the first inkling of any major roundball success for the university. The University of Louisville, on the other hand, had begun playing basketball in 1912. After an initial 0-3 campaign, the Cardinals had won their first game ever earlier in February 1913 over the New Albany YMCA.

The two schools met on the basketball court for the first time on February 15, 1913, in Lexington's Buell Hall, which would be the home of UK basketball until 1924. At one point, the gymnasium had the rare privilege of witnessing the Wildcats break the elusive half-century mark, in a 52-point outing against Centre College in 1912.

The University of Kentucky dominated the game from the outset, leading 18-4 at halftime, on their way to a 34-10 victory. R.C. Preston, a 5'10" center from Inez, Kentucky, paced the Wildcats with 13 points. Clarence Rogers was responsible for all of Louisville's points, including converting the Cardinals' only basket from the field in the final minute of the game. Dr. John J. Tigert, the head of the UK's philosophy department, coached the Wildcats to victory in his only season on the job. Von Wolther, who was missing two starters due to injury, was saddled with the loss as the coach of the University of Louisville.

While the game was clearly not one of the more competitive entries in the series, it was regarded by the universities as a roving success. A profit of $11.95 was reported after the expenses of the game were paid, and the two schools planned to match up again the following season.

Beginning in the 1913–14 season, UK and UofL scheduled an annual home and home series—with each team hosting the other once a season. The series lasted just three seasons.

In both 1913–14 and 1914–15, Alpha Brummage coached UK while the players themselves coached UofL. In Lexington, the games were played in Woodland Auditorium, also known as the Lexington City

Auditorium, apparently due to the size of crowds which the matchup attracted. The last of these four games, played in the Louisville YMCA, was the last game played by State University, as the squad became the University of Kentucky basketball team in time for the 1915–16 season. The University of Louisville won that contest, ending a streak of four straight losses to begin the series.

The 1915–16 season featured another split decision in the annual series. As this left unclear which school could claim bragging rights for the top school in the Commonwealth, apparently Louisville wanted a third matchup for that season. UK balked, and the lack of any real resolution of school superiority heated the rivalry.

However, World War I then intervened, and Louisville did not field a team in 1916–17. With cuts on athletics budgets throughout the land, the Bluegrass rivalry met a standstill. It was renewed in the 1921–22 season, with another home and home matchup scheduled.

In the meanwhile, the Wildcats had begun their rise to basketball prominence. The 1920–21 season culminated with Kentucky winning the SIAA championship (a forerunner of the modern Southeastern Conference). Basil Hayden had become the first All-America player in UK history. UofL, meanwhile, was coming off a 3-8 season. The teams played at St. Xavier High Gymnasium in Louisville and Buell Hall in Lexington, respectively.

UK swept the two 1921–22 games, winning 38-14 in Louisville, with Paul Adkins scoring 16 to pace the Wildcats, and pulling a 29-22 hard-fought rematch out back in Lexington. At this point, Kentucky led the series between the two schools 7-2. There was no apparent bad blood between the two universities or their respective teams. Kentucky was pursuing its ongoing rivalry with Centre College, but none of this provides any clue as to why basketball games between the University of Kentucky and University of Louisville suddenly stopped with no regular season meeting occurring for the next 61 years.

Eight years after the last matchup between the two schools, Kentucky cast its basketball fortunes with an untested young coach from the University of Kansas. Adolph Rupp revolutionized college basketball from top to bottom, and his legendary shadow is notably cast over the deep freeze in the UK/UofL rivalry. Simply stated, Rupp had no use for in-state opponents for his Wildcats. His fast-breaking style of basketball was designed to dominate the SIAA, and later SEC conferences, as well as the national scene—and not the regional scene.

As for the University of Louisville, its path to the top of college basketball was much more twisted. Coaches came and went, some with relative success and some without. Tom King turned in a 44-21 record in five seasons with Louisville shortly before Adolph Rupp arrived in Lexington. However, other succeeding coaches were less successful—Lawrence Apitz went 10-52 in 1936–40, as Rupp and UK were continuing their assent up the basketball mountain.

In 1944, Bernard "Peck" Hickman was hired at the University of Louisville. While none of the Cardinals' previous coaches had eclipsed Tom King's five-year tenure, Hickman would be the head coach of the Cardinals for more than twenty years, nearly outlasting Rupp's time across the state. Hickman inherited a team that had completed seven straight non-winning seasons and promptly led his first team to a 16-3 mark.

While Hickman was leading UofL out of mediocrity, Adolph Rupp found his bumper crop of recruits emerging from World War II as men rather than boys. Wildcat starter Cliff Barker, a former POW, was older than Claude Sullivan, the primary UK radio broadcaster of the era. In 1946, with Louisville sensation Ralph Beard leading the Wildcats, the team, at 28-2, won the National Invitational Tournament, the school's first real national title. At the time, the NIT was a more serious event than the five-year-old NCAA Tournament, which was still in its infancy.

Two seasons later, in 1947–48, Rupp's squad, then known as The Fabulous Five, simply lit up college basketball. UK suffered two losses— one at Temple in December and one at Notre Dame in February. Otherwise, they won, and they won big. Kentucky won 14 games that season by a margin of 30 or more points. They did not lose at home, they did not lose in the SEC, and most importantly, they did not lose in the NCAA Tournament. Kentucky outlasted Bob Cousy's Holy Cross team 60-52 in the semifinal and then beat Baylor in the championship game 58-42.

In the meanwhile, Peck Hickman's 1947–48 squad also had a fine season. The Cardinals, featuring star player Jack Coleman, went 29-5. UofL lost three times to in-state rival Western Kentucky, including once in the KIAC Tournament, but otherwise very rarely at all. The Cardinals participated in the lesser-known NABC Tournament after the season, and they won it cleanly, beating Indiana State 82-70 in the finals.

Since 1948 was an Olympic year, shortly after the respective schools won their tournaments, UK and UofL earned a spot traveling to New York and entered a small tournament for the right to represent the United States in the London Summer Games. Of course, they were immediately scheduled to play each other—for the first time in 26 years.

The game was no contest. Kentucky demolished Louisville 91-57, led by 22 points from Louisvillian Ralph Beard and 19 points from multi-sport star Wallace "Wah Wah" Jones. While UK eventually lost to the AAU Champion Phillips 76ers, the squad played well enough that the starting five were picked to join the US squad, and Coach Rupp served as an assistant coach. The team won gold in London.

While Kentucky went on to win the NCAA Tournament again in 1949, Louisville continued to be competitive under Hickman. The two programs next met in 1951, when the NCAA matched Rupp's No. 1 ranked 28-2 team and Hickman's 19-6 squad in the first round of the NCAA Tournament in Raleigh, North Carolina. Unlike the last matchup, Louisville fought gamely against the Cats. They held 7-foot UK sensation Bill Spivey to ten points and seven rebounds and induced him to foul out of the game. Meanwhile, a trio of Bobs (Brown, Naber, and Lochmuller) totaled 44 points for the Cardinals. Still, UK had too much talent, with Shelby Linville stepping up to score 23 points and grab 10 rebounds for the Cats in a 79-68 win. Three wins later, UK had its third NCAA title in four seasons.

Shortly thereafter, Kentucky was implicated in a point-shaving scandal and was banned from playing the 1952–53 season. While the program rebounded to win the 1958 NCAA title, there would be no more runs like those of 1948–1951.

There was one more matchup with UofL before the rivalry took a 24-year drought. In 1959, the NCAA again matched UK and UofL in the first round of the NCAA Tournament, with the No. 2 Cats and unranked Cards fighting it out in Evanston, Illinois. While Kentucky jumped out to an early lead, the Cardinals won the day. UofL overcame an eight-point halftime deficit with aggressive defensive pressure that led to a 76-61 victory. The Cardinals went on to upset another top-10 team (Michigan State) and appeared in the team's first Final Four. UofL lost to Jerry West's West Virginia Mountaineers in the semifinals but had enjoyed a historic season.

The Cats and the Cardinals would not play each other again for the next 24 years, and in that time, the landscape of college basketball would change greatly from these early games. It would be a long and strange trip to an annual rivalry game, and getting there would be half the fun.

Prelude 2—1960–1983: Reaching the Rivalry

AFTER 1958, RUPP never won an NCAA title again at Kentucky. He continued to field top-flight teams that dominated SEC play, but as time went on, it became more and more clear what was missing. In accordance with the unwritten policy of the Southeastern Conference, Rupp initially did not recruit African American players. However, whatever one thinks of Rupp's personal politics, there are few who would argue his primary concern was anything but winning. As African American players from Kentucky like Clem Haskins, Butch Beard, and Wes Unseld came of age in front of Rupp's eyes, he apparently realized that the lily-white SEC would have to change or fall behind. Rupp supposedly offered scholarships to Beard and Unseld. Both were understandably reluctant to become the Jackie Robinson of the SEC and chose to go elsewhere. All three players chose to attend Louisville (although Haskins became homesick and transferred to Western Kentucky, where Coach John Oldham was as progressive as the Cardinals).

Rupp had realized what the rest of college basketball saw in the 1966 NCAA Tournament, when Rupp's Runts, absent the athleticism of Beard or Unseld, lost the title game to Texas Western, which fielded an all-black starting five. The revolution, whatever the reasons may be, had moved on without the Kentucky Wildcats.

In 1962, Peck Hickman, coaching at a slightly more progressive institution in a slightly more northern city, broke the color barrier at Louisville by signing African Americans Eddie Whitehead and Wade

Houston. While Whitehead and Houston were solid citizens, but not All-America players, Beard and Unseld belonged to both groups. After the 1966–67 season, which ended with a trip to the NCAA Sweet 16, Hickman stepped down as the Cardinals' coach, giving way to his assistant, John Dromo.

Dromo continued the success of Hickman's program, feasting on a large amount of homegrown talent and going 68-23 as Cardinals head coach. His budding career was cut shortduring the 1970–71 season, however, when Dromo suffered a heart attack. After the season, he stepped down from the position because of his health. Louisville would have to choose a new coach in 1971 to lead them in their search for college basketball greatness. What a choice it would be!

Meanwhile, health was a problem in the UK coach's office as well. Rupp suffered from myriad illnesses and injuries in the late years of his tenure. He also did not return to another Final Four after 1966. His 1970 team, with Dan Issel and Mike Pratt, lost to Jacksonville and little-known but dynamic center Artis Gilmore.

In June 1969, Rupp, aided by recently hired assistant Joe B. Hall, became the second SEC coach to sign an African American player. Vanderbilt had integrated SEC basketball by signing Perry Wallace, and the Wildcats added Tom Payne, a 7' center from Louisville's Shawnee High School. Payne starred in one season at Kentucky, but he was a troubled person and has spent much of his life in prison.

The University of Kentucky had fallen behind. While the calendar indicates a seven-year difference between the dates of integration of UofL basketball and UK basketball, many African Americans, particularly in Louisville, were unable to foster benign feelings toward Rupp or Kentucky. It would be nearly a decade and a half before Kentucky could break into the inner-city Louisville recruiting scene in a significant manner. Many more difficult recruiting seasons would follow before the lingering spectrum of southern racism would be mostly purged from the program.

Trying to counteract Kentucky's failure to keep up with the times became the task of Joe B. Hall. In 1972, Rupp turned 70 and grudgingly allowed himself to be nudged into retirement. After seven seasons as his chief assistant, 43-year-old Hall replaced the institution who had been

Kentucky's head coach for 41 years. Few have faced such difficult tasks in the history of coaching.

The man who would become Hall's chief rival had taken a very different coaching path. Denny Crum had played under John Wooden at UCLA and later served as his assistant coach for eight seasons, but did not wait around in Westwood to follow his mentor. In 1971, a year before Hall was hired at Kentucky, Louisville was seeking a replacement for John Dromo. Thirty-four-year old Crum was a dynamic young coach who was an excellent recruiter and was well drilled in Wooden's championship tactics. He accepted the Louisville job, planning to return to UCLA whenever Wooden was ready to step down as the coach of the Bruins.

Crum had very defined viewpoints on a couple of crucial areas: playing intrastate opponents and recruiting. He feared no team and saw little reason not to take on the other Kentucky universities. "We wanted to be a school that, if we were going to give guarantees to someone . . . I'd rather see the money go to Kentucky schools than to . . . someone from the outside that really didn't do anything for your program," Crum admits. "Rather than Lousiville playing Fresno or San Jose State, we played Eastern, Western, Murray, or Morehead. It just made more sense to me."

Crum also wanted to play the toughest competition he could face—including his nearby big-shot neighbor in Lexington. Crum recalls that the University depended on men's basketball to fund the entire athletic department during most of his tenure. Crum had to attract fans and sell tickets—and in order to do so, he would play anyone, anywhere, anytime.

While Crum's aggressive scheduling drew in fans, it was his recruiting that built the modern Louisville program. "One of the reasons I took the Louisville job was that I felt like we were located in a central area," explains Crum, "You could recruit 360 degrees and find enough talent to be competitive. We made a living, in all honesty, recruiting good athletes from the South. You go down there and recruit and you were on television as a basketball school, it created interest in a lot of kids. We targeted kids in the South and tried to recruit as many of the better athletes as we could recruit. We felt like we could teach them about basketball. We knew how to do that. The more talent they had, the better they could learn to do it."

While Crum targeted the Deep South, where football was often king and a high-flying basketball program was an easy sales pitch for athletes whose hardwood exploits were overshadowed by the gridiron game, he knew he had to recruit at home as well. "We usually had to fight Kentucky for the better high school kids in the state," says Crum. "I think we did that fairly well. We didn't get them all, but neither did they."

As time went on, Crum got more and more of them. And the results transformed the relationship of UofL and UK.

Denny Crum makes a point to an official in Freedom Hall.
UofL played in one Final Four before Crum, but under his leadership, the Cardinals reached six more Final Fours, won two NCAA titles, and established their rivalry with Kentucky.
(Photo by Jamie Vaught, appears courtesy of the Somerset Commonwealth Journal)

✯✯✯✯✯

Louisville had appeared in one Final Four before Crum's arrival. In his first season, he doubled that total. Dromo had left a fine team—featuring All-America guard Jim Price. Three of Crum's starters were African American players from Kentucky: Price, who hailed from

Russellville, in western Kentucky, and Ron Thomas and Henry Bacon, who hailed from Louisville.

Louisville began the season ranked ninth in the nation and reached as high as second. They entered the NCAA Tournament with a 24-3 record, and after dispatching Southwestern Louisiana and Kansas State, reached the Final Four. In Los Angeles, Crum found the Cards matched up with the UCLA dynasty he helped shape. The Bruins won by 19, but Crum's first season could not be considered anything but a sterling success.

Louisville lost its entire starting lineup from that squad. Over the next few years, Crum thus had the opportunity to see his own recruits come of age. Allen Murphy came from Alabama, while Junior Bridgeman hailed from the Chicago area. Wesley Cox, the star from Louisville Male High, only had to commute across town, but all three starred for Crum's Cardinals. Crum's style of play was aggressive. He vested his players with a fair amount of freedom on offense, relying on defensive pressure and athletic creativity to dominate the opposition.

After two quiet seasons, in 1974–75, Murphy and Bridgeman were seniors and Cox was a rugged sophomore forward. Louisville again returned to the Final Four. The Cardinals sprinted through a 24-2 regular season. After three NCAA wins, Crum found himself matched up again with Wooden and UCLA. The game was a barn burner, but after UofL reserve Terry Howard, who had gone 28-for-28 on free throws for the season, missed a crucial free throw, UCLA edged the Cardinals by a point.

The loss was particularly disappointing for Louisville fans, because the winner of the other semifinal was Kentucky. But for some very bad luck, the 1975 NCAA Tournament would have ended with UK and UofL slugging it out for college basketball's ultimate prize.

After the semifinal with Louisville, Wooden announced that the following day's championship game would be his final contest with the Bruins. This was the day Louisville fans had feared. Crum had gone to two Final Fours in four seasons. He had expanded the recruiting efforts of Dromo and was making Louisville a national player. But he couldn't turn down his alma mater, a bigger power on the collegiate scene at that time. Or could he?

He did. In *Born to Coach*, Crum told author Billy Reed of a sleepless evening that resolved itself in a decision to stay at Louisville. Two years later, UCLA came knocking again, flying Crum to Los Angeles to formally offer him the job. But the love affair between Crum and Louisville was in full bloom, and again the Bruins did not get their man.

Louisville moved from the Missouri Valley Conference to the Metro Conference before the 1975–76 season. Crum and the Cardinals fielded good but not great teams over the next several seasons. Particularly with freshmen eligibility enacted, Crum spent more and more time trying to land the next great recruit—that player who could push Louisville over the top from really good to legendary.

In 1976, he landed him. Everybody in the nation knew that Darrell Griffith was special. The 6'4" scoring guard played basketball without limitations. He could slash to the basket with anyone and soar over anyone foolish enough to try to stop him. Best of all for the Cardinals, he was from Louisville. Male High School had already been kind to Crum, with Wesley Cox being one of several fine players from the school who formed a pipeline to UofL.

Griffith had seen all he needed to see in 1975. He briefly considered Maryland and Michigan, but his recruitment was quick and simple. The best player in the nation was going to Louisville. When Male star Bobby Turner, an NBA talent in his own right, elected to join Griffith, it seemed almost unfair to other coaches who would face the duo in the 1976–77 season.

However, Crum did not rest on his laurels. He continued to rely on evaluation as well as reputation in the recruiting game. In 1977, a little-known Georgia forward named Derek Smith was contemplating Furman or Gardner-Webb before the Cardinals got involved. He ended up being the leading scorer for two UofL squads.

It did take time for all of the talent to gel together. While UofL made the NCAA Tournament in three of the next four seasons, it did not win more than one NCAA game in any single year.

But in 1980, Griffith was a senior and the Cardinals were undeniable. Sadly, Turner left school and was not part of the season, but Griffith and Derek Smith were joined by center Wiley Brown, guard Jerry Eaves, and brothers/forwards Rodney and Scooter McCray. The

Cardinals were 26-3 in the regular season and were ranked second in the nation when the NCAA Tournament began.

The cardiac Cardinals needed overtime to win their first two games, but then beat a highly regarded LSU squad by 20. The Final Four was played in nearby Indianapolis and, after dispatching Iowa, Crum found himself matched up with UCLA yet again. Wunderkind coach Larry Brown held the job Crum had been assumed as likely to inherit, but Denny's judgment was upheld by the game's results—Louisville won 59-54 and was crowned NCAA Tournament champions.

If the rest of college basketball thought success would make Louisville complacent, they were wrong. Crum continued to build athletic squads of long-armed guards and undersized but athletic big men. In the aftermath of the UCLA dynasty, Crum's Cardinals were as good of a program as one would find.

In 1981, Mississippi guard Lancaster Gordon added his talents to the team. The following season, Camden, New Jersey, star Milt Wagner did likewise. In 1982, Crum again led his Cards to the Final Four. An NCAA Tournament showdown with Kentucky was a near-certainty, but the Wildcats were upset by Middle Tennessee State, and Louisville accordingly dispatched the Blue Raiders. In the Final Four, the Cardinals ran into Patrick Ewing's Georgetown squad and suffered an ugly 50-46 loss.

In Crum's twelve seasons, UofL had won a national title and had appeared in four Final Fours. They were a national power in recruiting and had the added mojo of being perceived as a fun program that players enjoyed. Crum delighted in an "anyone, anytime, anywhere" aspect to his annual schedule. And yet UofL had played their perceived intrastate rival Kentucky Wildcats zero times. Why and for how long could this continue? The answers lay with Kentucky.

*****

Joe B. Hall always had plenty on his mind in Lexington. In 1972, he inherited a roster with center Jim Andrews and forward Kevin Grevey. The squad was competent but devoid of sufficient firepower to contend for a championship. Hall almost immediately recruited Reggie Warford, an African American guard from Drakesboro, Kentucky. Warford provided no immediate help, but was evidence that Hall would waste no time to try to divest Kentucky of the negative connotations that had followed his illustrious predecessor.

UK went 20-8 in the first year, losing in the second round of the NCAA Tournament. The following year was a 13-13 season, and it took very little time for Hall's seat to become warm in the climates of Lexington. Hall was no less dogged in his pursuit of excellence than his rival down Interstate 64. Before 1974–75, he fine-tuned the skills of veterans Grevey, Jimmy Dan Connor, and Mike Flynn. He also brought in a great recruiting haul—with big men Rick Robey and Mike Phillips, and two superb forwards from Lexington, James Lee and Jack Givens. The sudden improvement of recruiting coincided with the hiring of Assistant Coach Leonard Hamilton. Many of the African American players who Kentucky signed over the next decade credited their relationship with Hamilton. Givens went on to become UK's first African American All-America player, and Lee, who is also African American, became a superb sixth man. While the recruitment of Givens and Lee from across town did little to ease Louisville's stronghold on the state's largest city, it did demonstrate visibly that times had changed in Lexington.

When Hall combined something old and something new in 1975, the results were impressive. UK was 22-4 in the regular season and began the NCAA Tournament ranked No. 6. After a dramatic Mideast Regional Final victory over top-ranked Indiana and coach Bob Knight, UK plowed through Syracuse to reach the NCAA title game. Instead of facing Louisville, UK took on UCLA. John Wooden announced his retirement before the game, and the Bruins rode the ensuing wave of emotion to the title, 92-85 over the Wildcats.

Still, Hall was established as a great coach in his own right. He favored power and crisp offensive execution over the freewheeling guard-oriented game plan that Rupp installed. Hall did not approach the game as an innovator, but as the protector of Wildcat glory. It would be a taxing job, but one in which Hall succeeded.

Three years after the NCAA title near-miss, in 1978, those freshmen from 1975 were now experienced seniors. Givens, Robey, Phillips, and Lee were joined by Purdue transfer Kyle Macy and defensive specialist Truman Claytor to form a basketball powerhouse. The expectations for the squad were so high that it was dubbed "The Season without Joy."

After a 25-2 regular season in which UK was generally the nation's top-ranked squad, the Wildcats fought through a tough NCAA field. They beat Magic Johnson's Michigan State team in the Mideast Regional in Dayton; in St. Louis at the Final Four, they outlasted Eddie Sutton's Arkansas Razorbacks before beating Duke 94-88 for the title.

Givens, who was a rock-steady forward, had the game of his life against Duke, scoring 41 points in leading the Wildcats to their first national title in two decades. He and Kyle Macy, the smooth shooting point guard, were the toast of Big Blue Nation. It had taken Joe B. Hall only six seasons to win his place in Wildcat history.

At Kentucky, Hall continued to face high expectations. Over the next few years, sometimes they were met and sometimes not. Hall recruited a superb athlete, Dwight "The Blur" Anderson, only to see Anderson transfer after a season and a half because of struggles to fit within Hall's system. In 1979, Hall added superstar center Sam Bowie, a 7'1" center who could run like a gazelle, handle the ball, and even shoot smoothly. With other talented additions like Lexingtonians Dirk Minniefield and Melvin Turpin, Kentucky was always relevant in the NCAA conversation.

However, Hall's squads did not return to the Final Four. In fact, in 1982, the NCAA set up UK to face UofL in the NCAA tournament, but the Wildcats blew the matchup by suffering an embarrassing 50-44 first-round loss in Nashville to lightly regarded Middle Tennessee State.

And so, the whispers had grown louder with every Louisville Final Four. They had become plain speech with the 1980 Cardinal NCAA victory. And by 1982, they were near scream level—why wouldn't Kentucky play Louisville?

Hall has always maintained that he was not interested in the series in part because of his role as guardian of the UK program, which necessitated upholding Wildcat traditions. Rupp did not schedule intrastate matchups with Louisville, Eastern Kentucky, Western Kentucky, Morehead State, or others. Perhaps this was because Rupp felt Kentucky had nothing to gain, perhaps it was because he preferred to play other opponents.

Denny Crum said in a recent interview, "Joe . . . wanted to do it the way Rupp did it and that's the way he should've been. There's no reason why you would expect him to think like I would. . . . They were on top and we had to get there."

Secondly, Hall noted the 18-game SEC schedule his teams faced, and the abundance of quality competition they were already committed to play. Even three decades later, Hall is angered by the assertion that the game didn't happen because he didn't want to play Louisville.

In Hall's defense, his UK squads weren't scheduling the Little Sisters of the Poor instead of the Cardinals. In 1981–82, Hall's pre-conference schedule was No. 1 North Carolina; No. 12 Indiana; traditional powers Ohio State, Notre Dame, and Kansas; two opponents for UK's Christmas Tournament, Jacksonville and Seton Hall; and a season-opener against Akron. The 1982–83 schedule was similar. Non-conference foes were No. 4 Villanova; No. 5 Indiana; traditional rivals Kansas and Notre Dame; two Christmas Tournament opponents, Duquesne and Tulane; and then Illinois, Butler, and Detroit. Either slate would make a current UK/UofL game participant blush.

*****

And so, in the early 1980s, there were two college basketball powers in Kentucky. They were located sixty miles apart and, on parallel paths, they slashed their way through the rest of college basketball. But they hadn't played in over two decades. It would take something special to change the situation. While no one knew it, something special was on the way. And soon, every year would have one date circled on calendars in Louisville and Lexington. But in the early '80s, that idea was just a dream. It would take a Dream Game to change things.

Chapter 1

The Dream Game . . . Finally!

No. 2 UofL 80, No. 12 UK 68 (OT)
NCAA Mideast Regional final
March 26, 1983, at Stokely Center, Knoxville, Tenn.

Pre-Game:

When 24 years of posturing, cajoling, and dealing amounted to nothing, the NCAA did what the fans, the politicians, and the pundits couldn't do—made the game happen. While MTSU had foiled the plan in 1982, this time around, UK and Louisville fought through the NCAA bracket like the matchup simply had to be played. UK took down No. 5 Indiana 64-59 in its Mideast Regional Semifinal, and in the other semifinal, Louisville rallied from a 16-point deficit to edge Arkansas 65-63 on a Scooter McCray tip-in.

The pair then matched up in the Mideast Regional Final in Knoxville, Tennessee's Stokely Center. A crowd of nearly 13,000 battled for tickets to watch basketball history.

It was on. And the state of Kentucky was soon to be in a frenzy.

The 1983 Wildcats were a good, but not great, squad. At 23-7, Joe B. Hall's team felt the loss of All-America star Sam Bowie, who missed his second consecutive season with leg injuries. UK entered the game ranked No. 12 in the nation. Junior center Melvin Turpin was the squad's high scorer and rebounder. Junior guard Jim Master provided outside shooting touch and was joined in the lineup by senior forward Derrick Hord, senior swingman Charles Hurt, and senior point guard Dirk Minniefield. Freshman forward Kenny Walker and reserves Bret Bearup and Dicky Beal provided depth. Kentucky was a patient and skilled team, shooting a staggering 55.6% from the field for the season, but without Bowie, they lacked explosive athleticism, barely outrebounding opponents (they only had nine more rebounds than their opponents on the season).

The 1983 Cardinals, on the other hand, were ranked second in the nation, and at 31-3, had the essential ingredients to win Denny Crum's second national title. Sophomore guard Milt Wagner led a balanced Cardinal attack. Junior guard Lancaster Gordon was a ball hawk and another scoring threat and was central to Louisville's March hopes. A front line of 6'8" shot blocker Charles Jones and senior brothers 6'7" Rodney and 6'9" Scooter McCray made Louisville an aggressive, athletic team that imposed its will on the competition. Freshman Billy Thompson led a short bench. Louisville shot 51% from the field and averaged four boards more per game than the opponent, also blocking three times more shots than their opponents.

If Kentucky's system was efficient and thoughtful, Louisville's style was aggressive and freewheeling. In his third season as a Louisville starter, Gordon, the 6'3" slashing scorer and pickpocket defender, explained to *Sports Illustrated*, "We play a loose style of ball, and Coach Crum lets us be creative." It was the loose, creative mode of play, and perhaps the 1980 championship banner, that had drawn Gordon from Jackson, Mississippi—what was once the heart of SEC recruiting country—to Louisville.

When 24 years of hype were boiled down, in the Mideast Regional Final in Knoxville's tiny Stokely Center, UK and UofL fans both had reasons to be optimistic. UK planned to play carefully and patiently, trying to lure UofL into defensive gambles and create easy opportunities for the veteran sharp-shooters. UofL hoped to speed up the game and force UK to hurry at both ends. There was certainly no question that each side wanted this game (and the ensuing Final Four berth) badly.

"You didn't really have much time to contemplate on it," said Coach Crum in a recent interview. "I think you only had one night in between [NCAA games], so you didn't have time to do any special preparations. . . . I don't know if we were a better team than Kentucky. I felt like we were as good as they were."

"We were confident heading into the game, for sure," UK coach Joe B. Hall recalled. "We were a good team and we felt we could take it to them. Obviously, they felt the same, and the fans and the media really built it up a whole lot bigger than it ever could be. But the game lived up to the billing."

Joe B. Hall leads the Wildcats in Knoxville's Stokely Center, where Dream Game I was played. Hall succeeded Adolph Rupp and took UK to three Final Fours and an NCAA championship.
(Photo by Jamie Vaught)

The Game:

Conventional wisdom held that if one team began thumping the other, Crum's Cards would be the aggressors. However, conventional wisdom didn't hold. Kentucky looked like the team that had looked forward to this game for 24 years, as the Cats bolted from the opening gate.

In the game's first five minutes, UK shot 6-of-9 from the field. No Cat started hotter than Derrick Hord, who was finishing a disappointing senior campaign. Hord, whose scoring average had dipped from 16.3 points per game a year before to barely over half that, shook off the offensive rust to can three consecutive mid-range jump shots. Meanwhile, Louisville was harried and uncomfortable, with Gordon surprisingly missing an open layup. Five minutes in, Crum had seen enough and called for time, trailing 13-6.

The flood did not stop, however, as UK surged to a 23-10 advantage after Hord canned another jumper, leaving Crum again asking for time. In addition to Hord's uncharacteristically strong start, Kentucky's outside shooter extraordinaire Jim Master was 3-of-4 on perimeter jump shots. Master was a 6'5" prototype Indiana jump shooter, who may have looked like he stumbled in from the movie *Hoosiers*, but who was eager to match up with his Louisville counterparts. With Master giving the Wildcat faithful superb perimeter play on which to base upset hopes and Mel Turpin holding his own with Louisville's bruisers inside, UK was outshooting UofL 65%-29% at the point of Crum's timeout.

With the roof of the Stokely Center threatening to come off due to the noise, Crum had to hope his team could survive and keep the game competitive. After all, the Cardinals had rallied from 16 points down against Arkansas. Though the Cardinals adopted their coach's cool attitude and hung in the game, Kentucky continued to play strong, leading 35-23 around the 3:00 mark in the half. However, Louisville closed well, with a late Jones basket trimming the halftime gap to 37-30. Rodney McCray managed nine first-half points. Charles Jones was battling Turpin for position and had chipped in six points of his own. Lancaster Gordon added six as well.

For Kentucky, the good news was that Hall's Cats shot 62% in the first half and turned the ball over only four times. Louisville had shot a mere 41%, but somehow trailed only by seven. Crum smelled blood. At halftime, he told the Cards that Kentucky had played as well as they could, but UofL only trailed by seven. Crum calmed his team and told them he felt they could beat UK, but they would have to tighten their press.

"There were no Knute Rockne speeches," Crum told the University of Louisville's alumni magazine. "The incentive was there."

It seemed unlikely that UK could continue its torrid pace, but as the second half began, the Wildcats did just that. Melvin Turpin went to war with two offensive rebound baskets and a post-up hoop, giving UK a 43-32 advantage with 16:38 to play.

And then, the switch was tripped. UofL caught fire, with the Cardinal press forcing five UK turnovers in the next minute and a half of game action. Two Rodney McCray dunks and a follow-up basket, as well as two jump shots from Gordon and Wagner, trimmed UK's advantage to 45-42 almost instantly. Not only was Louisville's defensive pressure suffocating, with UK throwing the ball all over the offensive backcourt, but suddenly the Louisville offense was getting high-percentage shots as opposed to contested jumpers. At the 15:00 mark, Joe B. Hall called for time and hoped to restore order.

However, just as UK seemingly could not miss in the first half, UofL was now on fire in the second stanza. Over the next seven minutes, Louisville shot 8 of 11 from the field. Gordon and Wagner were leaking out on fast breaks and Louisville's big men found them with timely outlet passes. Of those eight baskets, two were dunks for Lancaster Gordon and two others were short jumpers for the Louisville high flier. Kentucky tried to answer with Master, who drained three more mid- to long-range jumpers over the same span. But Louisville's press was wearing Kentucky down, and inside of eight minutes to go, UofL had staked itself to a 58-53 lead.

As dark as Louisville's chances had been when UK shot the lights out, the Wildcats looked even less likely to rally at this stage. In the pre-shot clock era, a team with athletic ball handlers could freeze the ball for minutes at a time. While Crum did not send Louisville into a deep freeze, he did clearly emphasize patience and finding high-percentage shots.

However, Louisville sandwiched a lone offensive rebound basket by Jones around three turnovers. After two Turpin foul shots and a Master jumper, Derrick Hord drew a UofL foul. With UK trailing 60-57 and

3:18 left, Hord drained the first shot. He missed the second, but Charles Hurt crashed the boards for a follow-up basket and a 60-60 tie.

It was now Louisville's turn to be frazzled and, at 2:24, Wagner overshot a pass to Gordon on the left baseline and UK had the ball back. Hall told Dirk Minniefield to hold the ball for the final shot. As Louisville continued to trap and reach for steals, Kentucky had to burn two timeouts to keep possession. With the clock running down and tension mounting, Minniefield suddenly saw a lane to the basket at around 0:20. He drove the left baseline past Gordon and rose for an arcing layup. Louisville's angst was short-lived as Jones hustled to the ball and leaped to tip it with a fingertip and send it grazing off the edge of the rim instead of into the basket.

Scooter McCray grabbed the rebound and the Cardinals were off. With no expectations of draining the clock, McCray threw another long outlet pass to his brother Rodney, who quickly swung the ball to Lancaster Gordon. The Mississippi missile wasted no time. Sensing he could send his team to a second consecutive Final Four, Gordon went up for a short jumper from the right shoulder. While Master challenged the shot, it was true and banked in off the glass with 11 seconds left.

UofL led, 62-60.

Kentucky inbounded the ball and called a final timeout with eight seconds to play, needing a timely bucket to extend the game. When play resumed, Minniefield shook off his heartbreaking miss by finding Master as the clock ticked down.

Master shook Scooter McCray and launched a midrange jumper near the left baseline as the clock reached zero.

All eyes in the arena followed the flight of Master's shot. How many times had each of the players in that game replayed a moment just like that, in a backyard, playground, or a community gym?

Unlike Minniefield's shot, Master's soared over the outstretched arms of Jones and dropped straight through the basket. Overtime!

It was bedlam in the Stokely Center.

The Dream Game had lived up to its billing and the denouement was pushed back for five more minutes. Kentucky felt a new surge of confidence.

"I could see a great look in our team's eyes," Hall admitted after the game to the *New York Times*. But just as they had answered UK's initial run, Louisville had one more burst left.

"We came out and played about as well as we could have," Denny Crum said.

On the first possession of overtime, Louisville held the ball for just over a minute and Gordon picked up where he had left off, sinking another jumper. He promptly stole the ball from Turpin and drained another.

Kentucky's next two possessions were also turnovers. Louisville, meanwhile, continued to push the game.

"It was like a cavalry charge," Master commented after the game.

When the dust settled, UofL had scored the first 14 points of overtime, and by the time Minniefield finally broke UK's drought with a driving layup, at 76-64 with under a minute left, the game was long since over. Gordon added two more dunks and when the buzzer sounded, UofL had won 80-68.

UofL had outgunned the Cats when it counted. In the second half and overtime, UofL shot an astounding 81.5%. Over the entire game, Kentucky had shot 56% in defeat. Louisville's Gordon and Wagner had proved to be the difference in the game, with their unflinching defensive pressure and timely scoring. Gordon tallied 24 points on his way to being the region's Most Outstanding Player. He was joined on the all-tournament team by Wagner (18 points in the game), Scooter McCray (7 points, 7 rebounds, 4 assists), and UK's Turpin (18 points and 9 boards) and Master (18 points on 9-of-13 shooting).

Postgame:

Lancaster Gordon had been the top Card in one of the biggest games in school history. His unflinching defense and clutch shooting wrote his name large in the annals of the rivalry. The significance of the game isn't lost on Gordon, who scored 1,614 points at UofL and went on to be the eighth pick in the 1984 NBA Draft. He played four seasons for the L.A. Clippers.

"I'd like to think that people remember me for the totality of my career," he told the Louisville *Courier-Journal* in 2012. "[B]ut the bottom line is that it's really about the UK game and what I did in the tournament. It *still* carries over."

Gordon has also been active in his community after his basketball career. Gordon has admitted to growing up in relative poverty in Mississippi, and today, he uses his influence to help other children in difficult circumstances. He is the Coordinator of Volunteers for CASA, a local program that provides advocates in the family court system for abused and neglected children.

✶✶✶✶✶

In the immediate future, UofL won a berth in the Final Four in Albuquerque and faced No.1 Houston and legendary Phi Slamma Jamma. The UofL/Houston game was viewed by most as the de facto title game, and when the Cougars outlasted the Cardinals 94-81, their championship coronation was an afterthought. No one told this to Jim Valvano's NC State Wolfpack, who pulled off a monumental upset with their shocking title game win over Clyde Drexler, Hakeem (then Akeem) Olajuwon, and their Houston teammates.

In the longer future, it was clear that UK could no longer ignore UofL.

Hall and Cliff Hagan continued with the party line and did not want to set a regular matchup with Louisville. But UK's athletic board had a highly charged meeting, and voted 10-5 to discuss a series. Simply put, the reality of a UK/UofL game had been so astounding that public pressure mandated it become an annual event instead of a once-every-quarter-century NCAA showcase.

Perhaps because this first meeting has led to three decades of annual matchups, its importance would be hard to overstate. Over time, much of the sting has lessened for UK.

Jim Master acknowledges, "There's always going to be stress and pressure playing in a game like [The Dream Game]. It's a great feeling, to know you performed well on such a big stage. It's a big, big deal."

Louisville's Rodney McCray concurred.

McCray, who was a starter on Louisville's 1980 NCAA title-winning team and won an NBA title with the Chicago Bulls, told the Louisville

Courier-Journal in 2012, "[O]n a scale of 1 to 10 for all the games I played in during my career, that game was a 10. If we don't win that game, the guys on that team really believe in our hearts that Kentucky never would have started the series. They would have kept ignoring us. They couldn't ignore us anymore."

When asked about McCray's comment, Denny Crum agrees. "That may very well be true." Crum remembers UK alum and Kentucky governor John Y. Brown being impressed with the game and feels that Brown's influence had a significant role in creating the annual series.

Indeed, if Dream Game I had been more hype than hoops, it might not have been a big deal. It wouldn't have been a testimony to the pride that Hall's Cats felt in defending their historical superiority and that Crum's Cards felt in bringing a modern flavor to the state's biggest matchup.

Instead, after a hasty round of negotiations, UK's next game, the first of 1983–84, would be a rematch with UofL—and would mark the transition of the game to an annual date to be circled on all of college basketball fans' calendars.

Louisville 80

NAME	MIN	FG-FGA	FT-FTA	REB	PF	AST	STL	BLK	TO	TP
S.McCray	40	3-6	1-1	7	3	4	3	1	2	7
R. McCray	42	7-7	1-2	8	3	2	1	2	1	15
Jones	38	4-9	4-6	7	1	2	0	2	2	12
Gordon	42	11-21	2-3	1	1	2	4	0	2	24
Wagner	39	7-10	4-4	2	2	4	2	0	3	18
Thompson	13	2-4	0-1	2	1	1	0	0	1	4
Hall	9	0-0	0-0	0	1	0	1	0	0	0
West	1	0-0	0-0	0	0	0	0	0	0	0
Valentine	1	0-0	0-0	0	0	0	0	0	0	0
TEAM				1						
TOTAL	225	34-57	12-17	28	12	15	11	5	11	80

Kentucky 68

NAME	MIN	FG-FGA	FT-FTA	REB	PF	AST	STL	BLK	TO	TP
Hord	30	4-9	1-2	2	1	0	0	0	0	9
Hurt	31	3-5	1-2	6	3	1	0	0	3	7
Turpin	36	8-13	2-2	9	4	1	3	1	3	18
Minnifield	37	6-13	0-0	3	4	5	3	0	6	12
Master	40	9-13	0-0	2	4	2	0	0	2	18
Walker	26	1-3	0-0	1	1	0	0	0	1	2
Beal	15	0-0	0-0	0	3	4	0	0	2	0
Bearup	9	1-1	0-2	3	0	0	0	0	0	2
Hardin	1	0-0	0-0	0	0	0	0	0	1	0
TEAM				1						
TOTAL	225	32-57	4-8	27	20	13	6	1	18	68

Chapter 2

Revenge Served Hot

No. 2 UK 65, No. 6 UofL 44
November 26, 1983 at Rupp Arena

Pre-Game:

In five minutes in March 1983, the Louisville Cardinals turned the rivalry with the Kentucky Wildcats on its head. No more was Louisville's claim of basketball superiority based on such abstract measures as winning the last NCAA title or obtaining a better record or a higher ranking. Louisville laid claim to being the top squad in Kentucky with a head-to-head win, and it did not sit well in Lexington.

The first regular season matchup between UK and UofL in 61 years was scheduled as the season opener for both the Cats and Cards. Dream Game II, as it was instantly dubbed, figured to match two very different UK and UofL teams than the first edition of the modern rivalry had. Gordon and Wagner, Louisville's brilliant backcourt, returned for another campaign, as did solid center Charles Jones. The McCray brothers, however, had moved on to the NBA, and were replaced by sophomore Billy Thompson and junior Manual Forrest. While Jones was a known quality at center, the rest of the Cardinal frontcourt was a bit of a question mark. Freshman Mark McSwain hoped to add depth, as did veteran guard Jeff Hall in the backcourt.

For Kentucky, from their previous season's lineup, only big man Melvin Turpin and shooting guard Jim Master returned. Hurt, Hord, and Minniefield had all completed their eligibility. Talented sophomore Kenny Walker manned the small forward spot, and pint-sized sophomore guards Roger Harden and Dicky Beal shared point guard duties. Freshmen Winston Bennett (a powerful forward from Louisville) and James Blackmon hoped to add depth. The fifth starter was 7'1" of pure game changer—oft-injured Kentucky center Sam Bowie.

Bowie was finally healthy—more or less—after missing two full seasons with a slate of serious leg injuries. When he was at full strength, Bowie's size and skills—including a smooth shooting touch, deft passing, and full-scale defensive intimidation—made him a force to be reckoned with. However, it had been 32 months since Bowie had played college basketball.

With UK at No. 2 in the preseason AP poll, behind only North Carolina, and UofL only a few spots back at No. 6, expectations were high for both squads. Louisville saw no reason that its veteran guards wouldn't have another field day at UK's expense and hoped to force Kentucky to run and gun against the Louisville defensive pressure, which had flattened the previous season's Wildcats. Kentucky fans valued the emotional edge of intended revenge—and the height of Sam Bowie. They hoped for a more controlled pace—and for Kentucky's size to carry the day.

Conventional wisdom said that the pressure was on Kentucky to answer Louisville's March dominance. Not entirely true, maintains UK's senior scorer, Jim Master. "I looked forward to the game," Master says today. "It was very exciting to be part of history in renewing the series. With Bowie back, basically we were number one, and I was ready for a new season—and to beat the Cards."

Kentucky had been lucky to nab Master, who had grown up as a Notre Dame fan. However, the Wildcat program had shifted his thinking, and in three seasons, Master had quietly put up 965 points. His former coach, Joe B. Hall, recalls him as "a smart ballplayer [who] did not take bad shots."

Master was the Wildcats' quiet assassin. The 6'5" shooting guard from Fort Wayne, Indiana, often got lost in the shuffle behind Bowie and Turpin. While he was not a physical marvel like Bowie, Master was deceptively athletic. He enjoyed the challenge of playing against the Cardinals and their NBA-ready backcourt. Master had come up big in the previous meeting in March, and he would be pivotal to the November meeting.

The Game:

In the opening minutes of Dream Game II, both squads looked tentative and a bit tight. Neither team began the game shooting well. Master had his first jump shot blocked and airballed his second attempt. Louisville missed several close shots, but just inside the 13:00 mark in the first half held a 12-9 lead on a Manuel Forrest jump shot.

Suddenly, the tables turned. Master caught fire. He drained a mid-range jumper to cut the Louisville lead to one, took a charge from Milt Wagner, and then knocked down a jump shot on the other end. He added a free throw after a technical foul was assessed to Louisville because Mark McSwain's uniform number was listed incorrectly in the official score book. After the teams swapped possessions, Master dropped in another perimeter jump shot, totaling seven consecutive points for him person-ally, and giving UK a 16-12 lead. UK never trailed again.

At the same time Master caught fire, Kentucky's defense locked down. "They forced us out of our offense," Lancaster Gordon told the *Lexington Herald-Leader* after the game. Milt Wagner agreed, "[T]hey made us force a lot of shots, go up off-balance," he admitted to the *Herald-Leader*. "They just outplayed us." Gordon and Wagner each had just two points in the first half, as Master the scorer showcased surprising defensive intensity.

Also central in the UK effort was Bowie, blocking some shots and changing others, shooting into passing lanes, and racking up assists with smooth passes in the half-court. Master admits that Bowie was a "very big" influence on the game. "Having Bowie helped us keep more pres-sure on the guards," he notes. "His presence, shot-blocking, and passing all were a big help."

After Louisville's 12-9 start, UK rolled by a 26-8 margin for the remainder of the half. Reserve James Blackmon twice picked UofL guards' pockets and raced in for easy layups. Rupp Arena was rocking, with Kentucky holding a 35-20 lead at the half.

Of course, Kentucky had held a halftime lead in the previous Dream Game, only to watch it evaporate under Louisville's second-half defensive pressure. In this edition of the game, however, any Cardinal dreams of a second consecutive comeback thriller ended very quickly. Kentucky's defense continued to be razor-sharp, as Bowie, Walker, and Bennett each jumped into passing lanes for quick steals. Offensively, the deluge continued. Walker had a reverse dunk, Master drained two perimeter jump shots, and Turpin dunked off of a beautiful touch pass from Bowie. With UK holding a 49-24 lead, TBS broadcaster Skip Caray deadpanned, "The Cardinals now know how General Custer felt."

Perhaps the most telling play of the game came a few moments later. Louisville got a rare look at the basket, as Charles Jones powered up with a post move, only to meet both Turpin and Bowie, either of whom could be credited with blocking his shot. Jim Master chased down the rebound and was fouled by Milt Wagner. When Master drained both free throws, UK led 55-26, courtesy of a 46-14 run in 22 minutes of basketball.

Louisville continued to fight, drawing to a more respectable 65-44 final total. Louisville was held to under 36% shooting, and Kentucky forced the Cardinals to commit 20 turnovers. Master totaled 19 points, including a perfect 9-of-9 from the foul line. Turpin and Walker added 16 and 13 points, respectively. Bowie did not make a basket, but did manage 7 free throws, and filled the stat sheet with 10 rebounds, 5 assists, 5 blocked shots, and 3 steals in 33 minutes of play. Louisville had few bright spots. Freshman McSwain was the lone Cardinal to score in double figures, with 10 points. Gordon and Wagner combined for 12 points on 6-of-21 shooting.

Joe B. Hall was proud of his victorious squad. "I've got to single out a great defensive effort. . . . We were dominating inside and our guards were pressuring them outside," Hall noted.

Denny Crum was philosophical in defeat. "I'm not sure, considering the relative talent levels and physical size, that we'll ever be able to beat Kentucky this year," he told the *Courier-Journal*. "But our young people are going to have to play every game and keep learning. . . . [G]ive Kentucky the credit."

Indeed, much of the credit had to go to the surprising defensive star, Jim Master. Not only had he been UK's high scorer in both of the first two Dream Games, but he had held Louisville's All-America backcourt firmly in check.

Postgame:

Jim Master had a typically solid senior season. He totaled 1,283 points in his UK career, which at the time ranked him in the top 20 in Wildcat history. Master was drafted in the sixth round of the NBA Draft by the Atlanta Hawks, but never played in the league. He served as a television color commentator at one point, but later settled into a role as a financial advisor in Lexington.

"I'm proud to have been a part of this great series," Master says of his Dream Game days. "I think it is very good for the state and the schools . . . and I enjoy rooting against the Cardinals," he laughs.

✳✳✳✳✳

The last time Kentucky and Louisville had met in a regular season matchup, Warren G. Harding was the US president and radio and automobiles were still relatively uncommon innovations. Dream Game II was the beginning of a grand experiment in annual rivalry, the culmination of a great deal of basketball success and political maneuvering.

For the second consecutive game in the series, the team that utilized defensive pressure to force a key run emerged as the victor. Kentucky had adapted to play a tenacious in-your-face man-to-man defense which looked, for all intents and purposes, like a half-court version of the full-court variation that Louisville had emphasized during its recent success.

Kentucky had served notice in other ways that it was not going quietly behind the Cardinals. Winston Bennett, who had two points and seven rebounds in his first collegiate game, was the crown jewel of Joe B. Hall's recruiting class. Bennett, who hailed from Louisville, was the first inner-city Louisville player whom Kentucky had signed in recent memory. The old lines were giving way, and in the brave new world, success was king.

The most immediate impact of Dream Game II, however, was much more direct. "Revenge did matter," Master admits. "It was a tough loss in the Dream Game, and it had not been that long ago. I was very excited for the win and ready for the long year." What neither Master nor anyone else knew was that the long year would not be complete without a third incarnation of the Dream Game—again, during March Madness.

Kentucky 65

NAME	MIN	FG-FGA	FT-FTA	REB	PF	AST	STL	BLK	TO	TP
Bowie	33	0-3	7-8	10	2	5	3	5	3	7
Walker	24	6-9	1-4	3	0	0	3	0	0	13
Turpin	33	5-11	6-8	9	2	1	1	1	2	16
Master	37	5-13	9-9	2	3	2	1	0	3	19
Harden	25	0-0	0-0	1	2	2	0	0	1	0
Bennett	23	0-6	2-4	7	4	1	1	1	3	2
Blackmon	16	3-5	0-1	2	3	4	3	0	2	6
Beal	4	0-0	2-2	0	0	0	0	0	0	2
Bearup	2	0-1	0-0	1	0	0	0	0	0	0
Andrews	1	0-0	0-0	0	0	0	0	0	0	0
Heitz	1	0-0	0-0	0	0	0	0	0	0	0
McKinley	1	0-0	0-0	0	0	0	0	0	0	0
TEAM				1						
Total	200	19-48	27-36	36	16	15	12	7	14	65

Louisville 44

NAME	MIN	FG-FGA	FT-FTA	REB	PF	AST	STL	BLK	TO	TP
Forrest	24	3-8	0-0	5	3	0	0	0	3	6
Thompson	25	2-6	0-0	6	4	2	1	1	5	4
Jones	36	2-8	2-2	8	2	1	1	0	2	6
Gordon	35	4-12	0-1	6	1	2	2	0	2	8
Wagner	22	2-9	0-0	3	5	3	0	1	2	4
Hall	25	3-9	0-0	1	2	1	1	1	2	6
Sumpter	15	0-2	0-2	5	3	1	0	0	1	0
McSwain	12	5-5	0-0	2	4	0	0	0	2	10
Mitchell	4	0-0	0-0	1	0	0	0	0	1	0
Valentine	1	0-0	0-0	0	0	1	0	0	0	0
Jeter	1	0-0	0-0	0	1	0	0	0	0	0
TEAM				4						
Total	200	21-59	2-5	41	25	11	5	3	20	44

Chapter 3

Dream Game III

No. 3 UK 72, No. 16 UofL 67
NCAA Mideast Regional Semifinals
March 22, 1984, at Rupp Arena

Pre-Game:

After not playing Louisville since the 1950s, Kentucky would face the Cards three times in a calendar year. The third time (just like the '83 contest) was held in the pressure cooker of the NCAA Tournament. Thanks to the NCAA selection committee, Kentucky was able to face UofL in the confines of their own home court.

In the infancy of the renewed rivalry, fans were spoiled. Kentucky and Louisville were to play on the biggest stage for the second year in a row. This time, the storylines were different.

In 1983, Louisville had wanted a piece of Kentucky anywhere and anytime. The following season, when the rivalry was renewed on the official annual basis, Kentucky wanted revenge, and got it—big time.

Now, the storyline had flipped again. Louisville, smarting from their whipping in November to the Cats, had decided they were a much better team than what they'd showed in the first meeting that season.

"You're gonna get beat sometimes, and sometimes you're gonna get beat bad," Louisville guard Jeff Hall (a native of Ashland, Kentucky) told the *Lexington Herald-Leader* after that game. "They were better than us. They deserved to win. But I guarantee we'll find things to learn from."

Louisville, ranked No. 16, learned well throughout the season. They came into the contest with a record of 24-10. They had played their typical tough schedule, besting four top-10 teams along the way (Iowa, UCLA, N.C. State, and Memphis State—twice) before upsetting No. 12 Tulsa on a last-second shot by Milt Wagner to reach the Sweet Sixteen.

Kentucky would certainly be ready this time. In his best opportunity to win a championship since 1978, Joe B. Hall had put together a dominant team. At 27-4, Kentucky was one of the best teams in the country. They won the SEC regular season and tournament titles, defeating No. 9 LSU (twice) and No. 4 Houston along the way. Overall, the team had everything it took to win a championship. They did not want Louisville to derail them for a second consecutive year in the NCAA Tournament.

When Kentucky and Louisville squared off on March 22, 1984, Kentucky fans thought one thing: *Not again.* Louisville, on the other hand, was confident. They had been here before. They had won.

The only difference? This time the Cards had to do it on Kentucky's home court. And that may have made all the difference in the world.

The Game:

From the beginning, fans knew this game would be different than the one in November. They called it Dream Game III.

First off, there was a lot of red in the stands, most holding signs that said BEAT KENTUCKY. But when the game started, Jim Master scored the first four points, and Walker scored the next four on putbacks. UK led early 8-2.

But it came down to Gordon and Wagner for UofL. The pair scored their team's first 13 points, which cut the lead to 16-13. (The duo had just 12 points in the year's first meeting). Beal, not normally known for his shooting, hit two 16-footers in the first six minutes, and Master hit another shot in that time.

Turnovers, offensive fouls, and the quick hands of the Louisville players got the Cards back in it. Gordon scored 14 points in the first 10 minutes, aiding a 12-0 Louisville run for a 22-16 Cards lead. Against the Louisville pressure, Kentucky constantly gave the ball to Sam Bowie, who either dribbled up court or gave the ball to a guard to do so. Sometimes it worked, and sometimes it resulted in a turnover. Kentucky had eight turnovers in those first 10 minutes.

Beal, who was still playing after three arthroscopic knee operations, led UK back. The pint-sized pride of Covington drove for a layup and then made a steal with 7:50 to play in the half. Beal fed Turpin inside for a turnaround jumper to cut the Louisville lead to two. Beal then got another steal, and as he sped to the hoop, he took a hard foul from Louisville's Barry Sumpter.

Evidently, one less-than-intelligent UK fan decided the foul was too hard and took out his frustrations on UofL coach Denny Crum—by throwing a quarter at the Louisville coach. The coin hit the coach in the forehead, cutting him, and forcing him to be treated on the sideline during the game.

Beal hit both free throws for his seventh and eighth points to keep UK in the game and bring his team within two. He would later find Bowie for an alley-oop slam. With 4:32 to play, Master hit a jumper for a 28-all tie—but he was soon forced to leave the half early with three personal fouls.

In the final ten seconds of the half, Beal trapped Wagner in the back-court as Louisville tried to hold for the last shot. The 5'11" Beal then tipped the ball away, recovered it, and streaked downcourt for a layup that cut the lead to 36-32 at the half. It was a harbinger of what was to come.

Louisville had injury problems coming into the game. Forrest hurt his leg against Tulsa, and Thompson had a bum knee. UK tried to take advantage, but those players weren't the problem. The tandem of Gordon and Wagner scored 26 of Louisville's 36 points. Gordon had 18 himself.

But Turpin and Bowie were too much on the boards for the guard-oriented Cards. The Wildcats held a 19-15 rebounding lead at the half. Still, Louisville shot 50% (UK shot 47%) and forced Kentucky to surrender 12 turnovers.

To start the second half, Beal stole the ball, which resulted in a Master jumper. Another Beal assist led to a bucket that tied the game—a layup by freshman James Blackmon gave UK the tie, 38-38.

Bennett came in to give a lift, and he was matched up mostly against the ailing Thompson. Bennett scored 10 points and grabbed 5 rebounds in the game.

Kentucky turned up the defensive pressure in the second half, and with Beal providing the spark, sped up the game. Beal consistently drove to the hoop and fed teammates time and again—sometimes with passes so deft his teammates could not handle them. As the second half went back and forth, neither team could pull away.

At the 9:40 mark, Louisville held the lead, 49-47. Kentucky then went on a 10-0 run to effectively take over the game. Two free throws tied the game, and Master hit another jumper to take the lead. Then Beal got another steal—one of six in the game for the guard—and scored a layup. During and after the run, the Wildcats went to a 2-3 zone that seemed to work against the Cards. But there were still fireworks reserved for the end of the game.

With under two minutes to play, UK led 67-61. But Bennett then made just one of a possible four free throws, and with 21 seconds to go, Louisville came back to within 68-65. The pressure was on—and Jim Master went to the line. He made the first free throw.

He then missed the second, but luckily, Bennett was there for the biggest rebound of his career. He tipped in the basket and was fouled. The crowd of blue roared its approval as Bennett made the free throw for the unusual four-point play. UK led 72-65 and the game was in hand for the first time all evening.

UK held on to win, 72-67. Gordon (25) and Wagner (22) would combine for 47 of their team's 67 points, but no other Cardinal would score in double figures.

For Kentucky, the Wildcats were led by Beal, whose statline was packed: 15 points, 9 assists, 6 steals, and 6 turnovers in 39 minutes. Master finished with 15 points, as Turpin scored 14 and Bowie scored 8 and grabbed 12 rebounds.

"I'm very proud of my team, needless to say," Crum said of his Louisville team afterward to the Associated Press. "This game proved you can play well against a good team and get beat. That's what happened."

Postgame:

Louisville's season ended at 24-11. It was the last amazing performance for Lancaster Gordon, who was chosen with the eighth pick in the NBA Draft by the Los Angeles Clippers. Fellow UofL senior Charles

Jones was a second-round NBA Draft pick and also had a solid NBA career.

Kentucky advanced to defeat Illinois for a spot in the 1984 Final Four in Seattle. There, the Wildcats squared off against mighty Georgetown and its center Patrick Ewing. After a dominating first half, which saw Kentucky lead by as many as 12, UK held a 27-20 halftime lead. The Wildcats shot 50% from the field (10-20). What followed was one of the worst second-half performances in Kentucky history. The team shot 3-for-33 in the second half, and lost 53-40. Kentucky did not score in the second half until almost 10 minutes had passed, and as a team, finished 13-for-53 from the field (24.5%).

It was the end of the line for seniors Dicky Beal, Jim Master, Mel Turpin, and Sam Bowie. After basketball, Beal has worked in several fields, including pharmaceutical and insurance sales. He has remained active in the Covington community. "It never ceased to amaze me, graduating from UK so long ago, the people who respect and love me," Beal told Kyforward.com in 2012.

Mel Turpin was the sixth overall pick in the 1984 NBA Draft by the Washington Bullets, who then traded him to the Cleveland Cavaliers. Turpin struggled with his weight while in the NBA and played six seasons before retiring. In the 2000s, he worked as a security guard in Lexington. At age 49, Turpin was found dead of an apparent self-inflicted gunshot wound. The reason for the suicide was never determined.

Sam Bowie was one of the most heavily sought-after big men ever to play at the University of Kentucky. Long and nimble, Bowie could do almost anything—as long as he was healthy. But after breaking his leg and then requiring two surgeries, he missed two full seasons at UK before taking part in the 1984 Final Four run. When he came back, few thought he was ever the same.

Still, he had potential. And even with the surgeries and injuries, the Portland Trailblazers selected Bowie No. 2 overall in that draft—one spot ahead of Michael Jordan. It is a decision that has been ridiculed ever since. Bowie was never a star in the NBA, but he did play 10 seasons, averaging just under 11 points, with 7.5 rebounds and 1.78 blocks per game.

Talented but oft-injured center Sam Bowie reaches high to pull
in a rebound as teammate Melvin Turpin watches.

(Photo by Jamie Vaught)

Today, Bowie lives in Lexington. He has served as a radio announcer
for UK sports and also works as an owner and horse trainer.

"I was blessed to make enough money for myself that I can be happy
and do what I want," Bowie says.

Kentucky 72

NAME	MIN	FG-FGA	FT-FTA	REB	PF	AST	STL	BLK	TO	TP
Walker	35	2-7	4-4	6	3	3	2	1	0	8
Bowie	38	3-9	2-2	12	3	2	1	3	5	8
Turpin	32	6-10	2-2	5	3	2	0	2	5	14
Beal	39	6-9	3-4	2	3	9	6	0	6	15
Master	30	6-10	3-4	4	3	0	0	0	2	15
Bennett	15	4-9	2-4	5	3	0	0	0	1	10
Blackmon	10	1-1	0-0	1	0	0	0	0	1	2
Harden	1	0-0	0-0	0	1	0	0	0	0	0
TEAM				1						
Total	200	28-55	16-20	36	19	16	9	6	20	72

Louisville 67

NAME	MIN	FG-FGA	FT-FTA	REB	PF	AST	STL	BLK	TO	TP
Thompson	27	2-8	0-3	5	4	1	0	0	4	4
Forrest	35	3-4	0-1	4	5	2	2	1	1	6
Jones	37	2-9	4-4	9	1	0	3	0	0	8
Gordon	34	10-18	5-6	3	2	2	1	0	6	25
Wagner	36	10-17	2-2	2	2	5	1	0	4	22
McSwain	15	0-1	0-0	0	1	1	0	0	0	0
Hall	11	1-4	0-0	0	3	0	1	0	0	2
Sumpter	5	0-0	0-0	0	2	0	0	0	1	0
TEAM				6						
Total	200	28-61	11-16	29	20	11	8	1	16	67

Chapter 4

A Leap of Faith

No. 14 UofL 71, UK 64
December 15, 1984 at Freedom Hall

Pre-Game:

Billy Thompson was struggling. In 1982, he had signed with Louisville as the most highly sought-after high school prospect in the nation. The 6'7" forward from Camden, New Jersey, could bang in the post with big men or step outside and handle the ball with a silky mid-range jump shot. What he could not do was equal the hype.

As a freshman, Thompson scored 7.3 points and grabbed 3.9 rebounds per game. He was a solid substitute on a veteran team that reached the Final Four. However, the following year, as a sophomore starter, his stats improved only slightly—9.2 points and 5.6 rebounds per game. Thompson was inconsistent and struggled to assert himself. In retrospect, this was because the man-child with the million-dollar skill set was finding himself.

Early in the 1984–85 season, Milt Wagner went down with a season-ending injury. Thompson was left as the centerpiece of an uneven UofL team, surrounded by Jeff Hall and a bevy of post players—including senior Manuel Forrest and sophomores Mark McSwain and Barry

Sumpter. If UofL would go anywhere in 1984–85, Thompson had to step up his game. Due to the lack of team depth, he even had to play shooting guard on occasion.

UofL began the year 3-1. Despite their No. 14 national ranking, the Cardinals seemed doomed to inconsistency—they won at Indiana, but two games later, lost to Louisiana Tech despite holding Tech's big man, Karl Malone, to just four points. The results were also mixed on Thompson—while he was the team's leading scorer, he also was committing more than five turnovers per game.

The good news for Louisville was that as bad as things had been for the Cardinals, it was worse for the Wildcats. After a season-opening win over Toledo, UK had lost three in a row leading into the annual tilt with UofL. Freshman guard Ed Davender had talent, and other Wildcats like Winston Bennett and Richard Madison were capable role players. But Kentucky had to pin its hopes on superb junior forward Kenny Walker. Walker, like Thompson, could bang in the paint or shoot mid-range jump shots and had gone from being one of several good players to the heart and soul of UK's program.

The Game:

When the game tipped off, UK's Walker was a man on a mission. As he would all season long, he fought through screens, grabbed loose balls, hustled and scrambled, and fought to create offense. In the first half, he managed 16 points, and his tip-in just before the buzzer gave Kentucky a surprising 30-28 advantage at the half.

As the game progressed into the second half, the two teams continually punched and counterpunched. Winston Bennett aided the Kentucky cause with 14 points and 9 rebounds. Guard Roger Harden tallied a dozen points for the Cats as well.

Louisville countered from all corners—five different Cardinals scored in double figures, including Mark McSwain (13 points), Manuel Forrest (12), Barry Sumpter, and Jeff Hall (10 each). But Billy Thompson was the man who made the difference.

Inside of 9:00 to play, Thompson grabbed a missed shot and converted the offensive rebound into a basket. At the time, it gave UofL a

Louisville's Billy Thompson prepares to rebound as Kentucky's
Kenny Walker shoots. Walker scored 32 points, but Thompson led
the Cardinals to victory.

(Photo by Jamie Vaught, appears courtesy of the Somerset Commonwealth Journal)

43-42 lead, but the lead proved to be one that would not be relinquished. Shortly thereafter, Forrest went to the bench with a leg injury. But Thompson was undaunted. He gave Louisville exactly what it needed— scoring 17 points, pulling down a dozen rebounds, dishing out 6 assists, and blocking 4 shots—each category representing a team high—while only turning the ball over only three times.

Kentucky hung close, drawing to within 51-49 on a three-point play by Walker. Thompson again came to the rescue, connecting on an inside bucket off of his own rebound. A few moments later, Winston Bennett cut the Louisville lead to 56-53.

This time, Jeff Hall lent a helping hand. First, the veteran guard drained a corner jumper, and then he stole Kentucky's inbounds pass. After a Kentucky foul, he added two more free throws. Kentucky never moved closer than five points from that time, as Louisville came up big on the foul line.

Louisville held on to win the game, 71-64. UofL rose to 4-1, and UK fell to 1-4.

Despite the loss, Joe B. Hall was optimistic about his team's effort. "It was a great effort," Hall told the *Lexington Herald-Leader.* "The players played about as well as they could." Kenny Walker finished with 32 points and 15 rebounds in defeat.

Walker was quick to admit that the Cats had been beaten by a relatively superior opponent. He particularly was impressed with Thompson. "Billy is a great athlete," he told the Louisville *Courier-Journal.* "I think for two years people were putting an awful lot of pressure on him. Right now you're seeing the real Billy Thompson."

With all respect to Walker, time has proven him wrong. That was about the only thing he missed all season long.

Postgame:

Despite Kenny Walker's approval, and Billy Thompson's huge performance in the Dream Game, there was still something weighing on Thompson's mind throughout the 1984–85 season. At home after the season, Thompson was into his recreational life—recreation that he has admitted included partying and drugs. The *Los Angeles Times* in 1987 noted that in those early days, Thompson's professional future had been clouded by reports that he was "into the nose candy."

Denny Crum says of Thompson, "I don't know if you've talked to Billy about it . . . but he will probably tell you until he found Christ in his life he never was comfortable with himself. He had ability and he was tough mentally, but he could never put it all together. But when he finally did . . ."

In the summer of 1985, Thompson had a wake-up call. Recalling that incident in 2012, Thompson told website Charisma News that during one early morning of partying, he had a vision of himself on a gurney in the back of an ambulance, and then a headline "Billy Thompson, Basketball Star, Dead of Drug Overdose." Thompson says that God then spoke to him, warning him, "You are going to die if you don't give your life over to me."

Thompson got the message. A year later, he had a horrifying look at what might have been his future when his high school friend Len Bias died of a cocaine overdose mere hours after being chosen second in the 1986 NBA Draft by the Boston Celtics.

Thompson's path extended instead through a born-again Christian faith. Not only were the best moments of his Louisville career yet to come, but Thompson went on to be a part of the L.A. Lakers' "Showtime" squads that won back-to-back NBA titles in 1986–87 and 1987–88. Thompson played three more seasons for the expansion Miami Heat and his professional career extended to Israel, where he managed to explore the roots of his Christian heritage while continuing his basketball career.

Thompson hung up his basketball shoes in 1998, and shortly thereafter began serving as associate pastor at Jesus People Proclaim International Ministries Church in Boca Raton, Florida. In 2001, he became senior pastor, and he has never looked back.

One of the intersections of Thompson's past and present is his side job—serving as chaplain of the Miami Heat, a capacity in which he has now won three more NBA championship rings.

Today, Billy Thompson preaches the gospel of salvation through a relationship with Jesus Christ both at home in Boca Raton and elsewhere across the nation. He told Charisma News in 2012, "I believe God has some things planned for me to take this gospel across the United States."

It is certainly a very different journey than the one on which Thompson believes he had initially been headed.

✳✳✳✳✳

In spite of Thompson's Dream Game heroics and UofL's top-15 national ranking, the Cardinals struggled through the rest of the 1984–85 season, finishing 19-18 and ending the season in the NIT. Thompson was consistently better—he averaged 15.1 points and 8.4 boards per game and led the team in assists, as well as finishing second in blocked shots and steals. But without Milt Wagner, the team's chemistry never jelled. At one point in January 1985, UofL lost four games in a row. It was a tough step back for the Cardinals.

Kentucky did a superlative job of making lemonade from its particular lemons of circumstance. Walker was everything Joe B. Hall could have hoped—he was a consensus All-America player after averaging 22.9 points and 10.2 rebounds per game. But with little help for Walker (Davendar was second in scoring at a mere 8.5 points per game), UK struggled to reach its 18-13 mark. The team surprised Washington and UNLV in the NCAA Tournament before losing in the Sweet 16. After the game, in a surprise move, Joe B. Hall announced that he was immediately retiring as Wildcat coach. He would leave an established rivalry with Louisville to his successor—and a difficult legacy to follow.

Kentucky moved quickly and nabbed Arkansas's Eddie Sutton. Sutton was a respected veteran coach who had coached at Arkansas for 11 seasons, reaching four Sweet 16 appearances and a Final Four with the Hogs. Sutton would derisively refer to Louisville as "little brother" in future years and would achieve the rare trick of eventually earning the scorn of both the UofL and UK fans in the rivalry. It was quite a changing of the guards.

Louisville 71

NAME	MIN	FG-FGA	FT-FTA	OR-REB	PF	AST	STL	BLK	TO	TP
Forrest	28	5-10	2-3	0-0	2	3	0	0	2	12
Thompson	39	7-13	3-7	3-12	1	6	1	4	3	17
Sumpter	30	4-8	2-3	1-7	4	1	0	2	0	10
West	33	1-6	3-4	0-3	1	4	2	1	1	5
Hall	33	3-8	4-4	1-2	2	1	1	0	5	10
McSwain	23	2-5	9-10	3-4	3	0	1	0	0	13
Jeter	11	0-0	4-4	2-2	0	2	1	0	2	4
Abram	3	0-0	0-0	0-1	0	0	0	0	0	0
TEAM				1-1						
Total	200	22-50	27-35	11-32	13	17	6	7	13	71

Kentucky 64

NAME	MIN	FG-FGA	FT-FTA	OR-REB	PF	AST	STL	BLK	TO	TP
Bennett	34	6-14	2-4	4-9	5	0	0	0	4	14
Walker	40	14-25	4-5	6-15	2	2	1	0	1	32
Bearup	36	3-8	0-0	2-9	4	1	1	0	4	6
Andrews	18	0-0	0-0	0-0	4	1	0	0	2	0
Harden	33	6-9	0-0	0-2	1	2	1	0	2	12
Blackmon	23	0-1	0-0	0-0	2	1	1	0	1	0
Davendar	8	0-4	0-0	0-0	2	1	0	0	2	0
Madison	6	0-2	0-0	2-2	5	0	0	0	1	0
Lock	2	0-0	0-0	0-0	2	0	0	0	0	0
TEAM				1-1						
Total	200	29-63	6-9	15-39	27	8	4	0	17	64

Chapter 5

Losing the Battle, but Winning the War

No. 13 UK 69, No. 15 UofL 64
December 28, 1985 at Rupp Arena

Pre-Game:

While the man ruling the sideline of the Wildcat program changed, most of the notable faces on his squad remained the same. Given another year of battle testing, the Wildcats Eddie Sutton inherited were a talented and balanced squad. Consensus All-America star Kenny Walker had returned for his senior season and he was supported by an experienced group of teammates, including guards Ed Davender and James Blackmon. Junior forward Winston Bennett provided the muscle for Sutton's first team, and the group began the year at 7-1, entering the Louisville game ranked 13th in the AP Poll.

Two spots below Kentucky was a 6-2 Louisville team. Milt Wagner, back from his redshirt campaign for his final season, joined durable seniors Billy Thompson and Jeff Hall. Sophomore Herbert Crook became a surprising starter opposite Thompson at forward, and freshman sensation Pervis Ellison manned the middle for the Cards. Between the return of

Wagner, the emergence of Crook, and the consistent excellence of the freshman center who would become known as "Never Nervous Pervis," Louisville bore little resemblance to the 19-18 team of the previous season.

With the modern rivalry tied at two games each, a new head coach in Lexington, and two talented squads, the 1985–86 edition of the Dream Game figured to be a war. It was exactly that, and the hero of the day was the strongest man on the court.

✳✳✳✳✳

When Winston Bennett, the latest in a long line of stars from Louisville's Male High School, spurned the hometown Cardinals for the Wildcats, then-Coach Joe B. Hall had pulled an upset that was almost as monumental as Louisville's win in Dream Game I. Bennett had been a ball boy for the Cardinals and had played at Coach Crum's summer camps. Outsiders thought the recruitment was a done deal, but they were wrong.

"Being a minority from Louisville, I think it was always expected that I would go to Louisville," said Bennett in a recent interview. "I grew up in a time where there was a racial cloud over the Kentucky program in terms of how African Americans in Louisville felt about UK. . . . But my parents had always taught me to go and see things for yourself, get an understanding for yourself."

When Bennett saw things for himself in Lexington, he bonded with Coach Hall and with Assistant Coach Leonard Hamilton. He chose to become a Wildcat. Hall was delighted.

"It had been very difficult in the past to get a top athlete from Louisville," said Hall. "We had gone through a dry spell and had not had success getting key players out of Louisville, and Winston was a big break through."

For two seasons, Bennett served a sturdy and reliable component part for the Wildcats. "I was a dirty-work man," he recalled in a recent interview. "I was the dive-on-the floor guy, get-the-rebounds guy." He had scored 6.5 and 7.2 points per game in his first two seasons respectively, but after the difficult 1984–85 campaign, Bennett would have to step up to keep defenses from sagging on Wildcat sensation Kenny Walker. Bennett was noted for his physical play and his intensity. Against Crook,

Thompson, and Ellison, Kentucky's front line was in grave danger of being outmuscled by the Cardinals. But Bennett knew otherwise.

"Physicality was my game," Bennett says, "I liked to get in there and mix it up a bit."

The Game:

As Eddie Sutton prepared for his first UK/UofL matchup, one thing jumped out at him about the Cardinals. Kenny Walker explained after the game to the Louisville *Courier-Journal*, "They have great athletes . . . but on offensive rebounds, they weren't putting their bodies on a guy to box out." So Sutton sent his Wildcats to the glass, and chief among them would be the man who did the dirty work, Winston Bennett.

The game hung tantalizingly within the reach of the Cardinals for much of the afternoon. Wagner again was superb, returning to form with 19 points and 4 assists. Crook and Ellison added 14 and 13 points respectively. But Louisville led only twice all day, by a 3-2 score moments into the game, and at 36-35 early in the second half. Otherwise, Kentucky held a slim lead throughout.

Walker, fresh off his monster game in the previous year's matchup, drew most of the defensive attention from Louisville. However, between pulling a back muscle and sustaining leg cramps late in the game, the Kentucky sensation was held to a meager 11 points, although he did contribute 14 critical rebounds. Davender, who had scored 20 points or more in three of Kentucky's first seven games, was held to 1-of-9 shooting and 6 points.

But Louisville had no answer for Bennett. Playing all 40 minutes, he slashed his way to 23 points, including 7-of-8 free throw shooting, and grabbed 8 crucial rebounds. Buoyed by his example, Kentucky outrebounded the Cardinals 36-24 (including an astounding 20 offensive rebounds) and shot 25 free throws, to only seven attempts for Louisville. Particularly in the first half, Bennett wreaked havoc on the Cards. He canned short jumpers, had a dunk and a tip in, and sank three free throws on his way to 15 first-half points.

When Louisville trimmed the Kentucky advantage to 61-58 late in the second half, Kentucky missed its ensuing shot, only to grab two consecutive offensive rebounds. The third UK shot was then goaltended by

Ellison, in a rare mistake. After a Louisville turnover, Kentucky added two more free throws, and the only question was the final margin. When the buzzer sounded, Kentucky held a 69-64 victory.

Bennett had been the difference. Coach Crum pulled no punches after the loss. "He played as good a game as I've ever seen him play," the Louisville boss admitted.

Postgame:

While the Dream Game battle had gone to Kentucky, the 1986 NCAA war ultimately went to Louisville. The Cardinals entered the NCAA Tournament ranked No. 7 in the nation. After beating Bradley and Drexel to reach the Sweet 16, UofL thumped North Carolina and beat Auburn to claim Crum's sixth Final Four berth as the Louisville coach. A week later, the Cardinals beat Duke 72-69 to claim the school's second NCAA title—and their second in the last six years.

Many of the stars Crum had assembled over the previous years hit hot streaks at the same time. Pervis Ellison, as a mere freshman, was Most Outstanding Player of the Final Four. Billy Thompson had been superb, shooting an astounding 75% from the field in the Tournament. Veterans Wagner and Hall had provided enough steady leadership to see the Cardinals to the title. In April 1986, Louisville was celebrating and Kentucky was fit to be tied.

Kentucky had one Final Four appearance to show during UofL's six-year run. The Wildcats were No. 3 in the nation at the end of the 1986 regular season, and had advanced to the Elite Eight, when they had to face a LSU squad they had previously defeated three times (with two of the wins coming by two and three points, respectively). The fourth time was not a charm, as LSU shocked the Wildcats, 59-57.

In a rivalry like Kentucky and Louisville, defeat does not breed just misery, but also a sense of desperation. In a few short years, Louisville had climbed into competition with Kentucky and now past the Wildcats as the top team in the Commonwealth. But Kentucky would not go down without a fight, and the next chapter in the rivalry would be a memorable one for the Wildcats.

✳✳✳✳✳

Winston Bennett had many more big games in his career at Kentucky, although it ended without an NCAA title. He totaled 1,399 points and 799 rebounds and parlayed his success into four seasons in the NBA, mostly with the Cleveland Cavaliers. After his playing days ended, Bennett became an assistant coach at Kentucky under Rick Pitino for three seasons. As an assistant coach, he then followed Pitino to the Boston Celtics before he was fired, in his own explanation, due to an inappropriate sexual relationship he had conducted with an employee of Brandeis University, where the Celtics practiced.

The extra-marital relationship was one of many, Bennett admits. He had struggled for years with sex addiction, and it jeopardized not only his career, but his marriage and family life. Bennett sought treatment and, thanks to his Christian faith, emerged as a changed man. While Bennett became a Christian as a young man, he admits that he backslid in his faith, or failed to conduct himself in accordance with the tenants of his beliefs. During his treatment, Bennett recommitted to his faith and his marriage, and later returned to coaching at Kentucky State University and Mid-Continent University near Paducah, Kentucky.

Bennett authored a book, *Fight For Your Life*, and found that he enjoyed sharing his message of redemption via public speaking. He has left basketball and is now bringing the same intensity that he brought to the backboards and the low post to the speaking circuit. Interestingly, one of Bennett's biggest memories of his most successful Dream Game was a tussle with Billy Thompson over a loose ball. Much like Thompson, basketball has now taken a back seat for Bennett to the challenges of sharing his mistakes and the ensuing life lessons with others. Just as in the scrap for the loose ball with Thompson that Bennett remembered, today he and Billy Thompson are each poised for war, fighting for their team, but instead of pursuing rebounds or steals, each is hoping to teach young people to focus on the teachings of Jesus Christ and to avoid the temptations of illicit sex or drugs, which once nearly ruined promising young lives. They were one Wildcat and one Cardinal, but today, in the ultimate picture, they are both on the same team.

Kentucky 69

NAME	MIN	FG-FGA	FT-FTA	OR-REB	PF	AST	STL	BLK	TO	TP
Bennett	40	8-13	7-8	7-7	3	2	3	1	1	23
Walker	36	5-13	1-5	7-14	3	0	0	0	0	11
Blackmon	28	3-12	3-4	3-4	1	1	0	0	1	9
Davendar	38	1-9	4-4	1-2	0	2	1	0	2	6
Harden	28	3-6	4-4	0-2	2	4	2	0	3	10
Madison	26	5-7	0-0	1-5	2	1	0	0	0	10
Jenkins	4	0-0	0-0	0-0	1	0	0	1	0	0
TEAM				1-2						
Total	200	25-60	19-25	20-36	12	10	6	2	7	69

Louisville 64

NAME	MIN	FG-FGA	FT-FTA	OR-REB	PF	AST	STL	BLK	TO	TP
Crook	30	7-9	0-0	0-1	4	4	1	1	1	14
Thompson	33	3-6	2-2	2-8	4	3	0	2	4	8
Ellison	38	5-10	3-3	2-7	2	3	0	4	0	13
Wagner	37	9-13	1-2	0-2	2	4	0	1	2	19
Hall	32	3-5	0-0	0-3	3	3	0	0	2	6
West	10	1-2	0-0	0-0	3	1	0	0	0	2
Kimbro	10	1-3	0-0	1-1	1	0	0	0	2	2
McSwain	8	0-0	0-0	0-0	2	0	0	1	0	0
Payne	2	0-2	0-0	0-0	1	1	0	0	1	0
TEAM				0-2						
Total	200	29-50	6-7	5-24	22	19	1	9	12	64

Chapter 6

The Boy King (or the One Who Got Away)

No. 18 UK 85, UofL 51
December 27, 1986 at Freedom Hall

Pre-Game:

As Louisville's drive toward the 1986 NCAA title had percolated, Kentucky struck back with its own thunderous counter-offensive in the other great rivalry sport—recruiting. In the spring of 1986, an exceptionally deep and talented group of recruits graduated from Kentucky's high schools. Reggie Hanson and Felton Spencer were both quality young players, who, in time, made their marks at UK and UofL, respectively. But the King of the Bluegrass, the recruit so talented that the memory of missing out on him stings like the name of an old girlfriend, was Owensboro's Rex Chapman.

"I love Rex Chapman," said Denny Crum in 2013. "I thought he was going to be a great player, and he was. We tried really hard to recruit him. We thought we had a good shot at getting him, and then we didn't. . . . Physically, he could play with anybody. He could run and jump. He had great stamina. He was just really good."

Before Chapman's senior season, recruiting analyst Bob Gibbons tabbed him as the third-best prep player in the entire nation. Rex could do it all—he could sky with the greatest of leapers, shoot with the best of scorers, rebound, pass, defend, and generally play the game not only with a high level of skill, but with an abundance of panache. This wonder recruit was just over 100 miles away from Louisville's campus and about 175 miles from UK's territory. The battle was hard-fought, and while Rex took official visits to Georgia Tech, North Carolina, and Western Kentucky, in the end, it was the Cats and the Cards.

In winning Chapman, UK stymied the Cardinal momentum. The Wildcats boasted one of the nation's premier backcourts, as Chapman was paired with steady junior guard Ed Davender, a New York prep star who had managed 11.5 points per game in his sophomore campaign. In the low post, Kentucky's outlook was much murkier. Winston Bennett sustained a serious knee injury and redshirted for the season. Richard Madison, Rob Lock, and Cedric Jenkins were left to man the post, with reserve guards James Blackmon and Derrick Miller adding extra punch. By December, UK was 5-1 and ranked No. 18 in the AP poll.

Louisville, meanwhile, was a very different team in December 1986 than the title winners of the previous April had been. Guards Milt Wagner and Jeff Hall and forward Billy Thompson had each been 1,000-point scorers. With 51% of the team's scoring gone, Crum was left to depend on Pervis Ellison and Herb Crook on the low blocks and a series of young guards, with sophomore Tony Kimbro being the best of the bunch. Senior Mark McSwain and sophomore Kenny Payne added further talent on the inside, but Louisville's steady veterans were gone. And while the Cardinal cupboard was far from bare, it was no match for "King Rex." The Cardinals entered the UK game with a 4-5 mark, a far cry from their title days.

The Game:

Not only did this edition of the Dream Game introduce Chapman, but it also introduced the three-point basket to the rivalry. All of college basketball was trying to determine how to deal with the changes in the game the three-point shot brought. At Louisville, it was a short discussion—Crum didn't like it. Louisville took very few three-point shots, preferring to power the ball into its talented inside players. Nearly three decades later, Crum says this was purely a pragmatic decision.

"It wasn't that I didn't embrace it; we didn't have any three-point shooters the first year. . . . I can remember telling [assistant] Coach [Bobby] Dotson, 'Go find me a three-point shooter. I don't have anybody that can make it.'"

Kentucky, in theory, was somewhat tentative about the shot as well. The Wildcats had four players who were given the green light to shoot the shot, and the entire rest of the team took only five three-point attempts all season. But on a given day, the reticence toward the new-fangled shot melted away.

As in most years, the game opened with both teams looking a bit nervous and unable to take control. Louisville scored the first two baskets, and a few minutes in, Kentucky led 14-12. But King Rex was about to unleash one of his greatest shows. A trio of three-point bombs obliterated the Freedom Hall crowd and brought Kentucky into the lead. Chapman was not only aggressive about the three-point shot, he didn't mind taking them from behind the much deeper NBA line. With his shooting bonafides established, Chapman turned things up a notch. He stole a pass from Ellison, raced toward the basket for a dunk, and when he was challenged by Louisville's Keith Williams, changed his mind in mid-move and settled for a smooth finger roll. Kentucky's lead was 29-18 at that point.

Louisville answered, pulling to within 36-28 with the first-half clock running down. Chapman responded with a spinning, twisting jump shot ahead of the halftime buzzer, which swished cleanly through the net as Chapman fell down, giving King Rex 18 first-half points. The Cardinals could only shake their heads.

The second half was a dream for Wildcat fans and a nightmare for their Cardinal counterparts. With Chapman draining a total of five three-point shots for the game and adding a vicious second-half dunk on Kenny Payne, Kentucky forged out to a bigger and bigger lead. James Blackmon made two three-point shots. Awkward center Rob Lock managed an open baseline drive and a power dunk. Kentucky finished the game 11-of-17 in three-point shooting, while Louisville managed a lone

Rex Chapman, the Boy King of UK, the one who got away
for UofL, looking on as backcourt mate Ed Davender
speaks to TV broadcaster Joe Dean.

(Photo by Jamie Vaught)

trifecta in eight attempts. By the time the final horn sounded, Chapman totaled 26 points and had been praised effusively by CBS Television's Brent Musburger and Billy Packer. Kentucky had won 85-51. Ellison had been held to 4 meager points, and Tony Kimbro and freshman Felton Spencer were the only Cardinals to score in double figures, with 10 points each.

Postgame:

As with Dream Game II, the Cardinals ascent above Kentucky on the basketball ladder was answered by a determined Kentucky beatdown. More significant than the initial game was the excitement of Chapman and the possibilities that the three-point basket offered. Crum gradually gained more confidence in the shot, but the basketball revolution the three-point basket triggered would reverberate around the nation, among other spots at tiny Providence College where an up-and-coming head coach named Rick Pitino managed to ride three-point shooting and full-court pressure defense all the way to the 1987 Final Four.

Kentucky's season was not as smooth as it had been against Louisville. Chapman was a consensus All-SEC selection and was honored as the Conference's Freshman of the Year, courtesy of his 16 point per game scoring average and general feats of basketball wizardry. With the exception of the solid Davender, Chapman's support was inconsistent. Kentucky went 18-11, made the NCAA Tournament as a 8th seed, and lost to Ohio State in the first round.

Louisville also struggled, sliding to 18-14. Crook and Ellison each averaged over 15 points per game, and Kimbro improved over the course of the season. Youth and inconsistency doomed UofL as well, and the Cardinals did not appear in the Tournament they had won the previous March.

With Chapman and Eddie Sutton's star-studded recruiting classes, the 1986–87 game, still the most one-sided in the modern series, looked like a turning point in favor of Kentucky. The swing would prove to be temporary though, as Chapman's career and Sutton's upswing were both gone in a moment.

✳✳✳✳✳

Chapman played only one more season at Kentucky before entering the NBA at roughly the same time the NCAA set up long-term digs around Lexington. Chapman was taken with the eighth pick in the 1988 NBA Draft by the Charlotte Hornets. He spent 12 years playing in the NBA, averaging almost 15 points per game for his career. Since that time, Chapman has held several front-office NBA jobs, including serving as Director of Basketball Operations with the Phoenix Suns and as Vice President of Player Personnel for the Denver Nuggets. He has also worked as a studio analyst for television during the 2013 NCAA Tournament.

Despite the positive outcome, Chapman has seemed a bit uncomfortable with his Kentucky legacy. Rumors have circulated since his playing days that he and Eddie Sutton had a relationship that was significantly fractured and that this divide helped push King Rex to the NBA. However, in 2005, Chapman was interviewed by the Louisville *Courier-Journal* and indicated that he had left Kentucky early in part because of too much scrutiny of his private life. Specifically, Chapman indicated that he had dated African American women and felt pressured to "keep it confidential and hide it." He recalled someone scratching a racial epithet onto his car during his time at UK. Chapman has always been careful to qualify that he loves the University of Kentucky, but it is clear that his collegiate experience was not always as picturesque as it may have seemed.

Conversely, his admiration for the coach who almost nabbed him is clear. When told at a recent autograph signing that we would be interviewing Crum, Chapman visibly brightened. "Tell him I said hello," he asked, before stating simply, "That's my guy."

In his office at the school he turned into a basketball powerhouse, nearly three decades after the lost recruiting battle, Crum mostly avoids being too wistful.

"When he left after his sophomore year, I was kind of sad to see him go, because I loved watching him play. I'm not a big NBA fan . . . but I always looked at the box scores to see how he was doing, because he was one of my favorite players that ever came out of the state of Kentucky."

The question hangs there, perhaps all the more palpably because he doesn't say it.

What if Rex had gone to Louisville?

It isn't hard to imagine Chapman running rampant through the NCAA with a frontcourt of Ellison, Crook, and Payne. Or to imagine him as the three-point shooter that Crum was missing. Or to see Louisville continuing the pace of four Final Four appearances in seven seasons. Maybe Allan Houston would've stayed in Louisville, and Cliff Rozier and Samaki Walker wouldn't have gone pro early. And maybe Louisville would've been the UCLA of the '80s and '90s.

This is the stuff of dreams for the Cardinal faithful, and the stuff of nightmares for the Wildcat faithful. But the question lingers there, as it always will.

What if Rex had gone to Louisville?

Kentucky 85

NAME	MIN	FG-FGA	3-3A	FT-FTA	OR-REB	PF	AST	STL	BLK	TO	TP
Chapman	35	10-20	5-8	1-3	0-0	2	4	2	0	2	26
Blackmon	24	4-7	3-3	0-2	0-1	2	2	2	0	1	11
Davender	35	5-13	1-3	5-7	2-8	1	5	0	0	1	16
Lock	25	4-5	0-0	1-1	0-7	4	0	1	1	2	9
Thomas	24	2-3	0-0	2-2	3-5	4	0	1	1	2	6
Madison	29	4-7	0-0	1-1	6-17	3	2	1	0	2	9
Miller	24	3-4	2-3	0-0	1-3	3	1	0	0	1	8
Shigg	2	0-0	0-0	0-0	0-0	0	0	0	0	0	0
Bruce	1	0-0	0-0	0-0	0-0	0	0	0	0	0	0
Jenkins	1	0-0	0-0	0-0	0-0	0	0	0	0	0	0
TEAM					0-0						
Total	200	32-59	11-17	10-16	12-41	19	14	7	2	11	85

Louisville 51

NAME	MIN	FG-FGA	3-3A	FT-FTA	OR-REB	PF	AST	STL	BLK	TO	TP
Payne	17	3-8	1-4	0-0	1-1	2	1	0	0	3	7
Crook	27	1-5	0-0	4-6	2-7	2	1	1	0	1	6
Ellison	26	2-8	0-0	0-0	1-4	0	1	0	3	3	4
Hawley	17	1-3	0-1	0-0	0-2	1	2	0	0	2	2
Kimbro	28	4-9	0-0	2-2	0-3	3	1	1	0	0	10
Abram	25	4-10	0-0	0-0	2-3	2	1	1	1	1	8
Williams	22	0-2	0-2	0-0	0-0	0	4	0	0	0	0
Spencer	15	4-7	0-0	2-6	3-5	0	0	0	0	1	10
McSwain	11	1-2	0-0	0-1	2-4	0	1	0	0	0	2
West	8	0-2	0-1	0-0	1-2	2	1	0	0	1	0
Marshall	4	1-2	0-0	0-0	1-1	1	0	1	0	0	2
TEAM					1-1						
Total	200	21-58	1-8	8-15	14-33	13	13	4	4	12	51

Chapter 7

A Matter of Inches and Seconds

No. 1 UK 76, UofL 75
December 12, 1987 at Rupp Arena

Pre-Game:

The 1987–88 rendition of the annual Dream Game did not appear likely to be a classic. Denny Crum's Cardinal squad was far removed from the group with which he had struck NCAA championship gold a year and a half prior. For only the second time since the renewal of the series, Louisville entered the game not ranked in the AP Poll's top-25. Tony Kimbro was academically ineligible for the season and Mark McSwain had completed his college career. Louisville was not without talent, however. Frontcourt standouts Pervis Ellison and Herb Crook were the centerpieces of the 1987–88 squad, and junior forward Kenny Payne joined them in the lineup. Talented freshman LaBradford Smith and solid sophomore Keith Williams rounded out the lineup. Louisville had lost their season opener 69-54, and coming off the previous season's difficulties, did not figure to provide much competition for Kentucky.

Eddie Sutton's Wildcats, on the other hand, were the top-ranked team in the nation. The Wildcats were 3-0, including a win in Indianapolis over No. 5 Indiana. Not only was Rex Chapman back for his sophomore season, but Winston Bennett had returned from his redshirt year, and he and Ed Davender promised steady senior leadership. Senior Rob Lock was a solid center, and the team rotated several players with that main group—including highly regarded freshmen Eric Manual and LeRon Ellis and journeymen seniors Richard Madison and Cedric Jenkins.

Jenkins was a tall forward from Georgia who had been a McDonald's All-America player in high school. He had nearly chosen Georgia Tech, recalling, "I really connected with Coach [Bobby] Cremins, [the then-coach at Georgia Tech], but the tradition and the exposure afforded at UK and all of that just kind of won out on me." Joe B. Hall's staff had recruited Jenkins, but Cedric had to adjust his game to fit Coach Sutton's style of play. Additionally, he had sustained a serious leg injury before the 1986–87 season—one that had both shortened his junior season and limited his effectiveness. Despite the adversity of his young career, Jenkins refused to give anything less than his best effort. "For me, the glass was always half-full," recalls Jenkins, "If not, why are you going to bother?" Coming into his senior season, Jenkins averaged just over a basket per game for his UK career. However, sometimes, one basket can make a world of difference.

The Game:

Kentucky came out of the gates in Rupp Arena looking like the No. 1 team in the country. While Winston Bennett was not primarily a scorer, on his final battle with his hometown opponent, he came out firing. Bennett put up 9 points in the game's first 8 minutes. Ed Davender also began the game with a scoring streak. Louisville hung in, and even led 19-17 before UK ran off 12 unanswered points. Davender had a three-point basket and a free throw during that run, and Eric Manuel added a pair of baskets as well. When Rex Chapman added two consecutive baskets, including a thunderous two-handed stuff off of a Louisville turnover, Kentucky's lead swelled to 45-29.

Just at the point when Kentucky seemed poised to blow the doors off, a funny thing happened. UofL's Kenny Payne drained a pivotal three-pointer seconds before halftime, trimming the lead to 13 points. When the second half began, momentum swung further toward the visitors, as Bennett and Rob Lock picked up quick fouls that relegated both to the bench. Against Jenkins, Madison, and Ellis, Louisville began to flex its interior muscle. While Kentucky had shot 46% in the first half, against the triangle-and-two defense Crum used to slow Davendar and Chapman, UK struggled to a 36% second-half mark. At the same time, UofL's shooting percentage went from 34% in the first stanza to a sizzling 64% in the second. Herbert Crook led the charge, totaling 24 points and 9 rebounds for the Cards. While Ellison started the game slowly, by the end, he managed 20 points, 13 rebounds, 5 assists, 4 steals, and 3 blocked shots. Kentucky's post players came unglued—with Bennett and Lock consigned to the bench, Ellis went into a tantrum after an offensive foul call and nearly lost his composure entirely. Only Jenkins continued to consistently battle with any success—the veteran endlessly hustled, screening, grabbing rebounds, and forcing Ellison into tough shots whenever possible.

Offensively, Kentucky countered with Chapman, who forced some difficult baskets against the triangle-and-two from Louisville. Fifteen of his 21 points came in the second half, and mostly on the strength of those baskets, UK clung to a 70-65 lead with just under three minutes remaining. Louisville went to its all-out pressure defense—forcing a trio of turnovers and answering with a basket from Crook and two from Payne—the latter another three-pointer, turning the count to 72-70 Louisville with 2:21 to play. Kentucky was understandably befuddled. "It would have been a travesty," Cedric Jenkins says, "to end up losing that game after controlling it for a good part of the first half."

Back and forth the game spun, as Louisville fought to make Jenkins's travesty a reality. Chapman made a foul shot to put UK ahead 74-73. On the ensuing Louisville possession, Ellison calmly sank a short baseline jumper to give UofL the 75-74 advantage. Kentucky ran down the clock and called for time with 11 seconds remaining.

"The exact play, I definitely don't remember," Jenkins admits. "But I think everybody in the gym knew who was going to be taking the last shot."

Rex Chapman, that intended shooter, concurs. "When we came out for the last play we'd drawn up a play that was supposed to go to me.

Pervis [Ellison] knew that. He actually came out and was ready to steal the ball if it came to me. So we had to end up getting the ball to someone else."

As the clock ticked down, Davender, stuck with the ball, dribbled right. Without a clear path, he leaned in from the right baseline and forced a short jumper as the seconds ticked away. The shot missed and a sea of hands went up, reaching, straining for victory. Cedric Jenkins was in the middle of that pack.

Cedric notes, "Being able to gauge how much time is really left is oftentimes a challenge, because what seems like a very little amount of time . . . is actually a very long time. So you go to the boards and there's still quite a few seconds and you know people are not boxed out, anything can happen."

Jenkins nudged the ball, and it hung on the rim tantalizingly before rolling off. With the internal clock pounding in his head, Jenkins stayed with the shot, skying once more. This time up, the roll of the ball off his fingertips was true and straight into the basket. Louisville frantically signaled for timeout as Jenkins's basket dropped through, but the clock expired. Cedric Jenkins had fought gamely for 32 minutes in his final UK/UofL game. He scrapped his way to 11 rebounds and even unselfishly handed out three assists. He also scored two points—the two points that made the difference between winning and losing.

Postgame:

For Jenkins, winning his last Dream Game carried "a sense of pride, a sense of bragging rights," he says. "You don't EVER want to lose that game." Today, Cedric has long since hung up his sneakers. He lives in Lexington with his family, where he is a realtor and owner of a nutritional supplement store.

The game isn't memorable only to Cedric. Of Denny Crum's dozen total Dream Game losses, the one that he admitted still sticks with him is Jenkins's big day. "You almost think, *I'd rather lose by twenty than get beat in a close one like that.*"

Joe B. Hall enjoyed the big moment of the young man he had recruited. "Cedric is . . . maybe too nice to be a competitive athlete, but he is a wonderful person," says Hall. "His timely basket that beat Louisville is a legacy that he'll carry with him forever."

✶✶✶✶✶

Kentucky won its first 10 games and hung around the top-10 for most of the season. The team won an SEC Tournament title and picked up two victories in the NCAA Tournament before a surprising Villanova team ended their season in the Sweet 16. Despite an 0-2 start, Louisville rallied to a 24-11 mark, winning a Metro Tournament title and also picking up two NCAA Tournament wins before bowing out in a Sweet 16 loss to eventual national runner-up Oklahoma.

Kentucky's biggest problems were of the off-court variety. Shortly after the season ended, an Emery freight package from the UK basketball offices to recruit Chris Mills apparently "fell open" in transit. The package allegedly contained cash, and began a very messy and acrimonious NCAA nightmare for the Kentucky program. As the investigation continued, Rex Chapman decided to forego his remaining NCAA eligibility and enter the NBA Draft. Eric Manuel was barred from NCAA college basketball, and Mills, after his freshman year, was not allowed to further play at Kentucky. These were dark days for Kentucky basketball, and in the short term, they would only get darker.

The Cardinals, however, returned Ellison, Payne, and Smith among others. While Kentucky struggled to survive, the Cardinals looked to thrive—and, more immediately, to gain some revenge.

Kentucky 76

NAME	MIN	FG-FGA	3-3A	FT-FTA	OR-REB	PF	AST	STL	BLK	TO	TP
Bennett	24	6-11	0-0	2-4	2-6	5	2	0	0	2	14
Jenkins	32	1-4	0-0	0-0	5-11	0	3	0	1	0	2
Lock	32	1-7	0-0	4-6	5-6	4	2	3	1	0	6
Chapman	37	8-15	2-7	3-4	1-3	1	2	1	0	3	21
Davender	34	7-14	2-3	4-4	0-2	3	3	2	0	2	20
Manuel	18	2-7	0-0	4-4	2-5	1	2	0	0	0	8
Miller	9	1-5	0-3	0-0	1-1	0	0	0	0	0	2
Madison	8	0-1	0-0	0-0	0-1	1	1	0	0	3	0
Ellis	6	1-1	0-0	1-2	0-1	2	0	1	0	1	3
TEAM					0-1						
Total	200	27-65	4-13	18-24	16-37	17	15	7	2	11	76

Louisville 75

NAME	MIN	FG-FGA	3-3A	FT-FTA	OR-REB	PF	AST	STL	BLK	TO	TP
Payne	36	4-9	2-5	0-0	1-5	5	1	1	0	0	10
Crook	36	10-16	0-0	4-6	4-9	3	1	1	0	3	24
Ellison	39	7-17	0-0	6-7	3-13	3	5	4	3	2	20
Williams	36	4-6	0-0	0-0	0-1	0	3	1	0	1	8
Smith	28	4-13	1-4	0-0	1-3	5	6	0	0	5	9
Abram	16	1-2	0-0	2-2	2-2	0	3	0	0	2	4
Spencer	9	0-0	0-0	0-0	0-0	2	2	0	0	1	0
TEAM					2-3						
Total	200	30-63	3-9	12-15	13-36	18	21	7	3	14	75

Chapter 8

A Never Nervous Whoopin'

No. 14 UofL 97, UK 75
December 31, 1988 at Freedom Hall

Pre-Game:

Pervis Ellison was meant to play at Louisville.

A long, lean, 6'9" center from Savannah, Georgia, Ellison ran an up-tempo style of basketball in high school, which enabled him to handle the ball and develop a quickness that most centers would not have.

The UofL offense, long based on featuring athletic big men, was an attractive option. Ellison decided to play for Denny Crum. And during the first practice in October, coaches knew what they had: a lethal combination of explosive player and the perfect system for him.

He also took a bit of Southern culture with him to the Louisville campus. His favorite food? Roast duck, according to *Sports Illustrated*. He played three instruments: piano, tuba, and trombone. But it was basketball that made him a star.

In his first year, Ellison's star grew brighter than any freshman's ever had. With Milt Wagner, Billy Thompson, and crew, Ellison led the Cards to their second national championship, defeating Duke. Ellison scored 25 points and grabbed 11 rebounds on the way to winning Most

Outstanding Player of the Final Four. His nickname was "Never Nervous" Pervis. Denny Crum's nickname was "Cool Hand Luke."

Clearly they were made for each other.

Ellison's presence would set the Cards up for four consecutive years of national prominence. In 1988, Louisville was 6-2, ranked No. 14 in the country, and rolling with the success that comes from a recent national championship. Still, they had extra motivations for wanting to beat Kentucky. Just two years prior, Kentucky had laid the worst of whoopings on the Cards— an 85-51 blowout that still smarted, according to the losing team.

For Kentucky it was a different story. Plagued by the swirling storm of a scandal, the Cats were trying to hold their team together. Still, there was talent. Chris Mills was a long, athletic forward. LeRon Ellis played big under the basket, and sharpshooter Derrick Miller provided relief from beyond the arc. But there was little depth in the UK lineup. Somerset native Reggie Hanson played forward while Sean Sutton, son of Coach Eddie Sutton, played the point. Mike Scott, Deron Feldhaus, and Richie Farmer rounded out the regulars.

It was not an overly athletic squad. Gone were Rex Chapman and Winston Bennett, off to the NBA. Rob Lock and Ed Davender were gone, too. Other stars were gone because of grades or the aforementioned scandal. UK sat at 5-6, with losses to Northwestern State and Bowling Green, and their record did not get much better.

If there was ever a time to take advantage of an undermanned UK team, this was it—December 31, 1988 at Freedom Hall. And Louisville was ready to do just that.

Pervis Ellison would lead the way, but he wouldn't be alone. Another star from Savannah would prove to be the only answer for UK.

The Game:

The list of UofL stars went on and on down the roster: Ellison, Kenny Payne, Tony Kimbro, LaBradford Smith, Everick Sullivan, Cornelius Holden, Felton Spencer, James Brewer.

They were athletic and deep. Coach Crum knew exactly how he would play Kentucky—he would wear them out. He would force them to play UofL's up-tempo style, and in the course of that play, Kentucky would wilt.

For this game, Crum could have been a prophet.

"We made them play our game," Crum told the *Lexington Herald-Leader*. "We didn't let them stand around. They had to play up-tempo. That was the most important thing. Make them play 94 feet."

"Anytime you play 94 feet, you've got to give some things up," Crum said. "We thought [Miller] would be their best and probably only guy that would take many shots out there. We didn't feel he could beat us alone. They'd have to beat us inside."

That was not something Kentucky could do.

Eddie Sutton tried to play a 2-3 zone defense to take away Louisville's athleticism. His thought was the Cardinal guards could not shoot well from outside—and the Cats would force Louisville to try. Citing a game against Vanderbilt earlier in the season where the Commodores employed the same strategy and beat UofL 65-62, Sutton thought it was UK's best chance to win.

But Kimbro and Sullivan proved the Kentucky coach wrong.

Five of Louisville's first six baskets (including their first four of the game) were three-pointers over that zone.

Kentucky could hit the three-ball as well. Sean Sutton hit one, and Derrick Miller, a 6'6" junior Parade All-America player from Savannah, hit two to keep things close with the Cards. With nine minutes to go, Kentucky had just one turnover and trailed by only four points, 27-23.

Then Louisville went on a defensive run, changing their pressure to more of a trapping style once the Wildcats crossed half-court. The Cards forced 8 turnovers over the course of the next 8 minutes, and converted those swipes into points, putting together a 17-6 run to effectively put the game away, 44-29. By halftime, Louisville was rolling, 50-35.

The question then was, could UofL best that 34-point blowout from two years before?

Twice in the second half, Kentucky rallied to within 12, led by the three-point shooting of Miller. But each time, Louisville's defense came up huge, forcing turnovers (Kentucky would give the ball away 17 times) and converting them into points.

Ellison led the way from the inside, scoring 20 points and grabbing 7 rebounds. Several times in the second half, the game looked like warm-ups for the NBA Dunk Contest. Kimbro and Sullivan combined to go 5-for-8 from behind the three-point line, single-handedly stopping the UK zone defense.

Louisville's game plan and overall athleticism were too much for UK. Miller poured in a nice effort, though—34 points on 13-of-26 shooting from the floor, including five three-pointers. Chris Mills added 13 points and 10 rebounds, as he was actively fighting for the ball on the inside. Ellison completely shut down UK center LeRon Ellis, who somehow managed 7 points.

Louisville's Pervis Ellison lives up to his never-nervous nickname. Ellison won a national title as a freshman, but had to wait until his senior season to win The Dream Game.

(Photo appears courtesy of University of Louisville Athletics)

Other players contributed for UofL besides just Sullivan and Kimbro. Payne dropped 16 points and Smith added 15. By the time the second half wound down, Kentucky hit free throws to cut the lead, but the Cards still recorded their worst beating over Kentucky, 97-75. It didn't quite match the 34 points by which UK had previously won, but this victory was sweet for Louisville.

Postgame:

Louisville went on to another successful year in what became a great run. They finished 24-9, won the Metro Conference tourney, and lost to third-ranked Illinois in the Sweet Sixteen. Kentucky struggled through its worst season since before Adolph Rupp was coach and finished with a 13-19 record. No NCAA Tournament. No postseason play of any kind.

Kentucky Coach Eddie Sutton, shown with Wildcat guard Roger Harden. Sutton was 3-1 in the Dream Game, but his Kentucky legacy lies mostly in the NCAA violations that forced him out of Lexington.

(Photo by Jamie Vaught, appears courtesy of the Somerset Commonwealth Journal)

At the end of the year the NCAA wrath would be felt with probation, the firing of a coach, and the departure of many of the program's best players, including Ellis, Sutton, and Mills.

It was the lowest point ever for the Wildcats. The road to basketball redemption would begin with a new head coach. Newly hired athletic director C. M. Newton studied the situation carefully, considering Arizona's Lute Olson and Seton Hall's P. J. Carlesimo, among others. But frankly, Newton struggled to find the right kind of coach who would accept what was then very much the toughest basketball job in America. As Newton was beginning to wonder if he might not have to coach the squad himself in the 1989–90 season, he instead found his man—a million-dollar coach with a penchant for flashy suits and city living. He hired Rick Pitino, and the rest is history.

Unlike many of his heralded teammates, Derrick Miller stuck it out to become one of the rebuilders of the Kentucky team under new Coach Rick Pitino. He scored more than 1,000 points and was named All-SEC First Team as a senior.

On the other side of things, Louisville was, inarguably, on top of the basketball world (at least in Kentucky).

Kenny Payne became one of the legends of Louisville basketball. He became a first-round draft pick of the Philadelphia 76ers and played 11 seasons professionally. He then went on to become one of the great recruiters in college basketball. For five years he recruited for Oregon, then, in 2010, he was hired at Kentucky. Under John Calipari, Payne helped UK land the No. 1 recruiting class for four consecutive years.

Pervis Ellison is generally regarded as one of the greatest players to ever wear the Louisville uniform. After becoming a first-team All-America selection in 1989, he was the No. 1 pick in the 1989 NBA Draft by the Sacramento Kings, but injuries plagued his career. He stayed in the NBA for 11 seasons, his best being his third, when he averaged 20 points, 11.4 rebounds, and 2.68 blocks per games.

After retiring from the NBA in 2000, Ellison went into coaching, first in the AAU leagues in Philadelphia, then at Life Center Academy in Burlington, New Jersey. There he began his career as an assistant before being named head coach in 2013.

"To have a coach with Pervis Ellison's experience is a wonderful benefit for our program and players," Life Center athletic director David Boudwin said in a press release. "We look forward to a great season and exciting future for Life Center basketball."

Coach Pervis will undoubtedly live up to his Never Nervous nickname if his teams can deliver the kind of beatings that Louisville did to Kentucky back on New Year's Eve of 1988.

Louisville 97

NAME	MIN	FG-FGA	3-3A	FT-FTA	REB	PF	AST	STL	BLK	TO	TP
Payne	33	5-8	1-3	5-6	5	2	2	0	1	2	16
Kimbro	27	4-7	3-4	0-0	3	0	1	2	0	0	11
Ellison	31	8-16	0-1	4-5	7	4	3	1	2	1	20
Williams	28	2-7	0-3	0-0	1	2	5	2	0	2	4
Smith	29	3-5	1-3	8-8	2	4	8	1	0	3	15
Sullivan	19	5-10	2-4	3-4	6	1	4	0	0	1	15
Holden	15	1-1	0-0	2-2	4	0	0	0	1	1	4
Spencer	10	1-1	0-0	4-4	1	5	0	0	1	1	6
Brewer	7	2-4	0-2	0-1	5	3	1	0	0	1	4
Hawley	1	1-1	0-0	0-0	1	0	0	0	0	0	2
TEAM											
Total	200	32-60	7-20	26-30	35	21	24	6	5	12	97

Kentucky 75

NAME	MIN	FG-FGA	3-3A	FT-FTA	REB	PF	AST	STL	BLK	TO	TP
Hanson	30	4-6	0-0	3-3	4	4	4	1	0	2	11
Mills	34	4-9	0-1	5-7	10	4	4	2	0	3	13
Ellis	36	3-7	0-0	1-4	5	5	1	1	2	3	7
Miller	39	13-26	5-14	3-3	4	4	1	1	0	4	34
Sutton	38	3-6	1-2	0-0	3	3	3	0	0	4	7
Scott	12	0-3	0-0	3-4	2	4	2	0	0	0	3
Feldhaus	9	0-1	0-0	0-0	1	1	0	0	0	0	0
Farmer	2	0-0	0-0	0-0	0	0	0	0	0	1	0
TEAM					2						
Total	200	27-58	6-17	15-21	31	25	15	5	2	17	75

Chapter 9

Cardinals Rule

No. 8 UofL 86, UK 79
December 30, 1989 at Rupp Arena

Pre-Game:

It doesn't matter, according to LaBradford Smith. The records? Disregard them. The level of talent? Pay no attention.

When two teams like Louisville and Kentucky meet in their annual rivalry, you can expect both squads—no matter how good they're supposed to be—to bring an extra level of enthusiasm into the game.

"You always just knew, if we were having a bad season or they were, it was going to be a tough game," says Smith, a former Louisville star. "You had to come ready to play. If you didn't, you'd find out real quick—the game against Kentucky meant more."

But what was interesting, Smith says, is how players from other parts of the country had to learn about the rivalry. And learn they did—quickly.

"I came from Texas, and I didn't know anything about Louisville and Kentucky," Smith says. "But when I came to play in Louisville, the fans tell you all the time, 'Beat Kentucky. Beat UK.' You learn how important it is to the fans. I think it's almost more important to them than it is to the players. And there's so many UK fans in Louisville, too. You hear about that game a lot."

Smith says he knew of the tradition of the two schools, but he knew very little about the rivalry. In the late 1980s and early '90s, as UofL and UK continued to recruit on a national level, high schoolers learned about the Louisville/Kentucky game thanks to national television. But they didn't know what it felt like to play in the game. That was entirely different.

After playing in previous UK and UofL contests, Smith learned what the game meant, specifically to the players. All wanted to win badly, whether they were supposed to or not.

"It's big bragging rights for the whole year, and we had friends on the UK team," Smith says.

*****

There was no better example of the haves playing the have-nots than when eighth-ranked Louisville came to Rupp Arena on December 30, 1989. Kentucky, on probation, had to make do with its depleted roster. Derrick Miller, the prolific scorer, led a ragtag group of players like John Pelphrey, Richie Farmer, Reggie Hanson, and Deron Feldhaus, all of whom hailed from Kentucky, with Sean Woods, who was from Indiana, but had spent time growing up with family in Lexington.

Their coach was not from Kentucky—far from it. Previously the head coach of the New York Knicks and Providence College, Rick Pitino accepted the task of rebuilding Kentucky in 1989. He employed a frenetic style of three-point shooting and pressing defenses. That ultimately won over the rabid fan base. Unfortunately for Kentucky and its fans, they did not have a wealth of talent. But, as LaBradford Smith said, it would be unwise to underestimate a rival.

Pitino said as much himself. The brash New Yorker knew he had to reunite a fractured fan base. Part of that included talking big—and believing it. In his first press conference he promised UK would win, and that they would win right away. Few fans thought it could actually happen. But then the Big Blue Nation started seeing the product, and immediately they fell in love with their new team. With the combination of this fearless new coach and his players, it seemed like anything was possible.

Louisville, on the other hand, was built for success. A top-10 team, led by a 7' center (and Louisville native) Felton Spencer, the Cardinals were ready to make a run in the NCAA Tournament. But Smith and teammates Tony Kimbro, Everick Sullivan, Keith Williams, Jerome Harmon, and Cornelius Holden came into Rupp Arena for the annual Dream Game with another goal: to become the first modern Louisville team to win in Lexington (the last time the Cards won there was in 1922).

Kentucky came into the contest with a 5-4 record, with losses to No. 14 Indiana (71-69), No. 24 North Carolina (121-110), and No. 2 Kansas (150-95). Still, most felt Pitino had done well in winning five ballgames (including victories over Ohio University and Mississippi State). Legendary UK broadcaster Cawood Ledford predicted the Cats would only win five games all season. They had lost two games in a row before playing Louisville.

Louisville was 8-1 with victories over Vanderbilt and 19th-ranked Notre Dame. Their only loss was by three points to 11th-ranked Missouri in the Maui Classic. Denny Crum always wanted to play the best teams, and the 1989–90 season would be no different. But they did have 12 days since their last game.

As the Cards traveled to Lexington, they did not expect that one of their toughest tests that season would come from the down-on-their-luck Wildcats. But as LaBradford Smith says, they should have.

The Game:

Kentucky made the first basket to take a 2-0 lead. That did not make Louisville very happy, but it did excite the 24,089 mostly UK fans in attendance. The aggressive Cards—and Smith in particular—played defense a bit too well, and Sean Woods of UK took exception. With 17 minutes to go in the first half, Derrick Miller apparently took offense to Smith's defense and told him so.

Smith then responded with taunts of his own. "You don't just let someone say anything they want," Smith explained in a recent interview.

Woods then shoved Smith, who responded with a shove, and both were given technical fouls. No one was ejected.

"[The Cardinals] have an attitude that they're not going to be pushed around," Miller told the *Lexington Herald-Leader*. "Well, we're not going to be pushed around, either."

Louisville's strategy was simple: limit the UK three-point shooting. If they were going to shoot them, make it difficult. Defensively, be aggressive. And let Smith handle UK's press.

It was all Cards at the start, as they rushed out to a 19-8 lead. Louisville was bigger and more athletic, and their defense suffocated UK early, especially from beyond the arc, as UK missed its first eight shots. In fact, the Wildcats made only 1 of their first 14 threes, but eventually, Kentucky heated up. It made sense when high school legend Farmer hit a three. It made less sense when Kentucky's pseudo-center Reggie Hanson hit one—the first of four threes he would hit that night.

But it was Smith for Louisville who could probably lay claim to being the best athlete on the floor. He navigated UK's press, drew fouls from the Cats, and guarded Woods.

Kentucky's three's cut the Louisville lead to two, 32-30. UK combated the Cards' defense by using Princeton-style backdoor cuts to the hoop and beating Louisville on the boards—especially the offensive end. The problem for Kentucky? Not enough players. Kentucky had just two reserves who played more than one minute—Farmer and Jeff Brassow.

Crum noted his team played good initial defense, but the Cards looked to fast-break too much on missed shots and gave up offensive boards. By halftime, Louisville had again established control, 42-35.

The three-point shot then helped UK again. Another three by Hanson regained the lead for the Cats with 17:00 to play. For the next six minutes, Louisville would find itself in a dogfight.

Down 60-59, Keith Williams beat his man and drove to the hoop to take the lead back for the Cards. Cornelius Holden added two buckets as part of an 11-2 Louisville run. With less than five minutes to go, the Cards led just 70-66—much too close for comfort.

Then Jerome Harmon drove to score 2 of his 16 points, and Smith stole the ball twice from Hanson to keep the lead a two-possession game. Smith, who finished 10-of-11 from the free throw line, helped clinch the win as Louisville went 8-for-8 over the final three minutes. The Cards finally got their victory in Lexington, 86-79.

Kentucky, which had taken as many as 53 three's in a game, was held to 29 attempts, and they only made 9.

Smith led his team with 22 points and 4 assists, while Sullivan scored 16 and Williams added 15.

Hanson led all scorers with 24 points, and also chipped in 6 rebounds and 3 steals. Derrick Miller added 13, and Deron Feldhaus scored 9 points, grabbed 16 rebounds, and had 3 steals. Louisville did out-rebound Kentucky, but only by two, 35-33. The Cards also had a season-high 24 turnovers.

Still, as the Louisville players said, a win is a win.

"To come away with a victory, by 1 point or 50, doesn't make much difference; I'm pleased," Denny Crum told the *Lexington Herald-Leader*. "It's a good victory. There aren't any bad victories. I didn't know how my team would play coming in here after 12 days off. Certainly, we didn't play as well as we're capable. I think we can play a lot better. But we won."

In an odd occurrence, the coach of the losing team was also pleased.

"The only thing we had a problem with was we had guys like Reggie Hanson, Derrick Miller, and Deron Feldhaus play too many minutes," Rick Pitino said. "You can't play that aggressive and that hard with a press for that long. I feel bad how I'm getting after them during the timeouts to reach back and suck it up. I don't think I've had a group work so hard. I can't tell you how proud of them I am. It's almost not human to do what they're doing."

Postgame:

Afterward, every new player on each side knew what it was like to play in the Dream Game.

Kentucky would go on to finish their season 14-14, with memorable wins over No. 25 Alabama and No. 9 LSU. All in all, Wildcat supporters had to view the season as a success. Pitino had started things off right.

For Louisville, the Cards finished an impressive 27-8 on the season before being upset by Ball State in the second round of the NCAA Tournament, 62-60.

LaBradford Smith went on to become one of the great guards in UofL history. He was selected in the first round—19th overall—by the Washington Bullets in the 1991 NBA Draft and played in the NBA until 1994. He even became famous for once scoring 37 points on Michael Jordan in 1993. Smith played in various pro leagues until 2000, and now he runs several companies in the Louisville area, including a car detail shop, a lawn service, and an apartment complex.

"My dad always told me, 'Why have one paycheck when you can have two?'" Smith says, laughing.

Smith loves recalling those rivalry games and how tough they were.

And not a day goes by, he says, without someone asking about basketball.

"It was especially big to beat [UK] in Rupp," he says. "To beat them on their turf, that's a little extra—that gives all the fans a little something more to hold on to."

Louisville 86

NAME	MIN	FG-FGA	3-3A	FT-FTA	REB	PF	AST	STL	BLK	TO	TP
Sullivan	37	4-11	2-5	6-8	6	2	2	0	0	5	16
Kimbro	13	1-2	0-0	0-0	2	1	0	0	0	2	2
Spencer	26	3-4	0-0	1-2	6	4	3	0	4	3	7
L. Smith	38	6-9	0-1	10-11	0	3	4	2	0	4	22
Williams	33	7-8	1-2	0-0	5	4	2	3	0	4	15
Harmon	29	7-14	0-1	2-2	6	0	3	3	0	3	16
Holden	23	3-4	0-0	2-4	7	1	0	0	1	3	8
T. Smith	3	0-0	0-0	0-0	1	0	0	0	0	0	0
TEAM					2						
Total	200	31-52	3-9	21-27	35	15	14	8	5	24	86

Kentucky 79

NAME	MIN	FG-FGA	3-3A	FT-FTA	REB	PF	AST	STL	BLK	TO	TP
Pelphrey	22	4-8	0-2	3-4	4	4	0	1	0	1	11
Feldhaus	37	3-13	1-3	2-2	16	5	2	3	0	4	9
Hanson	39	8-21	4-11	4-6	6	3	2	3	1	5	24
Miller	36	5-14	2-8	1-2	2	2	0	0	0	0	13
Woods	25	3-7	0-0	0-1	1	1	7	4	0	3	6
Farmer	20	4-7	2-4	0-0	1	2	9	3	0	2	10
Brassow	19	3-7	0-1	0-0	2	4	1	1	0	1	6
Davis	1	0-1	0-0	0-0	0	0	0	0	0	0	0
McGaw	1	0-0	0-0	0-0	0	0	0	0	0	0	0
TEAM					1						
Total	200	30-78	9-29	10-15	33	21	21	15	1	16	79

Chapter 10

Back on Top

No. 18 UK 93, UofL 85
December 29, 1990 at Freedom Hall

Pre-Game:

A mere year and a half before the December 1990 edition of the Dream Game, the rivalry appeared likely to be dead in the water. An 11-19 Kentucky team that had lost by 22 points to Louisville lost most of its best players and was placed on probation for two years. Meanwhile, the Cardinal program that had amassed four Final Fours and two NCAA titles in the last decade seemed unshakable. But a funny thing happened on the way to the Freedom Hall matchup four days after Christmas 1990.

For one thing, Pitino had revitalized Kentucky in record time. Not only had his system of full-court pressure and three-point bombing made the Wildcats surprisingly competitive, but now, his recruiting touch was also paying dividends. Freshman forward Jamal Mashburn was UK's first legitimate NBA prospect since the pre-probation era.

This is not to say that Pitino did not have his own recruiting issues— mostly his program's ghosts more than his team's current situation. He was locked in a fierce recruiting battle over Louisville star Dwayne Morton. Pitino later told Eddie Einhorn in the book *How March Became Madness*,

"The one big problem we had in recruiting at Kentucky was a bitterness about race. . . . [W]hen we were trying to get Dwayne Morton . . . I went to talk to his family and gave his big speech about why he should play for us. His grandmother was listening and she said, 'Coach Pitino, I'm a big fan of yours.' I smiled, thinking we were in, and then she said, 'But every time I see those boys go on the court and step on that man's name, we applaud in this household.'" Pitino continued, "She meant Adolph Rupp . . . and that was when I really understood the opinion of African Americans locally about Kentucky. . . . We lost Morton to Louisville."

Recruiting snafus aside, in year two, Pitino's squad still bombed away from three-point range, attempting an average of just over 25 long-distance attempts per game. When the shots went down, Kentucky's relative lack of talent and depth were neatly camouflaged. The Wildcats, who were 7-2 on the season and ranked 18th in the AP poll, returned senior Reggie Hanson, an all-SEC pick, as well as juniors Sean Woods, Richie Farmer, Deron Feldhaus, and John Pelphrey, who was also tabbed for all-SEC honors. All five of those players were native Kentuckians, with the exception of Woods. The speedy point guard from Indianapolis had watched Dream Game I as a pre-teen and recalled, "I liked those guards that Louisville had. Louisville was a real electrifying, exciting team to watch back then." Louisville had been one of the first teams to recruit Woods, but his mother hailed from Lexington and his grandmother still lived there. Due to his strong family ties, Woods landed with the Wildcats.

Down Interstate 64, Denny Crum was having his own recruiting problems. Recruiting guru Bob Gibbons had ranked UofL's recruiting class as No. 3 in the nation. However, that was before Louisville's top four recruits—all ranked within Gibbons's top-45 listing of the best incoming freshmen in the nation—all failed to qualify academically. Forward Dwayne Morton, guard Greg Minor, and center Brian Hopgood all enrolled as Proposition 48 casualties and were forced to miss the season. But the class's crown jewel, Gibbons's second-best player in the nation, forward Anthony Cade, would never play a minute at Louisville, transferring to a junior college and later entering the NBA Draft, where he was not chosen. Cade, who was projected as a better player than Mashburn,

Grant Hill, or Anfernee Hardaway, among others, could have been the poster child of Louisville basketball in the 1990s. But it was not to be.

Louisville entered the annual Dream Game with a 5-1 record, but the squad was unranked. Guards LaBradford Smith and Everick Sullivan returned, and with forward Cornelius Holden, totaled three Cards who had each averaged double-figure scoring totals during the previous season. Sophomores James Brewer and Troy Smith rounded out the UofL lineup. Louisville's squad would have been even stronger had it included Jerome Holden, a prep superstar who had missed two years due to academic ineligibility and back surgery before turning in a fine campaign in 1989–90 and bolting to the NBA as the first "one and done" in the history of this rivalry. Also, Crum's squad, which shot less than 13 three-point shots in an average game, could have used the long-range gunning of Alan Houston, who instead drained 99 treys and scored 23.7 points per game in his sophomore season at Tennessee. Houston had initially signed with the Cardinals before his father, UofL alum Wade Houston, was hired for the Tennessee head coaching position.

And by the combination of Pitino's upward momentum and Crum's bad luck, instead of Louisville gaining a permanent foothold in the rivalry, after two consecutive losses, Kentucky entered Freedom Hall intent on moving back on top of the rivalry. Sean Woods particularly looked forward to the challenge. Playing Louisville was fun, Woods says. "It was my type of game; it was going to be up and down."

The Game:

When the game began, Louisville moved out on the offensive, with LaBradford Smith taking flight. Smith established himself early and finished the game with game highs of 26 points and 11 rebounds. Cornelius Holden also played a formidable game in the post, totaling 22 points and 8 rebounds despite foul trouble, which limited him to 26 minutes. Louisville jumped out to an 11-7 advantage in the game's opening minutes.

As for Kentucky, the Wildcats had hit just 14-of-66 three-point attempts in their last two games, and missed their first three long-distance shots in this game. Center Reggie Hanson dropped in a triple from the top of the key to end that streak. And with that, Kentucky was off. Deron Feldhaus banked in a three-pointer. Sophomore guard Jeff Brassow knocked down three first-half treys, and Richie Farmer got into the act, draining 4-of-5 shots from deep to give Kentucky a 39-28 halftime advantage. The Cats were 9-of-19 in the first half from three-point range and led despite scoring only 12 points from inside the three-point arc.

In the locker room at the half, Louisville changed its defensive strategy. Enough sagging off the three-point shooters; it was time to challenge Kentucky on their jump shots. This was exactly the opportunity for which Sean Woods had been waiting. The senior had been scoreless in the first half. That changed quickly in the second stanza. Woods was not a three-point threat—he recalled Pitino limiting him on three-point shots and admits, "I still liked to score, so my thing was, if I could get layups, that's what I tried to do. . . . If [Louisville] stayed on the shooters, I could get to the rim."

While Kentucky made only four three-point shots in the second half, Woods had a field day, driving the ball relentlessly to the basket. At one point, he scored eight consecutive points, as Kentucky's lead bulged to 59-39. The two teams raced up and down the Freedom Hall floor, scoring almost at will in a 57-54 second half.

When the dust settled, Kentucky won 93-85, and Woods had totaled 20 second-half points. Louisville had out rebounded the Cats 42-35 and attempted 31 free throws to 17 for Kentucky. But in the end, Louisville had been beaten in the first half when they took away the drive, and thanks to Woods, beaten in the second half when they tightened up on UK's shooters. Rick Pitino admitted to the *Lexington Herald-Leader* after the game, "I don't think this team can play any better."

Louisville's winning streak was over, and Kentucky's had just begun.

Postgame:

Kentucky went on to a 22-6 record, finishing with the best record in the SEC. While the Wildcats were ineligible for the official SEC crown, the season represented another step in Rick Pitino's quest to return his team to their rightful place at the top of the heap of college basketball. The team would be off probation in 1991–92, and Woods, along with

Farmer, Feldhaus, and Pelphrey would finally get their shot in the NCAA Tournament.

Louisville's season, however, turned into a near nightmare. The Cardinals lost their next five games, and after squeaking past Tulane and South Alabama, they lost five more. However, with the season almost totally ruined, Louisville nearly snuck into the NCAA Tournament, upsetting No. 22 Southern Miss and Metro Conference rival Memphis State before falling in the tournament Final to Florida State. The 14-16 season was Louisville's first losing campaign since 1941–42. The Cardinals took solace in the impending return of Morton, who had been the subject of a fierce recruiting battle with Kentucky, and Minor. There were brighter days ahead.

For Sean Woods, after two tough years at Kentucky, the brighter days had arrived. Two decades later, Woods can take the long view of the rivalry now. "We always were ready for that game," he says. "It was a state deal—the Kentucky fans against the Louisville fans."

Woods is now the head coach at Morehead State, and he created a small firestorm within the UK community when he was critical of Kentucky's players and their lack of appreciation of the heritage of the program before his Eagles played the Wildcats in 2012. Woods explains that his comments were more general than they were taken. "That's across the board. Young kids—period—don't know the history of any school they're playing for, for the most part." Of course, Woods and his Unforgettable teammates form a significant part of UK history. When asked about that team, Woods comments, "We were a bunch of guys that loved each other and played for each other, and it gets better and better with time now."

Kentucky 93

NAME	MIN	FG-FGA	3-3A	FT-FTA	REB	PF	AST	STL	BLK	TP
Mashburn	21	1-5	0-0	4-4	10	4	1	0	0	6
Pelphrey	32	3-10	1-5	0-0	7	3	5	1	0	7
Hanson	29	7-13	1-2	2-4	8	4	2	0	2	17
Woods	32	7-13	0-0	6-6	2	3	4	1	0	20
Brassow	24	6-12	6-11	0-0	2	3	0	4	0	18
Feldhaus	24	2-5	1-2	1-1	2	3	1	0	0	6
Farmer	20	5-8	4-5	0-0	3	3	3	0	0	14
Braddy	11	2-4	0-1	1-2	0	1	2	1	0	5
Martinez	6	0-0	0-0	0-0	0	0	0	0	0	0
Bearup	1	0-0	0-0	0-0	0	0	0	0	0	0
TEAM					1					
Total	200	33-70	13-26	14-17	35	24	18	7	2	93

Louisville 85

NAME	MIN	FG-FGA	3-3A	FT-FTA	REB	PF	AST	STL	BLK	TP
Holden	26	9-12	0-0	4-5	8	4	0	0	1	22
Sullivan	30	2-13	1-6	2-2	5	3	3	0	1	7
T. Smith	28	2-3	0-0	0-0	3	2	0	1	1	4
Brewer	19	2-7	1-3	1-2	2	1	2	0	1	6
L. Smith	38	9-19	1-4	7-9	11	2	3	4	0	26
Stone	21	1-4	0-0	9-10	5	2	4	0	0	11
Wingfield	15	1-2	0-0	1-2	3	0	1	0	1	3
Webb	13	3-3	0-0	0-1	2	2	0	1	0	6
Case	10	0-2	0-2	0-0	1	1	0	1	1	0
TEAM					2					
Total	200	29-65	3-15	24-31	42	17	13	7	6	85

Chapter 11

Pelphrey, Motivated

No. 17 UK 103, No. 21 UofL 89
December 28, 1991 at Rupp Arena

Pre-Game:

"You cannot put into words what it's like to play in that game," says John Pelphrey, the native of Paintsville and former Mr. Basketball who grew up a Wildcat fan. "Kentucky fans expect to win every single game. But if there was one game, for lack of a better way to put it, that they would rather win, it would be that game versus Louisville. And certainly that trickles down to the players. Players on both sides figure that out.

"But when you have players on either team who are from the state, they really, really understand how big it is."

Pelphrey remembers when he was 14 and watched the original Dream Game in the NCAA Tournament in 1983.

"Myself, and a lot of other players . . . grew up watching those games on TV," he said. "When they played in the '83 NCAA Tournament, I can still remember plays that were not made for us that lost the game for us that day. I remember it being held in the old field house down in Tennessee. These things leave a lasting impression, especially for me as a kid wanting to grow up and play at Kentucky."

Pelphrey got to live his dream. He led his Paintsville team to the state Final Four before losing to eventual state champion Ballard; then he accepted a scholarship to play for the Wildcats.

Of course, it turned out to be a difficult time at UK. Kentucky was found to be paying recruits, among other misdeeds, and the school was placed on probation. Pelphrey would have one chance to play in an NCAA Tournament—his senior year of 1991–92. Things began to turn around when Rick Pitino was hired. A talented player from New York named Jamal Mashburn came into the program. Suddenly, UK was good again.

By December 28, 1991, the team was 7-2, ranked No. 17, with wins over No. 9 Indiana and Coach John Calipari's up-and-coming UMass squad and losses to Pitt and at No. 13 Georgia Tech.

Louisville was in rebuilding mode. Coming off a 14-16 season, the Cards needed an influx of talent, and while the 1991 squad was young, it did indeed have talent. There was homegrown star Dwayne Morton, who chose to play at Louisville over UK. Greg Minor, Cornelius Holden, Everick Sullivan, and James "Boo" Brewer made up a nice core of players who were ready to get the program back on the right track.

The Cards were ranked No. 21 and sat 6-0, with close wins at Notre Dame and LSU. It was clear this team had the chance to be very, very good. It could win on the road, but traveling to Rupp Arena can often be a different matter.

Kentucky's chances, as always, depended on their outside shooting and the inside-outside play of Mashburn. Over their past few games, the Cats had connected on only 11-of-43 three-point attempts. But everyone knew they would just keep shooting. Louisville wanted to use its athleticism and strength on the inside to its advantage.

But this game had an even deeper meaning to Pelphrey. In the week leading up to the matchup, there was the normal amount of trash-talking and media coverage. Then, Henry Hoening, a journalist from the University of Louisville student newspaper, wrote a column saying Louisville would be playing "the lowest form of life" in Rupp. He then directed his ire to Pelphrey, describing the player as "pointy-headed and limp-wristed."

"It was poking fun at our team," Pelphrey said. "It called us out. The coaches made a ton of copies of that and put it everywhere."

In a game where players needed no further motivation, Pelphrey had gotten an even bigger dose.

"You've gotta understand something else: the last three years for us, our fans showed up and cheered like everything was a championship," Pelphrey said. "They knew that with everything going on—players leaving, coaching changes—for us to have a chance to win, they were going to have to be a huge part of the game.

"So I can't even tell you the emotion and excitement and energy that was in that building—I vividly remember that."

The Game:

It started off poorly for Kentucky. Point guard Sean Woods earned two fouls just four minutes into the game, forcing him to the bench for the rest of the half.

Enter Pelphrey, who made his presence known immediately. Pel, as he was known to teammates, had hit just 1-of-10 from behind the arc in his past two games. Frustrated and motivated, he hit four threes in the first seven minutes against Louisville.

"It seems like against Louisville, they seem to make them," UofL Coach Denny Crum told the *Lexington Herald-Leader*. "That's a mark of a good team. They rise to the occasion."

The third-largest crowd to ever watch a game in Rupp Arena (24,295) saw Kentucky earn 15 personal fouls in the first half. And, as expected, Louisville used its size to control the boards. On their first five possessions, the Cards got offensive rebounds.

But UK once again found its shooting eyes against its intrastate foe. The previous season, Kentucky had hit 13-of-26 from three. Pelphrey led the way again, as the Cats hit 7 of their first 8 treys in Rupp.

"We came out and did exactly what we did not want to do," Louisville senior Everick Sullivan told the Associated Press. "We did not want to give them open three-pointers."

After two consecutive threes by Pelphrey, and a dish to Mashburn for a dunk, UK held a 29-19 lead at the 12:59 mark, and the Rupp Arena crowd was ravenous.

"It was so loud," Cornelius Holden told the *Herald-Leader*. "A lot of times we were talking and [our teammates] didn't hear."

In the next minute, Pelphrey was sent to the bench with his second foul. But the deluge continued, as UK center Gimel Martinez canned the first three of his career.

With under 7:00 to play in the half, Kentucky had its biggest lead, 47-33. But the shooting cooled, and Louisville went on a 10-0 run to cut the lead to 4 with 2:00 to go. Richie Farmer then hit a three to give the Cats more breathing room.

Louisville's massive rebounding edge kept them in the game. At the half, Kentucky led 54-45.

In the second half, the hot shooting continued. Pelphrey poured in a game-high 26, while Mashburn added 25. Dale Brown scored 16 of his own and Richie Farmer chipped in 10. Overall, UK hit 11-of-21 three's and shot 54 percent overall.

But the young Cards wouldn't go away. Nine Cardinals scored at least five points, with Greg Minor leading the way with 18. Sullivan added 14, Morton scored 13, and Troy Smith notched 11.

They out rebounded Kentucky 48-34. But the Cards could never quite get over the hump.

Leading 79-71, UK's Sean Woods drove the lane and into the Cards' Brewer, who caught Woods and held him on his shoulder for a split second. Brewer was called for the blocking foul, and he then let Woods fall awkwardly to the ground. Woods got up and was restrained by teammates as Brewer was called for the technical foul. Travis Ford made two free throws for the technical, Woods hit one for the foul, and Mashburn canned a shot when UK got the ball back.

Yet even then, the Cards clawed back, closing to within six with under 7:00 to play. They even had three possessions to draw closer but never could. Louisville came to within seven at 88-81.

On a fast break, Dale Brown found himself open behind the arc and drained the shot, just as his teammates had done all day long, effectively ending the game.

Kentucky won, 103-89.

Postgame

After the Louisville game, Pelphrey felt vindicated. His 26 points led all scorers in the win.

But he had another score to settle. In the postgame press conference, he sought out the Louisville student reporter who had trash-talked him in the student newspaper.

When he found the student's seat, Pelphrey gave the person sitting there an earful. There was only one problem.

"Whoever it was there, I need to apologize," Pelphrey told the *Herald-Leader*. "I understand the guy [Henry Hoening] wasn't here."

$$*****$$

Louisville rebounded from its poor 1990–91 season, finishing 19-11 and returning to the NCAA Tournament when the team thrashed Wake Forest in the first round, 81-58. The Cardinals were overmatched in the second round against fourth-ranked UCLA, but clearly, they were competitive again.

In its first season off probation, Kentucky finished 29-7, won the SEC Tournament, and made its way to the NCAAs for the first time since 1988. It became a memorable trip, as Kentucky lost to Duke 103-102 in overtime in the East Regional finals in what many call the greatest NCAA game ever played. While UK missed out on a trip to the Final Four, the same was true for both Kentucky and Louisville: the teams were back and competitive again.

$$*****$$

John Pelphrey became one of the most beloved UK players in history. His jersey was retired, along with that of the other three seniors on that team—Sean Woods, Deron Feldhaus, and Richie Farmer. He went on to assistant coaching jobs at Oklahoma State, Marshall, and Florida, before taking head coaching positions at South Alabama (where he earned a Sun Belt Coach of the Year Award) and Arkansas.

Now he is back as an assistant to Billy Donovan at Florida.

"Yeah, it is a good feeling to play and win a game like that, in front of all of our fans. It's a special memory, playing that game," Pelphrey said. "Words don't do it justice in terms of what it means to the state.

"The players, the coaches, how good the teams have been, it's pretty remarkable—one of the best games we have in basketball, and it's not going to go away anytime soon. Sometimes you have these really deep rivalries of teams that play twice a year or whatever—but this is a one-shot deal. That is a big part of it.

"You just can't understand the lasting memory," he said. "It puts an impression on you for a lifetime."

Kentucky 103

NAME	MIN	FG-FGA	3-3A	FT-FTA	REB	PF	AST	STL	BLK	TO	TP
Pelphrey	26	7-11	4-5	8-10	5	3	3	2	2	6	26
Mashburn	39	9-17	1-4	6-7	7	4	3	1	1	1	25
Martinez	12	1-3	1-1	2-2	1	5	0	0	3	1	5
Woods	20	2-3	0-0	5-8	0	3	5	3	0	3	9
Brown	30	5-10	3-7	3-6	9	4	2	2	0	4	16
Feldhaus	31	1-4	0-2	0-0	3	2	5	0	0	2	2
Farmer	17	4-6	2-2	0-1	1	4	1	3	0	0	10
Timberlake	11	2-3	0-0	0-0	3	1	0	0	0	0	4
Toomer	4	0-0	0-0	0-0	2	0	0	0	0	1	0
Braddy	4	1-2	0-0	0-0	0	0	0	1	0	0	2
Harrison	3	0-0	0-0	0-0	0	0	0	0	0	0	0
Ford	1	0-0	0-0	4-4	0	0	0	1	0	0	4
Riddick	1	0-0	0-0	0-0	0	0	0	0	0	0	0
TEAM					3						
Total	200	32-59	11-21	28-38	34	26	19	13	6	18	103

Louisville 89

NAME	MIN	FG-FGA	3-3A	FT-FTA	REB	PF	AST	STL	BLK	TO	TP
Minor	34	6-17	0-3	6-6	6	2	2	2	2	3	18
Morton	23	4-6	0-0	5-6	4	3	0	1	0	0	13
Holden	25	2-8	0-0	3-6	8	4	0	0	1	1	7
LeGree	27	3-7	0-1	2-4	3	3	0	2	0	4	8
Sullivan	30	5-13	2-8	2-3	5	4	0	0	0	5	14
Smith	18	4-12	0-0	3-4	8	1	2	0	1	1	11
Webb	14	3-3	0-0	1-2	3	2	0	1	0	1	7
Stone	11	3-7	0-2	0-0	2	1	1	3	1	3	6
Brewer	10	1-3	1-3	2-2	1	5	3	0	1	0	5
Hopgood	8	0-1	0-0	0-0	1	2	0	0	0	0	0
TEAM					7						
Total	200	31-77	3-17	24-33	48	27	8	9	6	18	89

Chapter 12

Monster Mash

No. 3 UK 88, No. 9 UofL 68
December 12, 1992 at Freedom Hall

Pre-Game:

Jamal Mashburn has said he did not dream of playing in the NBA when
he was a child.

Instead, the gangly kid from New York City would sit inside his parents' apartment and watch the people scurrying to work, all of them
looking professional in their dress shoes and overcoats. And then there
were the briefcases—they all had briefcases with shiny buttons and leather
handles—and they carried those into the subways, which they rode to the
skyscrapers in the city.

Someday, little Mashburn thought, *I'm going to have a briefcase too,
and I'm going to be a famous businessman, riding that subway to an important job in a big building. Someday.*

But Mashburn's life followed a different storyline. By the time he was
a high school senior he had grown to 6'8" and become a top-10 player in
America. He was coveted by a number of prestigious college basketball
schools, including Syracuse (his favorite team for years), Wake Forest,
and Kentucky.

'Cuse seemed the likely destination. They had tradition, along with a stable coach and a real shot at winning a national championship in the early '90s. But Wake Forest was a possibility, too—it was the favorite of Mash's mother.

Then there was the Wild Card—Kentucky. It was a traditional power, yes, but it was also a school on probation—barred from any postseason play for what would be Mashburn's freshman season. If he were to go to UK, he would be punished for something he had no part in. But Kentucky had Rick Pitino, also a New Yorker, and a coach that was famous for accepting nothing less than everything from his players.

Mashburn had developed a reputation as a great potential talent, but one who scouts agreed needed to be pushed to reach his full potential. Mashburn liked that Pitino could push him. But it really came down to a numbers game.

He visited Wake Forest, but didn't quite gel with the team. But his visit to Syracuse went better; he liked everything about it—except how the team was loaded with talent.

"I didn't really see where I was going to fit in and play," Mashburn said. "That was a problem."

Kentucky just, well—fit. He got along with the players and coaches, and Pitino seemed to be the man for the job. UK was a big-time stage to prove his work ethic and sitting out one year seemed like a small price to pay. Mashburn was sold. He committed to Kentucky.

*****

The transition to college was not easy. Legendary strength coach Rock Oliver made UK practices grueling. Mashburn had never worked out like that before, and at least at one point he decided he wanted to quit. But little Richie Farmer, the guard from Manchester, Kentucky, told Mashburn to keep going. He said working hard was the only way to get better.

So they worked, and they got better, and by 1992 they were off probation and part of the best team in the SEC. Their style and shooting were feared throughout the land. That year—Richie's senior season—it took them all the way to the brink of the Final Four. Only a miracle shot by Christian Laettner kept UK from marching on. Mashburn ended a truly splendid sophomore season by fouling out in overtime—with 28 points and 10 rebounds.

By the start of the next season, he was a preseason first team All-America selection.

*****

Pitino was building up to this—a team led by a superior talent in Mashburn, fortified with shooters in Dale Brown and point guard Travis Ford (who hailed from Madisonville, Kentucky), held down in the middle by beefy center Rodney Dent, and capped off by an influx of young stars. The fresh faces comprised the No. 1 recruiting class in the country, including overall No. 1 player Rodrick Rhodes, guard Tony Delk, and forward Jared Prickett. Many tabbed Kentucky as the favorite to win the national title. Nearly everyone had the Wildcats reaching the Final Four.

Louisville was a team in transition, but ready again for the spotlight. Coming off the disastrous 1990–91 campaign, in which several Cardinal recruits never made it to campus due to academic ineligibility, followed by the comeback year of 1991–92, Louisville looked to return to the national scene in 1992–93. By the end of 1992, the Cards were back in the NCAAs, dropping out in the second round to fourth-ranked UCLA.

UofL was re-loading. Anchored by the post presence of Cliff Rozier, and rounded out by the talents of Greg Minor, Dwayne Morton, Keith LeGree, Troy Smith, James "Boo" Brewer, and Brian Hopgood, Louisville was once again formidable. When they hosted No. 3 Kentucky (3-0) on December 12, 1992, Louisville (1-1) had moved up to No. 9 in the country.

And the Cards had a plan. Their thought was to ignore Kentucky's three-headed monster at center: Dent, Andre Riddick, and Gimel Martinez. Instead, UofL would double-team Mashburn and help on his teammates, leaving the center on his own. That player, they figured, would not beat them.

It was a good idea, and it worked—for a while.

The Game:

At the start of the game, Louisville's guards had a field day dribbling through Kentucky's supposedly vaunted press. They ran right past the defenders, beating their men and throwing over the top. They laid off the UK big men inside and sent help defenders to guard the deadly scorers on the wings, which tended to be Mashburn and Rhodes. The Cardinals got four fastbreak baskets to jump out to a 10-point lead at 26-16 with 11:35 to go.

The lead stayed at 10 by a score of 30-20 with 9:00 to play in the first half. Those who wore red in the record crowd of 19,663 in Freedom Hall were delighted.

Then came the confrontation between Rozier, the talented Louisville big man, and Rhodes, the precocious Wildcat freshman. Rozier, a 6'11", 245-pound coveted transfer from North Carolina, blocked a shot by Rhodes, who had come to UK as a 6'6" lithe small forward. Rhodes could not get his shot over Rozier, however, who promptly pitched the pill back into the seats. None of that mattered to the refs.

But when Rozier taunted Rhodes by standing over him and yelling like a conquering hero, it earned the Card a technical foul. All the momentum changed. Kentucky hit a free throw, got the ball back, and ratcheted up their team defense.

Mashburn started a 22-5 run by hitting a trio of three-pointers and helped to outscore Louisville 28-10 over the remainder of the half to seize a 48-40 lead. The halftime talk involved one thing:

"All we talked about at halftime was picking up the defense," UK Coach Rick Pitino told the *Lexington Herald-Leader*. "This was about as good as our team has zeroed in since the Duke game."

What he is referring to is the dominating performance the Wildcats displayed in the second half. Mashburn was, of course, a star. Rhodes played well beyond his years. But the real difference may have been the production Kentucky got from unheralded big man Gimel Martinez, who managed to score 14 points in just 20 minutes of action.

With Martinez at center, Louisville was then forced to play defense on all five UK players. They could not keep up.

The Wildcat full-court press, along with Martinez, fueled a 26-7 run to break the game wide open in the first seven minutes of the second half. Martinez chipped in seven points during the stretch.

Louisville then began to turn the ball over, which was converted immediately into points. Both Morton and LeGree finished with

5 turnovers apiece, and Brewer had 4. In all, the Cards committed 19 turnovers.

Uncanny shooting helped Kentucky as well. The Cats made 11-of-21 from three-point range (Mashburn went 5-for-7 while Martinez hit 2-of-2), and it is worth noting that Louisville would have stayed closer if not for horrid free throw shooting: 16-for-34.

With 9:00 to go, fans started heading for the exits. Travis Ford found Rhodes for a breakaway dunk that pushed the lead to 13. It would balloon to 27.

"Kentucky played about as well as you can play—at both ends of the floor," Crum told the *Herald-Leader*. "They capitalized on every mistake we made."

Kentucky went on to win, 88-68. Mashburn led the way with a monstrous 27 points and 7 rebounds. Rhodes added 20 and 7 rebounds himself. Troy Smith scored 15 for Louisville and Greg Minor was the only other Louisville player in double figures, with 14. Rozier finished with a disappointing 8 points, but did pull down 14 boards.

"It's a great feeling to beat them on their home floor," Mashburn told the Associated Press afterward. "We took the fans out of the game and turned it into our gym. We took control of the game."

Pitino called his star the premier player in all the land.

"Mashburn is an awesome player," he said. "He can hurt you in so many ways with his dribbling, shooting, and passing."

Postgame:

"An amazing game for Mash was pretty normal," his former teammate, John Pelphrey, said, reminiscing. "He always had amazing games against everybody."

Both Kentucky and Louisville went on to have similar successful seasons. Kentucky marched all the way to the Final Four for the first time since 1984. There, they bowed out to a powerful Michigan squad in overtime and finished 30-4. Louisville made it all the way back to the Sweet 16, where they lost to No. 1 Indiana. Still, they were 22-9 and back in the top-20 where they belonged. In all, it was a very successful year for basketball in the Bluegrass State.

Kentucky fans had to wait another three years for their first national title since 1978. Instead of making another deep NCAA Tournament run in 1994, Mashburn decided to forgo his senior year of college and enter the NBA draft. He was selected fourth overall by the Dallas Mavericks—and he became an instant millionaire.

For Mashburn, his plan for success worked. He chose an unconventional path to Kentucky, but it led him all the way to the NBA. He looked to be earmarked for superstardom, but Mashburn never quite realized that potential in the professional League. Mashburn played in the NBA for 12 seasons and was an All-Star once—though he was known as a player who could score in bunches, once dropping 50 points in a single game. Due to chronic knee problems (which required dangerous microfracture surgery), he was forced to retire when he was still playing at a very high level. He averaged 19.1 points per game for his career.

What Mashburn did very well was manage his money. Mashburn invested wisely, pumping money into businesses such as pizza chains, steakhouses, and car lots. He was so wise with his money that by the time his body forced him to retire, he was very comfortable in his lifestyle and finances. He was even interviewed as one of the subjects of an ESPN documentary on athletes who need help managing their money. Mashburn was seen as the example all athletes should follow.

By the time he retired in 2004, Mashburn was a successful businessman as well as a former professional athlete. He also landed a gig as an in-studio analyst and commentator for ESPN. Most impressively, he also gave back to his university. Mashburn set up a scholarship specifically earmarked for athletes to be able to come back and finish their degrees at UK.

Many UK fans see Mashburn as the most important recruit (and one of the most important players) in the program's storied history. Had it not been for the player from New York City, Kentucky basketball would have never come back so quickly. Mashburn gave the program immediate legitimacy—something it had lacked since its probation era.

Now, Mashburn can say he has reached his own dreams. After all these years, he can now finally go to work in a big building—and carry his own briefcase.

Kentucky 88

NAME	MIN	FG-FGA	3-3A	FT-FTA	REB	PF	AST	STL	BLK	TO	TP
Rhodes	34	8-16	2-5	2-4	7	2	3	2	0	2	20
Mashburn	31	10-15	5-7	2-4	7	5	4	1	0	1	27
Dent	14	2-4	0-0	0-1	3	4	0	0	1	1	4
Ford	25	1-4	1-3	3-4	2	4	7	4	0	2	6
Brown	29	2-5	1-2	3-6	3	2	3	2	0	2	8
Martinez	20	6-8	2-2	0-1	1	3	0	0	1	1	14
Brassow	17	0-1	0-1	0-0	3	1	1	0	0	0	0
Prickett	13	2-4	0-0	1-2	5	4	1	1	1	2	5
Delk	8	1-2	0-1	0-0	0	1	0	0	0	3	2
Riddick	3	0-0	0-0	0-0	0	0	0	1	0	0	0
Harrison	3	0-0	0-0	0-0	0	0	1	0	0	0	0
Timberlake	2	1-1	0-0	0-0	0	0	0	0	0	0	2
Braddy	1	0-0	0-0	0-0	0	0	0	0	0	0	0
TEAM					4						
Total	200	33-60	11-21	11-22	35	26	20	11	3	14	88

Louisville 68

NAME	MIN	FG-FGA	3-3A	FT-FTA	REB	PF	AST	STL	BLK	TO	TP
Smith	25	6-9	0-0	3-8	7	4	2	0	0	1	15
Morton	17	1-5	1-1	1-5	6	4	1	0	1	5	4
Rozier	30	3-8	0-0	2-6	14	0	3	1	4	0	8
LeGree	35	2-5	0-0	2-5	2	4	4	0	0	5	6
Minor	38	5-11	1-4	3-4	4	2	2	0	0	1	14
Brewer	20	3-9	0-2	2-2	2	3	0	1	0	4	8
Hopgood	10	3-5	0-0	3-4	4	1	0	0	2	2	9
Kiser	10	1-3	0-2	0-0	2	0	1	1	0	0	2
Webb	9	1-1	0-0	0-0	0	3	1	0	0	1	2
Rogers	4	0-1	0-0	0-2	1	0	1	1	0	0	0
Case	2	0-1	0-1	0-0	0	0	0	0	0	0	0
TEAM					1						
Total	200	25-58	2-10	16-36	43	21	15	4	7	19	68

Chapter 13

Tony Delk Arrives

No. 2 UK 78, No. 7 UofL 70
November 27, 1993 at Rupp Arena

Pre-Game:

The 13th edition of the Dream Game was the season opener for both schools. It was appropriate, then, that the game raised a fair number of questions. Who would step up for Kentucky in the absence of Jamal Mashburn, who was starting for the Dallas Mavericks instead of the Wildcats? How would star frosh Jason Osborne fit in for Louisville? And had the Cards jumped the Cats again?

This Kentucky team, while still a talented group, would be nowhere near as consistent as the previous year's squad. Without Mashburn to draw the attention of opposing defense, Travis Ford's open three-point attempts became more and more scarce. Highly talented but combustible sophomore Rodrick Rhodes was probably the most talented Wildcat, but whether Rhodes would score 20 points or 2 on a given night was an open question. Jared Prickett and Rodney Dent joined Rhodes in the Wildcat frontcourt, and Kentucky's fifth starter—Tony Delk—was perhaps the biggest mystery on the team. The sophomore from Brownsville, Tennessee, had been highly regarded as a recruit, but played little as a freshman. The word from insiders around the UK program was that Delk would surprise with the extent of his improvement. But in the preseason, talk is plentiful and cheap. Results are what matters.

Louisville countered with a talented veteran core and a pair of new additions. The Cardinals were No. 7 in the AP poll at game time, while the Cats were No. 2, but the rankings could easily have been reversed. Seniors Dwayne Morton and Greg Minor gave UofL two veteran scoring options who could play with anyone in the nation. Center Cliff Rozier was the returning Metro Conference Player of the Year and had notched 18 double-doubles in 1992–93. Louisville's other two starters were freshmen. Guard Jason Osborne, a silky smooth player, had been the subject of an intense in-state recruiting battle before the Cards had kept him home in Louisville. Osborne was the latest standout from (Louisville) Male High and a McDonald's All-America selection, the lone representative of UK or UofL in that year's game. DeJuan Wheat, a (Louisville) Ballard High School product who was much less heralded, but who had ceaselessly improved his game and would continue to do so, joined Osborne.

In case the matchup of two top-10 rivals was not hot enough, early in the week leading up to the game, top-ranked North Carolina was defeated. Kentucky faced Louisville with the knowledge that a win would vault them to No.1 in the nation. The Wildcats had spent a single week at No.1 in 1992–93, but otherwise had not held the top spot since the 1987–88 season.

For Tony Delk, being part of the game figured to be an improvement. He had been a McDonald's All-America selection but had logged just under ten minutes per game as a freshman, averaging four points per game. "Because I didn't play a lot my freshman year, I had a lot to prove," Delk recalled in a recent interview. "I wanted to show people that I wasn't a McDonald's All-American who was kind of a flop."

The Game:

While the game was played on November 27, it may have really begun earlier that week for Delk in UK's practice. Delk, who had struggled to an 8-of-24 shooting performance in UK's two exhibition games, missed a shot and hung his head. Rick Pitino told the *Lexington Herald-Leader*, "I went into a tirade. . . . I asked him 'Are you so one-dimensional?'" Pitino went on to tell Delk that he needed to focus on defense and rebounding and make up for missed shots there. "If you don't want to do that," Pitino reportedly said, "I'll play Brassow."

Delk listened and relaxed. The first shot, once the game began on the 27th, was Delk, for three. And it was good.

"That," Delk recalls, "might have been my coming-out game."

In his first starting assignment, Delk totaled 19 points, which included 5 three-point baskets. He also grabbed 10 rebounds, dished out 5 assists, and grabbed 2 steals.

A trio of Dream Game legends—on Senior Day for Kentucky's Tony Delk, he is congratulated by Coach Rick Pitino and Assistant Coach Winston Bennett. *(Photo by Jamie Vaught)*

Louisville fought valiantly to stay in the game. Rozier, who had been embarrassed by the turn-around of the previous season's game, was sharp for the entire game this time around. He exposed UK's relatively thin frontcourt with 29 points and 13 rebounds as well as 3 blocked shots. Morton and Minor put up 14 and 13 points respectively, playing solidly to keep UofL in the game.

But Kentucky led 39-28 at the half, and UofL could not overcome the early charge. The two new Louisville starters were apparently intimidated by opening their careers in Rupp Arena, as Osborne had just one point and turned the ball over six times. Wheat had six points, but shot 1-of-8.

Bench help from junior Andre Riddick was an important contribution for Kentucky. Rodney Dent spent the game in foul trouble, but Riddick managed 15 points and 8 rebounds. While Louisville won the rebounding battle 40-34, Riddick kept it close enough that Delk and senior Travis Ford, who totaled 14 points, could pull Kentucky away. Louisville stayed close, climbing to within 6 points on a Dwayne Morton three-pointer with just over 8:00 left. But they could climb no closer.

UK won 78-70 and moved to the top spot in the nation. In his postgame press conference, Pitino expressed some skepticism, ultimately admitting, "I think Kansas deserves the No. 1 ranking. They can have it. We don't want it."

Postgame:

Tony Delk never looked back. He made 95 three-point shots in 1993–94, only 6 shy of UK's single-season record, which Travis Ford had set the previous year. He averaged 16.6 points per game, leading the squad. In his four seasons, Delk totaled 1,890 points, then good for fourth on UK's career scoring list.

Tony went on to put together a solid NBA career, spanning ten seasons. When he was hot, he could still dominate games—as he showed in early 2001, when he scored 53 points for the Sacramento Kings against the Detroit Pistons. After his playing career, Delk was an assistant coach at New Mexico State. He has since left coaching and hopes to become an executive in the NBA.

Meanwhile, his family has kept Delk occupied. "I thank God for my three daughters," he says. "It's such a blessing to have daughters." Two of Delk's daughters have been diagnosed with sickle-cell disease, a hereditary blood disorder with numerous serious medical consequences, including a reduced life expectancy. With the support of his wife, Margie,

Delk established the Taylor Delk Sickle-Cell Foundation, a charity established to improve the quality of life of children and families affected by the disease. "It means a lot to me to help families out," Delk admits. "It humbles me when I see families that are going through tough times when they have kids that are sick."

In less serious matters, Tony's family threatened his basketball loyalties as well—but only a bit. His nephew, Reginald Delk, first played at Mississippi State and transferred to Louisville to finish his career under Rick Pitino. Tony says of his nephew "I love him to death," but recalls, "Even when he was at Mississippi State and they played Kentucky, [I told him] 'I hope you have a good game, but I hope you lose.'"

*****

Delk's 1993–94 UK teammates lacked his consistency. This was the sort of Kentucky team that could lose two games in a row and fall down by 31 to LSU in the second half of the third game. It was also the sort of UK team that could rally to win that LSU game. Kentucky finished 27-7, as Ford struggled in the absence of Mashburn, and Rhodes remained enigmatic. Rodney Dent blew out his knee before Christmas, and frontcourt depth was extra-thin thereafter. After winning the SEC Tournament, UK was upset in the second round of the NCAA Tournament by Marquette, 75-63.

Louisville ended up being more consistent than their intrastate rivals, posting a 28-6 mark and never sinking below No. 15 all season long. Rozier was the driving force behind the Cardinal attack, earning first team consensus All-America honors by averaging over 18 points and 11 boards per game. Morton and Minor were again as advertised, and Wheat became the team's fourth option, scoring 12.6 points per game as a freshman. Like UK, the Cardinals won their conference tournament and earned a No. 3 seed in the NCAA Tournament. The Cardinals won two games in the Tournament, losing in the Sweet 16 to Arizona, 82-70. Unfortunately for the Cardinal faithful, after the season, Rozier turned down his last year of college eligibility to play in the NBA. With Morton and Minor also finished with their careers and UK having won four consecutive games in the series, UofL fans wondered what it would take to beat UK. It would clearly take a special effort, one that would rank among the most memorable performances in the history of the rivalry.

Kentucky 78

NAME	MIN	FG-FGA	3-3A	FT-FTA	REB	PF	AST	STL	BLK	TO	TP
Rhodes	23	3-8	1-6	2-3	0	3	1	2	1	4	9
Prickett	33	2-5	0-1	0-0	2	2	4	0	0	2	4
Dent	14	3-5	0-0	0-0	4	4	0	0	1	0	6
Delk	34	6-14	5-11	2-5	10	1	5	2	2	0	19
Ford	39	4-11	2-5	4-4	2	2	5	0	0	2	14
Riddick	21	7-10	0-1	1-2	8	5	1	0	1	0	15
Brassow	17	2-3	2-3	0-0	2	2	2	1	0	0	6
Martinez	9	0-5	0-1	0-0	2	2	0	1	0	0	0
Sheppard	6	0-0	0-0	0-0	1	1	1	1	0	0	0
McCarty	3	2-3	1-1	0-2	1	0	0	0	0	1	5
Epps	1	0-1	0-1	0-0	0	1	0	0	0	0	0
TEAM					2						
Total	200	29-65	11-30	9-16	34	23	19	7	5	9	78

Louisville 70

NAME	MIN	FG-FGA	3-3A	FT-FTA	REB	PF	AST	STL	BLK	TO	TP
Osborne	33	0-6	0-2	1-2	7	3	1	1	0	6	1
Morton	35	5-10	2-2	2-5	6	2	1	0	0	2	14
Rozier	38	11-15	0-0	7-12	13	4	0	0	3	3	29
Minor	35	4-12	1-3	4-5	5	2	4	2	0	2	13
Wheat	29	1-8	1-3	3-5	2	1	1	0	0	1	6
Rogers	17	1-2	1-1	0-2	2	1	2	3	0	0	3
Kiser	8	2-3	0-0	0-0	2	0	1	0	0	1	4
Simons	2	0-0	0-0	0-0	0	0	0	0	0	0	0
Sims	2	0-0	0-0	0-0	1	2	0	0	0	0	0
TEAM					2						
Total	200	24-56	5-11	17-31	40	15	10	6	3	15	70

Chapter 14

Samaki's Triple-Double Surprise

UofL 88, No. 5 UK 86
January 1, 1995 at Freedom Hall

Pre-Game:

Four years in a row. Cards fans couldn't stand it. Cats fans couldn't stop talking about it.

It had been four years of Kentucky dominance over Louisville in their annual rivalry, four years since Louisville had notched a win. Largely it was a matter of Rick Pitino and Kentucky just having more talent: Jamal Mashburn, Rodrick Rhodes, Tony Delk, Travis Ford, and Walter McCarty, among others, contributed to big victories over their archrivals.

But the talent gap had narrowed by New Year's Day 1995. Louisville had gotten more athletic by the time this installment of the Dream Game, held in Freedom Hall, came around. They already had hometown hero DeJuan Wheat, who was proving to come up large again and again in clutch situations. They had other homegrown talent in Jason Osborne, Alvin Sims, Tick Rogers, and walk-on B.J. Flynn (son of former UK star Mike Flynn). But the difference in 1995 was a stout, shot-blocking freshman forward from Columbus, Ohio.

He was a 6'9", 240-pound defensive menace. His name was Samaki Walker.

*****

Samaki Ljuma Walker was born February 25, 1976, the youngest of seven children. His name is Swahili, and per his NBA biography, it loosely translates to "fish of the beautiful river." In Columbus, Walker attended Whitehall Yearling High School, where he was named a third team Parade All-America selection, but his reputation could have been hurt by multiple ankle injuries.

Walker chose to be a Cardinal because of the coach, the fans, and the opportunity to play right away.

"The reason I chose Louisville over any other school was that I believed in Denny Crum and his coaching abilities," Walker told website Cardinalsportszone.com. "Having a great visit didn't hurt the recruiting process either, and the fact that Cliff Rozier was leaving . . . it was the perfect fit for me.

"Coach Crum was the ultimate teacher and believed in details," he continued. "If there is one thing that sticks out in my mind about the many things Coach Crum has taught me, it is to use the backboard, and he was indeed a firm believer in that. Because he was a firm believer in the high-post offense, I really became comfortable facing the basket at that position, which helped my career tremendously."

Many would agree that Walker's career really began New Year's Day 1995.

As the Cardinals desperately wanted to beat UK, they realized they needed players who could match the skill level in Lexington. Walker could do that. Louisville was coming off a 28-6 season that saw them lose to ninth-ranked Arizona in the Regional of the NCAA Tournament. The 1994–95 campaign looked to be a rebuilding season, but Walker gave fans hope for the future.

For Kentucky, it seemed like the tracks were laid for a magical year. UK was deep with experience, talent, and shooters. They played frenetic defense and had a legitimate star in guard Tony Delk. Freshman forward Antoine Walker was a matchup nightmare. Entering the game, UK was ranked fifth in the nation with a record of 6-1, the lone loss coming at third-ranked UCLA by one point.

Louisville was 6-3 and still learning to play with Walker and without star post man Cliff Rozier. They started off 1-3, with losses to BYU and top-25 foes Villanova and Michigan State. But then the Cards righted the ship, defeating five consecutive teams, including No. 14 Georgia Tech in Atlanta in the Kuppenheimer Classic, where Walker was named MVP. Denny Crum's philosophy of playing any team, any place was paying dividends—and Walker was leading the way, averaging 16 points and 9 rebounds.

It all added up to one huge game for Louisville when Kentucky came to Freedom Hall to celebrate the New Year. According to CBS broadcasters Jim Nantz and Billy Packer, Crum—who during the previous May had been named to the Naismith Basketball Hall of Fame—had never lost to an opponent five straight times.

The streak of four losses to UK would come to an end, courtesy of the freshman from Columbus. For Samaki Walker, the greatest moment in his Louisville career occurred in that game.

"The memory that stands out the most for me is the Kentucky Wildcats [game] on New Year's Day, which is still one of the most memorable times of my life," Walker said.

The Game:

It seemed like the book on Kentucky was to force them to shoot. If they were making threes, you were toast. If they missed? Well, then you had a chance. No made shots equaled nopressure defense. Then again, teams that had no fear, that pushed Kentucky around and played good defense, and those squads that made enough shots of their own, could earn a victory over Kentucky too.

It was a blueprint the Cards created—and then showed to a national television audience.

Louisville came out red-hot on New Year's Day, while Kentucky just looked hungover. Louisville muscled UK around, blocking shots and scoring baskets to the delight of at least half of the Louisville-record 19,841 fans in Freedom Hall.

Walker hit his first shot, a short jumper, over the outmatched UK center, Andre Riddick. He then blocked a putback attempt by Walter McCarty, rebounded a miss by Louisville's Eric Johnson, and scored on a bank shot to put the Cards up 4-1.

Walker then blocked another UK shot, but it fell into the hands of Delk, and Tick Rogers, who was leading the nation in steals, almost knocked the ball away. It was a suffocating, pestering defense, and Kentucky looked lethargic.

"This is the worst team but the best players I've had since the first year [at UK]," Pitino told the *Lexington Herald-Leader*. "I think part of it is national TV and the hype."

Louisville blocked 5 of Kentucky's first 11 shots en route to a 21-11 lead. Then the pressure seemed to get to the Cards, who turned the ball over 5 out of the next 6 possessions, and Kentucky closed to within 21-20 as their rebounding kept them in the game.

But time and time again, Louisville's Wheat dribbled right through UK's signature press and passed off for easy layups. Louisville forced the Cats to shoot 2-10 from the three-point line, just 33% overall from the field, and held UK supposed star Rodrick Rhodes to zero points. UofL led 40-36 going into halftime. They had played the perfect half.

UK made a statement to start the second half. They scored six straight points, and when Rhodes hit his first shot (a three), Kentucky had a 42-40 lead. Louisville threw the ball away on the ensuing possession, and for the first time in the game, the Cards looked rattled. With 13:48 to play, Kentucky inched forward 54-49.

"The last three years, their team would have folded," Pitino said afterward.

It didn't happen. Instead, Wheat took over, scoring back-to-back three pointers and getting eight straight points overall in a 14-2 Louisville run.

"We didn't lose our poise when we lost our lead," Denny Crum told the media. "That's a hard thing for a young team. Usually, things get worse."

What did happen is the fans saw a great game. Kentucky continued to claw and Louisville continued to keep a lead. Louisville led by as many as seven points down the stretch. Flynn seemed to be everywhere on the court, and drove past four defenders for a layup and a 78-72 lead. Sheppard responded with a three for UK, but Samaki Walker then took a pass inside the post, shimmied, and sunk a hook shot for his 13th point. It was Cards, 80-75.

With a minute to go, the Cards led 82-77. Rhodes, who only had five points on the night, forced two shots down the stretch, fouled out, and with Louisville leading by three, Kentucky stole the ball with 58 seconds to play. Delk missed a long three to tie before Anthony Epps caught the long carom and fed McCarty. He tried a three, which was blocked out of bounds by UofL's Osborne.

UK had the ball, down three, with 50.4 seconds to play. After the inbound was passed around the perimeter, Jeff Sheppard drove and attempted a layup, which was promptly rejected by Samaki Walker. Sheppard got the rebound though, and his putback cut the lead to 1 with 42 seconds left.

Tick Rogers hit two huge free throws to push the lead back to three, and UK again tried to attack the inside, but it was a futile attempt. Sheppard tried to drive on Walker, who again swatted the shot, and this time Walker got the rebound and was fouled. The block gave him a triple-double, with 13 points, 10 rebounds, and 10 blocked shots for the game.

He even banked in a free throw to extend Louisville's lead and make it a two-possession game. His second attempt missed, and Louisville rebounded the ball, effectively ending the contest. Wheat nailed two free throws with 8 seconds to go (which gave him a game-high 23 points), and with Louisville holding a four-point lead, Kentucky hit a meaningless layup to end the game.

Wheat and Walker were the stories of the game.

"I had no idea I had that many blocks," Walker told the Associated Press after the game. "It's something to be proud of. Kentucky has a lot of big people. It was really important for me to play aggressive and meet the challenge. I think I did."

Louisville ended the streak, 88-86. As the clock ran out, Osborne and Wheat jumped into the air, arms raised. Crum sought out UK players to shake their hands.

Years later, Pitino (now coaching Louisville) downplayed the UK/ UofL regular season rivalry, saying most of the games did not matter that much.

"Except for Samaki Walker getting a triple-double against us, there's not really a game that sticks out for me in all those years," he told CN2 television in a 2012 interview. "Because I remember so many times during timeouts, [saying] 'Stop driving on that guy!'"

"To me, that's what college basketball is all about," Denny Crum said. "Two teams playing hard. It's a shame one team had to lose. Anyone who likes basketball—who didn't have their heart out there—had to enjoy the game."

Postgame:

Louisville fans could finally rejoice after four years of losing to Kentucky. But both fan bases suffered disappointments by the end of the college basketball year.

Kentucky finished an impressive 28-5, winning the SEC regular season and tournament titles. By the end of the conference schedule, it was the No. 2 team in the nation and earned a No. 1 seed in the NCAA Tournament. But the Wildcats fell one game short of the Final Four, losing to No. 2 seed North Carolina in the Elite Eight, 74-61.

Louisville finished the season 19-14. They earned a No. 11 seed in the NCAA Tournament before matching up with rival Memphis in the first round. The Tigers dispatched the Cards, 77-56.

Both Walker and Wheat went on to the NBA. Wheat left Louisville after his senior season, when the L.A. Lakers drafted him with the 51st pick. Wheat was cut by the Lakers but caught on for one season with the Minnesota Timberwolves. He then played a season with the Vancouver Grizzlies before playing overseas. He retired from hoops in 2010, but left college as Louisville's second all-time scoring leader (2,183 points) while finishing third in assists (498). In an interview with Louisville's *The Paper* in 2011, Wheat fondly remembered his Cardinal days.

"I loved playing at Freedom Hall," he said. "People can say it was old or whatever, it was probably built before I was born, but every time I stepped on the court it felt new to me. Every time it felt new. Louisville fans love their team. Sometimes it's like the last 11 or 12 years or whatever never happened. There's definitely something special about it."

Walker left college after his sophomore season and declared for the NBA Draft. He was chosen by the Dallas Mavericks with the ninth overall pick, and while Walker never emerged as an All-Star, he went on to play in the NBA for 10 years before continuing his career overseas. In 2002, he won a World Championship with the Lakers, where he averaged 6.7 points and 7 rebounds per game.

"Having over 19,000 screaming UofL fans is like being at a Lakers game," Walker told Cardinalsportszone.com. "It was always exciting to see who was there and chat with the season ticket holders on the lower level just before tipoff. It is without question that [the state of] Kentucky is basketball heaven, and seeing 19,000 fans all pumped up on New Year's and beating the Kentucky Wildcats ranks right up there with winning an NBA Championship with the Lakers."

Louisville 88

NAME	MIN	FG-FGA	3-3A	FT-FTA	REB	PF	AST	STL	BLK	TO	TP
Johnson	14	4-8	0-0	0-0	2	4	0	0	0	1	8
Osborne	32	3-7	1-4	5-6	6	3	2	2	3	6	12
Walker	33	5-8	0-0	4-7	10	3	1	2	11	0	14
Rogers	31	2-9	0-1	7-8	3	3	2	2	1	3	11
Wheat	31	7-9	3-4	6-8	4	1	5	3	0	1	23
Sims	19	2-4	0-0	0-0	5	2	3	0	1	2	4
Flynn	17	3-9	0-0	3-4	5	0	2	1	0	4	9
Kiser	15	1-3	1-2	0-0	2	3	1	0	0	0	3
Smith	8	2-3	0-0	0-0	0	3	0	1	1	0	4
TEAM					1						
Total	200	29-60	5-11	25-33	38	22	16	11	17	17	88

Kentucky 86

NAME	MIN	FG-FGA	3-3A	FT-FTA	REB	PF	AST	STL	BLK	TO	TP
Rhodes	19	1-9	1-3	2-2	1	5	0	0	1	3	5
McCarty	23	5-11	3-5	4-5	9	1	1	0	0	1	17
Riddick	16	1-3	0-0	0-0	4	2	1	0	1	0	2
Delk	37	9-19	3-8	2-3	8	3	1	1	0	2	23
Sheppard	33	6-17	2-4	5-6	4	4	3	0	1	3	19
Pope	24	4-10	0-3	1-3	10	2	1	1	0	2	9
Prickett	17	0-1	0-0	3-4	4	2	0	0	0	2	3
Walker	17	2-9	0-3	2-2	6	4	2	0	0	1	6
Epps	8	0-2	0-0	2-2	0	3	0	0	0	1	2
Edwards	4	0-1	0-1	0-0	1	1	1	0	0	1	0
Harrison	2	0-0	0-0	0-0	0	0	0	0	0	0	0
TEAM					5						
Total	200	28-82	9-27	21-27	52	27	10	2	3	16	86

Chapter 15
Pitino's Dream Team

No. 4 UK 89, No. 25 UofL 66
December 23, 1995 at Rupp Arena

AS THE 1995–96 season approached, Rick Pitino had one goal to accomplish. He had led UK back to the Final Four, had claimed a No. 1 ranking, and had garnered top recruiting classes. But it had been 17 years since the Cats had claimed college basketball's ultimate prize, the NCAA championship. In the meanwhile, Denny Crum's Cardinals had claimed two titles and made two additional Final Four appearances. Well-known Kentucky baiter John Feinstein, on National Public Radio just before the season tipped off, cracked that while Pitino had written two books and won no championships, he believed that the trend might change—if Pitino wrote a third book.

However, by the time the season began, it was apparent that Pitino had assembled one of the greatest teams in modern college basketball history. Six players from the squad went on to be NBA first-round draft picks, and three more Cats went on to play in the league. Kentucky had lost Rodrick Rhodes, guided out the door to Southern California by Pitino. However, they had replaced him with silky-smooth freshman forward Ron Mercer. Freshman guard Wayne Turner and junior transfer Derek Anderson were also new additions for the Wildcats. Seniors Tony Delk, Walter McCarty, and Mark Pope anchored the squad, with other talents like sophomore forward Antoine Walker and junior guards Anthony Epps and Jeff Sheppard helping the team. Not only was this Pitino's most talented collegiate team, but also it was by far his deepest—as Kentucky's second unit probably could've been a top-10 squad in their own right.

The Louisville Cardinals did not intend to go gently into the good night. Not only did Denny Crum's team hold the victory in the series's last meeting, but they also had an impressive array of talent. Kentucky killers Samaki Walker and DeJuan Wheat returned to wreak havoc on another UofL/UK matchup. Fearless perimeter players like Alvin Sims and Tick Rogers, and gritty shooter Brian Kiser, gave Louisville a fighting chance to pull a second consecutive Dream Game upset. However, the Cardinals missed forwards Jason Osborne and Alex Sanders, who were academically ineligible for the annual matchup.

Louisville entered the game with a solid 7-3 mark and No. 25 in the nation. Kentucky had begun the season as the nation's top-ranked squad, but after a second-game upset loss to Massachusetts, keyed by All-America center Marcus Camby and a spry young head coach named John Calipari, UK had slipped in the polls. The 6-1 Wildcats were ranked No. 4, but anyone who witnessed them winning by 64 points over Morehead State a week before the Dream Game realized that Pitino's team was showing signs of finding another gear.

For Pitino, a championship would mean vindication. His system of full-court pressure and three-point barrages had made bad teams good, but had failed to make good teams great. While he had taken Providence and Kentucky to the Final Four, he was 0-2 on college basketball's biggest stage. The road to basketball glory wound through the Dream Game, and the Untouchables, as Pitino's squad would later be known, saw the game as a proving ground.

"We owed them from the previous year," remembered Tony Delk in a recent interview. "When they came down to Kentucky, we hadn't forgotten about that. . . . [W]e were going to give them our 'A' game."

The Game:

Game day for Kentucky received an added boost when prep football sensation Tim Couch announced that morning that he would stay home to quarterback the Wildcats in college. Accordingly, he would duel Louisville's local favorite son, freshman QB Chris Redman, in an attempt to add some interest to the burgeoning football rivalry between the two schools.

Once tipoff came around, Kentucky looked like they could have used Couch, who was also an all-state basketball player, on the hardwood. Both UK and UofL began the game playing tight and missing open shots. Eight-and-a-half minutes into the game, Louisville led an ice-cold UK squad by a 10-4 count. One of the main culprits was Tony Delk, who started the game on a 0-for-6 shooting streak.

Would Pitino lose track of his talented Cats in the annual intrastate war? Simply put, no. While Louisville hung close for much of the first half, behind a particularly sharp game by Alvin Sims, who set a new career high with 23 points, Kentucky held a 22-20 lead late in the first half. Delk then caught fire, scoring UK's last 12 points of the half and leading the Cats to a 36-24 halftime advantage.

Kentucky, in an uncharacteristic move for a Pitino squad, crushed Louisville's frontcourt on the backboard, nabbing 20 offensive rebounds, which resulted in 21 second-chance points. Louisville-battled valiantly, pulling within 61-54 on a three-point basket by DeJuan Wheat, who scored 17 points in the game.

Enter Delk again. During a 12-4 run, Delk contributed a basket inside, a pair of free throws, and another three-pointer. In the end, Kentucky simply had too much firepower. Delk shook off his rough start by finishing the game on a 10-of-11 run, totaling 30 points for the game. Antoine Walker added 20 points and 12 rebounds. Kentucky beat Louisville, 89-66.

Postgame:

Louisville recognized it had little to hang its heads about. "Our kids played hard, but they just physically dominated us," noted Denny Crum to the Louisville *Courier-Journal* after the game.

Forward Brian Kiser admitted to the *Courier-Journal*, "When you shoot the ball like they do and hit the boards like they do, it makes for a long night."

DeJuan Wheat developed into the Cardinals' team leader, and Samaki Walker, who was held to 17 points by Kentucky, continued to be a dominant post presence. Tick Rogers was as steady as ever, and Alvin Sims developed into a double-figure scorer. Louisville ended its season at 22-12. The Cardinals were a single basket away from bringing about another Elite Eight Dream Game with Kentucky. Wake Forrest and Tim Duncan edged the Cardinals in the Sweet 16, 60-59.

For Kentucky, the Dream Game beating of Louisville was another step in the validation of this talented group. Lebanon, Kentucky native Anthony Epps, who had 14 points for the Cats, left little doubt on his feelings. "It's very sweet," he told the *Courier-Journal*. "This was a very, very big victory."

Tony Delk remembers his triumph fondly. "Being a scorer, you have to have amnesia when you miss four or five shots," he said of his poor start against Louisville. Delk fondly recalls the other half of his performance. "That particular game, it was just a matter of guys finding me," he says. "I was feeling it and sometimes you have games like that."

Delk and his fellow Wildcats had lots of games like that in 1996. Kentucky ran through an undefeated SEC season before being upset by Mississippi State in the SEC Tournament Finals. The whispers returned. *Could Pitino ever win the biggest games?* wondered Kentucky's fans and foes alike.

"Coach Pitino said something at the start of that season—'You guys can be a part of history.' Being young men, we didn't understand that," says Delk. "Coach Pitino did a great job of managing us and managing the egos and knowing how to massage players the right way."

This certainly came to fruition in the postseason. Pitino benched Antoine Walker in an SEC Tournament loss to Mississippi State, and then watched the versatile forward help lead Kentucky's stretch drive. As the team powered into the Final Four and won a hard-fought revenge win over John Calipari and UMass in the national semifinals, Pitino was again at work managing his players. Freshman Ron Mercer, content to stay in the background for much of the season, scored a season-high 20 points in the 1996 NCAA Championship game between Kentucky and Syracuse. Delk added a steady 24-point outing, and Kentucky held off the Orangemen 76-67 to win the school's first title since 1978.

Pitino had done it. In seven seasons, he had led Kentucky from its lowest point in basketball history back to the top of the NCAA mountain.

He had run an unfailingly clean program and had blended big-name recruits and underrated overachievers into a basketball powerhouse. With rumors of NBA teams scouting Pitino as hard as his Kentucky players, what could he do for an encore? In the tunnel after the NCAA title game, Derek Anderson was overheard by a *Courier-Journal* reporter giving his answer—"Repeat," Anderson said, still chewing on a piece of the net from the title game.

Pitino would nearly deliver on that request. But if you had asked a Louisville fan what he could do next for his ultimate encore, few if any would have ever posited, "Switch sides." But that is rivalry—a sublime mix of the triumph of the expected (Pitino's 1996 Untouchables) and of plot twists to come that absolutely no one expected.

Kentucky 89

NAME	MIN	FG-FGA	3-3A	FT-FTA	REB	PF	AST	STL	BLK	TO	TP
Walker	32	8-17	0-2	4-6	12	2	2	0	1	4	20
Mercer	20	1-5	0-3	2-2	2	2	3	1	1	0	4
McCarty	30	6-9	0-1	0-0	9	3	2	2	1	3	12
Delk	28	10-17	4-8	6-6	6	1	2	2	2	3	30
Epps	31	5-9	1-2	3-4	5	1	3	4	0	3	14
Pope	18	1-3	0-1	0-0	3	3	1	0	1	1	2
Anderson	13	2-6	0-2	0-0	3	2	3	2	0	2	4
Sheppard	12	0-3	0-0	0-0	1	2	1	0	0	0	0
Turner	9	0-1	0-0	0-0	0	0	1	0	0	1	0
Edwards	7	1-2	1-2	0-0	1	0	0	1	0	1	3
TEAM					2						
Total	200	34-72	6-21	15-18	44	16	18	12	6	18	89

Louisville 66

NAME	MIN	FG-FGA	3-3A	FT-FTA	REB	PF	AST	STL	BLK	TO	TP
Kiser	31	2-6	1-3	0-0	2	0	1	1	0	6	5
Sims	34	9-14	0-1	5-9	2	4	1	3	0	2	23
Walker	35	7-12	0-0	3-5	8	4	2	1	4	6	17
Rogers	31	0-4	0-2	0-0	3	4	4	1	0	2	0
Wheat	37	5-13	3-10	4-4	3	4	2	1	0	3	17
Dantzler	10	0-2	0-1	2-2	1	1	0	0	1	1	2
Taylor	8	0-1	0-1	0-0	1	1	2	1	0	1	0
Smith	7	1-1	0-0	0-0	2	2	0	0	0	1	2
Flynn	7	0-0	0-0	0-0	0	1	2	1	0	1	0
TEAM					2						
Total	200	24-56	4-18	14-20	24	21	14	9	5	23	66

Chapter 16

Two Words: The Dunk

No. 3 UK 74, No. 16 UofL 54
December 31, 1996 at Freedom Hall

Pre-Game:

Derek Anderson always dreamed of playing in the Louisville/Kentucky game, ever since he was just a poor kid growing up on the west side of Louisville.

But in those dreams, something was different. Anderson was playing for the Louisville Cardinals. He was a sweet-shooting guard, an amazing talent leading an amazing backcourt for a national champion Louisville team.

Something happened on the way to that dream. Instead, Anderson wound up at the University of Kentucky. There he would suit up for the Wildcats in the annual Dream Game rivalry.

Anderson will be the first to tell you that he never hated Kentucky. Kentucky just wasn't on his radar. His family was comprised of Louisville fans, so he was a Louisville fan. As an All-State guard at Doss High School, Anderson expected to play for the Cardinals.

"I was Louisville all the way," he said. "I expected to play for them."

It didn't work out that way. Ohio State recruited Anderson the hardest, and due to that advantage, coupled with the school's pharmacy program, Anderson became a Buckeye. For two years, he was a star in the Big Ten—that is, until recruiting violations placed the Buckeyes on probation. In 1995, he again had to decide where he would play college basketball.

"For me it came down to where I could win the national championship," he said. "I am all about winning."

The choices were UCLA and Kentucky. Louisville didn't have the pharmacy program Anderson was interested in, plus they never recruited him as hard as he thought they should have. Kentucky seemed to be on the verge of a championship and they were right down the road from where he grew up. The choice was easy. He would be a Wildcat.

"I really had a good relationship with the coaches and players at Kentucky," he said. "I felt comfortable there and I thought I could be a part of the national championship team."

Anderson turned out to be a prophet. In 1996, his first season playing with the team, Kentucky finished 34-2 and won the national title. But Anderson, ever the confident player, immediately said after the title game that UK would repeat when he was a senior in 1997.

Entering the 1996–97 season, it could be said that Kentucky fans had somewhat tempered their expectations. The same was not true at Louisville. Coming off a 22-12 Sweet 16 season the previous year, when the team lost to No. 9 Wake Forest by just a point, the Cardinals returned much of the same squad in 1997, including senior leader DeJuan Wheat. When the two teams matched up on December 31, 1996, in Freedom Hall, the Cards were ready. It was still Kentucky. It was still the biggest rivalry in college basketball. And no one knew that better than Derek Anderson.

"The day before the game me, and some friends were walking through the mall in Louisville," Anderson said. "And who should we run into, but a bunch of Louisville players."

Included in the group was one of Anderson's friends, Louisville forward Nate Johnson.

"We had known each other for a while," Anderson said. "We didn't talk. But somebody said something to us, something like they knew they were going to beat us the next day."

Anderson's friends heard the comment and relayed it back to the UK player.

"I told them all to just wait," Anderson said. "I told them that we would take it to them the next day."

That night, Anderson had a dream. But it was strange. Anderson was playing in the Dream Game, but he was playing for Louisville—just like he had always dreamt of when he was a kid.

"I remember I just woke up and laughed," Anderson said. "I knew what that dream meant. It meant that for UofL to win, they needed me on their team. But they didn't have me. Kentucky had me."

The Game:

The No. 3 Wildcats (10-1) came in to Freedom Hall ready for a close game. Louisville (10-0) had athletes, the team was well coached, and they always wanted to beat Kentucky. With victories over ranked teams like Arkansas and Boston College, the No. 14 Cardinals were faring even better than most had expected. Many thought Louisville could defeat these 1997 defending national champion Wildcats.

Then came The Dunk.

Whatever motivation, whatever excitement Louisville had coming into the game, Derek Anderson made sure to replace it with a healthy dose of doubt.

"I remember we were on a fast break—the game had really just started," Anderson said. "[Anthony] Epps hooked me up with a nice little bounce pass as I was streaking to the baseline. Then everything went to slow-motion. I looked up, and who was in front of me but Nate Johnson. I just wanted to dunk it hard."

What followed has been called by many college basketball analysts as one of the best dunks of that season—or of any season. With Kentucky leading 7-2 in the first three minutes of the game, Anderson rose up, and at one point looked to be almost parallel to the ground—because as Johnson came over to undercut the Wildcat, Anderson reared back and flushed a right-handed jam right on his head.

The whistle blew. It was an "And One." The bucket counted as Johnson earned the foul.

It was nasty, and the Wildcat faithful, which made up half of Freedom Hall's crowd, rose to their feet in excitement. The play sent a message.

"That was my town," Anderson said. "I wanted to go in there and I wanted to perform well. They should have recruited me and they didn't. I was mad. I wanted to win, and I wanted to get them back."

But Louisville bounced back. The Cardinals, led by the athleticism of Wheat, Johnson, and Alvin Sims, stayed in the game, leading the majority of the way. At halftime, they enjoyed a one-point lead, 28-27.

"It was just quiet at the half," Anderson said. "We just wanted to go back out and finish them."

The teams fought back and forth throughout the second half. With 10:00 to go, Louisville led by three, 42-39. They were grinding and defending, and Cards fans believed in their team, roaring approval. But the relentless Wildcat pressure eventually wore Louisville down. By turning the Cards over and forcing the tempo, Kentucky went on a punishing 35-12 run. Anderson got a steal, hit a free throw and a bank shot, canned a three, and found a teammate for a layup. Suddenly the score was 59-47, UK. The rout was on.

The close game became a 74-54 Kentucky victory. Kentucky forced Louisville into 25 turnovers and outscored the Cards from the free-throw line 24-12. It was a major win over a tough opponent on the road.

Anderson and Ron Mercer led the Wildcats, as they would for most of the season. Anderson led all scorers with 19 points and 6 rebounds, while Mercer added 16, Louisville native Scott Padgett scored 15, and forward Jared Prickett and center Nazr Mohammed scored 10 apiece. Guard B.J. Flynn, son of Wildcat great Mike Flynn, led all Louisville scorers with 12 points.

Louisville would have to wait to get their revenge.

Postgame:

For the 1997 Wildcats, the celebration would again last until the final game of the year. But Anderson would have to watch from the bench. Shortly after the start of the conference schedule, in a game against Auburn, Anderson suffered a major knee injury, which kept him out the rest of the season. He could only watch as Kentucky lost to Arizona in overtime of the national championship game. The Wildcats somehow finished 35-5, as players like Mercer, Epps, Padgett, and Nazr Mohammed overachieved to within an inch of a second consecutive NCAA title.

Perhaps more important to the rivalry, shortly thereafter, as had become an annual Kentucky tradition, the NBA came knocking on Rick Pitino's door. This time a mountain of cash was accompanied by a mountain of prestige and Pitino was given, as they say, an offer he couldn't refuse by the Boston Celtics. He took it, ending what he would refer to in his induction speech for the Basketball Hall of Fame as "eight years of Camelot." After 219 wins, three Final Fours, and an NCAA title, Pitino and UK were finished. His successor would inherit some rather large shoes to fill.

Meanwhile, Louisville went on to have an even better season than its previous one. With a record of 26-9, Louisville fared well in the NCAA Tournament, defeating UMass, No. 11 New Mexico, and Texas on the way to the Elite Eight. There they matched up with No. 4 North Carolina for a spot in the Final Four. But the Tar Heels were too much, besting the Cards 97-74. Still, Cards fans had to be pleased with the successful year.

Derek Anderson, the Louisville native, finished 2-0 against the Cardinals for his career. It's a badge of honor he wears proudly.

"For me, growing up in Louisville, there was nothing bigger than the Dream Game," Anderson said. "For me to go to play for Kentucky and beat Louisville twice, that was the ultimate. If I didn't beat them, I wouldn't have been able to go home."

Kentucky 74

NAME	MIN	FG-FGA	3-3A	FT-FTA	REB	PF	AST	STL	BLK	TO	TP
Mercer	36	5-13	2-4	4-5	2	2	1	3	0	2	16
Padgett	33	3-6	1-4	8-8	6	3	3	2	0	5	15
Mohammed	22	5-8	0-0	0-0	5	1	0	1	1	3	10
Anderson	34	8-13	1-3	2-4	6	3	2	2	1	1	19
Epps	32	0-6	0-4	3-4	4	1	4	1	1	1	3
Prickett	20	2-4	0-0	6-8	9	3	1	0	1	0	10
Edwards	12	0-1	0-0	1-2	2	2	2	1	0	3	1
Turner	8	0-1	0-0	0-0	0	2	0	1	0	2	0
Magloire	3	0-0	0-0	0-0	0	1	0	1	1	1	0
TEAM					1						
Total	200	23-52	4-15	24-31	35	18	13	12	5	18	74

Louisville 54

NAME	MIN	FG-FGA	3-3A	FT-FTA	REB	PF	AST	STL	BLK	TO	TP
N. Johnson	25	2-6	0-0	0-0	4	2	1	0	0	1	4
Dantzler	29	1-2	0-1	4-4	7	3	2	1	1	6	6
Sanders	26	4-7	0-2	0-0	5	5	2	0	0	5	8
Sims	32	3-14	2-4	1-3	8	4	4	3	1	5	9
Wheat	31	3-8	1-5	1-2	1	2	2	0	0	4	8
Flynn	28	3-8	1-3	5-5	3	4	0	2	0	2	12
E. Johnson	16	1-4	0-1	0-0	3	4	0	0	0	1	2
Smith	8	0-3	0-0	1-2	2	1	0	0	0	1	1
Williams	4	2-3	0-1	0-0	3	0	0	0	0	0	4
Akridge	1	0-0	0-0	0-0	0	1	0	0	0	0	0
TEAM					1						
Total	200	19-55	4-17	12-16	37	26	11	6	2	25	54

Chapter 17

UPSET

UofL 79, No. 4 UK 76
December 27, 1997 at Rupp Arena

THE THING IS, former Cardinals star Tony Williams says, there really isn't a lot of hate between players in the Louisville and Kentucky rivalry. Sure, maybe for a game they want to beat each other's brains in, but that's all. After that, it's possible you may see players from each team rooting for one another in certain situations. Or in some cases, rivals just may not care about the other team.

It's the AAU environment, players say. In the late 1980s and early 1990s, great high school players began to travel across the country and play one another. While they continue to be competitive, they also become friends, and it carries over to their college teams. Hatred is then diluted.

"Of course it meant more to me," says Williams, a shooting swingman and Louisville native. "I grew up with it. I knew it was big to beat Kentucky. But still, I liked those guys. Scott Padgett was a friend of mine. Nazr Mohammed was a friend of mine."

In 1997–98, Padgett (a Louisville native) and Mohammed were in the middle of a dynastic period for Kentucky: in '95, a regional final, in '96, a national title, in '97, a national runner-up finish. But 1997–98 was a different story altogether. Gone were some stars: Ron Mercer, Derek Anderson, and Anthony Epps. Gone was the championship coach: Rick Pitino decided to take the money ($70 million over 10 years), and he bolted for the Boston Celtics. Gone was the familiar hectic style of play: there was less of an influence on bombing three-pointers and pressing defense.

Instead, Tubby Smith was hired as the new Kentucky coach. He brought with him a new style and philosophy. Less pressure defense. More half-court focus. The same was true for the offense. At first the fans and the remaining players didn't seem to know what to think. It was an adjustment, to say the least. But there was still a lot of talent in Lexington. At 10-1 when the team met Louisville, Kentucky was No. 4 in the nation, with wins over No. 13 Clemson, No. 6 Purdue, and No. 24 Georgia Tech. Their only loss was by 15 to No. 1 Arizona in Maui.

The Wildcats were still figuring out their transition when they hosted unranked Louisville on December 27, 1997. The Cards were victims of their typical brutal schedule and arrived with a 2-6 record, with losses to No. 3 North Carolina, No. 6 Purdue, No. 15 Arkansas, and No. 18 Mississippi. Normally those schedules would make a team tougher and better. These Cards, however, were rebuilding. Gone were senior stars DeJuan Wheat and Alvin Sims. Gone was any semblance of an inside game. No player was taller than center Alex Sanders, who was 6'7".

Against Kentucky, the Cards would do the unthinkable—they would put it all together and prove they could defeat any team in the nation. How? With guts, hustle, and a bit of luck.

The Game:

Louisville came into Rupp Arena that day as a 16-point underdog. Clearly, Vegas and the gamblers thought the smart money was against an upset.

But UofL used a 2-3 zone to force Kentucky into uncomfortable situations. To a man, UK was more athletic. Man-to-man would not work. Instead, Louisville would roll the dice and essentially turn the game into a shooting contest from long range.

Instead of attacking, UK decided early on that they would beat the zone by shooting over it. It was a strategy Kentucky teams had lost in the past (most notably in a 1995 NCAA Regional Final meltdown against North Carolina). Against the Cards it would again prove ineffective.

Still, Louisville's game plan took a while to work. What the zone defense did early in the game was keep Louisville close. Early on, Kentucky used its height to its advantage, neutralizing Louisville's quickness with rebounding and inside play. With eight minutes to play in the first half, UK led 20-12, and fans in Rupp Arena felt as if the game was beginning to get out of control for the Cardinals.

Enter the jump shot. The Cards started to hit, and eventually they cut the lead to 35-31 by halftime.

"We let them back in the game," Padgett told the *Lexington Herald-Leader*. "When we didn't put them away, it gave them confidence. From that point on, they pretty much controlled the game."

"That run did it," Tony Williams said. "That made us feel like we could hit everything, that we could really win."

And in the second half, UofL really did almost hit everything.

During the second half Louisville point guard Cameron Murray (who had previously played two years at USC before transferring) showed his mettle as he successfully navigated UK's defense without erring. In all, Louisville turned the ball over just five times in the second half. But it was their shooting that changed the game in their favor, as they shot 17-of-27 from the field for 63%.

The game went back and forth until the 8:00 mark. Down 61-59, the Cards nailed three consecutive three-pointers to take command. The lead would swell from there.

With 2:13 to play, Kentucky trailed by 9. At the 1:23 mark it was 7. UK had one last gasp, largely due to poor free throw shooting by the Cards, who looked spent, as if they were inching their way to the finish. They hit just 5-of-12 freebies to end the game, almost giving away a victory.

With 20 seconds to go and a dwindling shot clock, Louisville's 78-76 lead looked to be in peril. Murray forced a shot, which was deflected by Wayne Turner. Louisville's Alex Sanders tipped the rebound back out to the foul line. Both UK's Jeff Sheppard and Louisville's Nate Johnson ran for it, and—symbolic of the entire game—Johnson got there first. Sheppard crashed into him, earning a foul. Johnson went to the free throw line and hit one, which made for the final score: 79-76.

Scott Padgett and Turner passed the ball between them and Padgett launched a long three for a harmless airball at the buzzer.

Louisville had done it, hitting 12-of-22 three-pointers along the way. Kentucky was an ice cold 5-of-23 from outside the paint.

Eric Johnson hit all three of his three-point attempts on the way to 20 points, which led all scorers. Sanders, the undersized center, held his own with 10 points and 10 rebounds. Williams hit for 16 and Murray had 15 and 6 assists.

For UK, Jeff Sheppard led the way with 18. Allen Edwards added 13, Wayne Turner scored 12, and Nazr Mohammed tallied 12 points and 9 rebounds in the loss.

"Everyone was against us—no one thought we could win," Williams said. "We loved that underdog role."

Postgame:

For many Kentucky fans, this was the lowest of lows. There was a feeling that Kentucky was better than they had shown against Louisville. Still reeling from the loss of their beloved Pitino, who had brought Kentucky back from the depths of probation to dominate most foes—including Louisville—UK fans were depressed. How had their team fallen so far?

Louisville had won in Rupp Arena and become the first non-conference opponent to do so in six years—over a span of 40 games. One would expect such a victory to catapult a team to greater heights, correct?

Not in this case. Louisville's lack of height and skilled players caught up with them. They finished 12-20. But for one night they had their magic working against UK.

Kentucky, though, had a much higher ceiling. With a roster of future NBA players, and two consecutive Final Four appearances, the Cats ended up winning a showdown with Duke in the NCAA Tournament to make another Final Four. Two wins later, the Wildcats were the unlikely national champions. Kentucky finished 35-4, and Sheppard was named the Most Outstanding Player of the tournament.

For Louisville fans, it provided the necessary ammunition to needle the followers of the Big Blue.

"I remember the T-shirts," Williams said. "Kentucky was the national champs—No. 1 in the nation but No. 2 in the state."

Many Louisville fans took solace in the fact that their team was the state champion. Louisville players, though, including Williams, were happy for UK.

"Yeah, I guess a lot of people don't know this, but we were rooting for them," said Williams, who went on to play in Europe for ten years before returning to Louisville, where he now coaches St. Francis High School's hoops squad. "We couldn't make the tournament, so as they kept going we watched them and we thought they had a great chance to win. They started playing so much better. As I said, we had a lot of friends on UK's team."

But for one night in Lexington in 1997, the future national champs were no match for the unranked Louisville Cardinals.

Louisville 79

NAME	MIN	FG-FGA	3-3A	FT-FTA	REB	PF	AST	STL	BLK	TO	TP
N. Johnson	21	1-3	0-0	2-4	3	2	0	1	0	1	4
Dantzler	27	3-8	0-0	0-2	6	3	2	0	1	2	6
Sanders	29	4-9	2-4	0-1	10	1	1	0	1	3	10
Maybin	22	3-5	2-4	0-1	1	2	2	2	0	1	8
Murray	33	4-9	2-4	5-6	3	4	6	0	0	4	15
Williams	26	5-9	3-7	3-6	6	2	0	0	0	2	16
E. Johnson	21	8-10	3-3	1-1	1	5	2	0	0	3	20
Best	10	0-1	0-0	0-0	1	0	2	0	0	1	0
Jackson	9	0-1	0-0	0-0	2	2	1	1	0	0	0
J. Johnson	1	0-0	0-0	0-0	0	0	0	0	0	1	0
TEAM					4					1	
Total	200	28-55	12-22	11-21	37	21	16	4	2	19	79

Kentucky 76

NAME	MIN	FG-FGA	3-3A	FT-FTA	REB	PF	AST	STL	BLK	TO	TP
Edwards	33	4-10	1-4	4-4	4	2	1	4	0	0	13
Padgett	25	3-13	0-5	1-2	6	4	4	3	2	1	7
Magloire	16	1-6	0-0	4-6	8	2	0	1	0	2	6
Sheppard	34	7-14	3-5	1-5	6	4	2	1	0	3	18
Turner	15	4-6	1-1	3-6	2	3	2	0	0	2	12
Smith	23	1-6	0-4	0-0	0	2	2	2	0	1	2
Evans	19	1-5	0-2	0-0	6	3	1	1	0	3	2
Mohammed	15	5-6	0-0	2-2	9	2	2	0	3	1	12
Anthony	10	0-1	0-0	2-2	1	0	0	0	0	0	2
Mills	7	1-4	0-2	0-0	1	2	0	0	0	0	2
Bradley	2	0-1	0-0	0-0	0	1	0	0	0	0	0
TEAM					0						
Total	200	27-72	5-23	17-27	43	25	14	12	5	14	76

Chapter 18

M&Ms: Maybin and Murray

UofL 83, No. 3 UK 74
December 26, 1998 at Freedom Hall

Pre-Game:

It wasn't an option for Marques Maybin. He had to go back to school.

He didn't want to disappoint the Louisville family, he says. With the support and motivation he had from them, he wanted to graduate. *But how would he do it?* he wondered. He needed help, of course.

Ever since the accident, things were definitely not the same. He would have to rely on the family.

*****

When it came time to choose a university, Marques Maybin, a smooth 6'3" 185-pound shooter from Clarksville, Tennessee, chose Tennessee. He thought it would be perfect. But when he found out he had not qualified academically, he chose to sit out a year, work on his game and academics, and then look again.

By 1997, he had decided on Louisville.

✻✻✻✻✻

In 1998, UK—ranked No. 3 in the nation—had already played a "Who's Who" of basketball powerhouses and fared pretty well. They sported a record of 10-2, with wins over No. 10 UCLA, No. 8 Kansas, No. 11 Indiana (in overtime), No. 2 Maryland, and Georgia Tech (whom they demolished 80-39). Their losses came to No. 2 Duke and unranked Pittsburgh on a neutral court.

Louisville was 4-2, and the Cards fans were much more optimistic about the kind of season they were going to have. They felt it would be nothing like the horrific 12-20 year they just completed. Of course, they did defeat the national champion Kentucky Wildcats, which made that pill a little easier to swallow. The Cards had lost to Mississippi and at No. 7 North Carolina. Louisville was supremely confident coming into the game with Kentucky, as they had knocked them off the previous year in Rupp Arena.

Now they had the Wildcats in their own house, and they had experience and swagger. But Kentucky had experience, too, and an influx of new talent who would eventually become stars. Championship players like Heshimu Evans, Scott Padgett, Wayne Turner, and Jamaal Magloire mixed with role players like Jules Camara, Ryan Hogan, and Saul Smith. Throw in Desmond Allison, Michael Bradley, and freshman Tayshaun Prince, and the Wildcats were loaded with a great combination of talent, skill, athleticism, depth, and shooters. They were long and could rebound. They had leaders.

They also had a desire for revenge. Take Padgett, for one. He was a senior from Louisville who said that even though the Wildcats won the national title in 1998, it was difficult to go home. UofL fans kept telling him his Wildcats were No. 1 in the nation but No. 2 in the state after their loss to Louisville earlier in the year. Padgett also took grief from fans because he'd had his own rough road at UK, missing the team's 1996 title run because he was academically ineligible.

And then there were the Cardinals. Just like the previous season, Louisville had a chance to again make waves in the basketball world. Point guard Cameron Murray wanted to go out a winner. So did Louisville native Tony Williams. Nate Johnson and Alex Sanders had tasted what it was like to beat UK, and they wanted to do it again. Plus, it would mean a step back into the limelight for the Cardinals. Could they beat No. 3 UK in Freedom Hall?

"Right now we're not even on the map," Louisville forward Eric Johnson told CBS before the December 26, 1998 game. "But if we win, we'll be on the map."

The sophomore guard named Marques Maybin would help a bit, too.

The Game:

Tubby Smith threw every defense he could at Louisville: a man-to-man, a 2-3 zone, a full-court press, back to a man-to-man, a 1-2-2 zone.

Few things worked for the Wildcats' head coach. The Cardinals were too quick.

And in those times when it required diving for a loose ball, or stretching for that elusive rebound, or playing that extra little bit of defense, it seemed like Louisville just wanted to win more than their opponents.

Cameron Murray spent the summer running the beaches of his native California, and it showed. The Louisville point guard had shed 20 pounds, and was—at times—the quickest player on the court. He controlled the tempo, breaking Kentucky's press early on for easy baskets.

After Scott Padgett hit a runner in the lane to start the game, the track meet was on. Murray found Maybin on the break for a layup and the foul—it was a theme UK should have gotten used to seeing. Countless times, Murray and Maybin would beat the Kentucky pressure, and they would find their big men for layups and dunks. Or, one of the pair would just hit a jumper.

At the 14-minute mark, UofL led 14-10, and Louisville forwards Alex Sanders and Dion Edward were winning all the hustle points.

Then, Kentucky seemed to wake up. Call it a Christmas hangover, or some other feeling of malaise, but for a bit the pressure seemed to rattle Louisville. UK looked inside to Michael Bradley and Jamaal Magloire, and little-used bench player Ryan Hogan chipped in 9 of Kentucky's first 17 points. Heshimu Evans got a dunk and Wayne Turner a layup, and in 4 minutes, UK had turned it around, and led 23-16 with 10:30 to play.

Enter Murray. Again. His layup, followed by a Tony Williams three, plus three free throws and a layup from Nate Johnson, regained the lead for Louisville, 26-25. With 6:00 left, it was all tied at 28.

The Freedom Hall crowd of 20,051 was alive. This was the game the fans in red were hoping to see.

Wayne Turner, Kentucky's all-everything point guard, was sent to the bench at the 5:00 mark with his second foul. Not surprisingly, Kentucky's offense was out of sorts. Two offensive fouls later, Eric Johnson hit a jumper and a three, and like that, the Cards went into halftime with a 47-40 lead.

They shot 63% from the field, compared to UK's 52%. The rebounding was tied at 15 apiece. For 20 minutes Louisville had done more than just hang with the defending champs—they had also out-played UK.

It turns out Christmas was actually extended a day for Cardinals fans.

Maybin hit a three to start the second half, and Williams followed with another. Two Sanders free throws extended the lead to 55-46 at the 15:00 mark.

Then Dion Edward committed his fourth foul, and Louisville missed his energy, as the Cards actually went six minutes without a field goal. But the fireworks were ready to begin. With 13:00 to play, Nate Johnson fouled Magloire and the two got tangled up in elbows. Both started jawing and both were awarded technical fouls. The personal and the technical gave Johnson four fouls and sent him to the bench. UK, sparked by the technicals and the implementation of a 1-2-2 zone defense to attempt to contain the Louisville guards, went on a run, cutting the lead to 55-51.

Michael Bradley, Scott Padgett, and Jamaal Magloire worked the inside against Louisville and hung with them for a while. Then an unlikely hero emerged in big man Tobiah Hopper. In the span of two minutes, Hopper hit a layup, got a steal off the press and hit another layup, and then blocked two shots to start a new Cardinal run.

"Oh yeah, they got frustrated," Tony Williams told the media afterward. "You could see it on their faces."

The score stood at 68-58 when the signature play occurred. Murray found Maybin in the corner in transition, right in front of the Louisville bench. The Clarksville, Tennessee, sophomore shooter didn't hesitate. Even with the 6'11" Magloire flying at him to block his shot, Maybin pulled up and fired, giving his shot extra arc to push it up over the outstretched arms of the Kentucky big man.

Maybin drained it. Magloire crashed into him, earning the foul. The UK player fell into the Louisville bench as the Cards celebrated and Maybin was mobbed.

It effectively ended the game.

Maybin hit the last two free throws of the game as the crowd chanted "U OF L!" The Cards won 83-74—their largest margin of victory since their 22-point win in 1988.

The contest was marred only by its last play. Maybin found Nate Johnson all alone under the hoop for what most thought would be an uncontested jam as the clock ran out—that is, until Magloire came over and blocked the shot out of bounds.

Johnson came up yelling at Magloire, and the UK player then walked over and got into Johnson's face. Players from both squads then got involved, even as the game was officially over. Pushing and shoving occurred, much of it by UK player Scott Padgett, who wisely got between the two players and muscled Magloire back toward the UK bench. It could have been much worse if Padgett had not gotten involved.

That said, the UofL team had gotten the last laugh.

Postgame:

Padgett finished with 13 points to lead UK. Eight Wildcats scored at least 5 points, including Bradley's 12-point, 7-rebound effort. Turner scored 11 points and dished 4 assists, but also committed 6 turnovers. Of Kentucky's big three of Padgett, Evans, and Turner, none made much difference in the game. UofL turned Padgett into a driver, Turner into a shooter, and kept Evans out of transition.

"Those were the guys we wanted to shut down," Maybin told the *Herald-Leader* after the game. "We knew they were the heart of the team. We knew how to play those guys."

Maybin led all scorers with 19 points. Murray was the other half of the dynamite backcourt, finishing with 14 points, 10 assists, and just 3 turnovers. Williams, also a Louisville native, was the only other double-figure scorer on the team, tallying 14 points and adding 4 assists. All together, eight Cards scored at least 5 points, including surprise performances from Hopper (6 points) and Dion Edward (8 points).

Kentucky finished 28-9 and again pulled together at just the right moment. Only a narrow loss to Michigan State in the regional finals, 73-66, kept them from their fourth consecutive Final Four appearance. Scott Padgett, Wayne Turner, and Heshimu Evans had completed their Wildcat careers, and thus ended one of the greatest runs in Kentucky basketball history.

After the disastrous 12-20 season in 1998, Louisville improved to 19-11 and made it back to the NCAAs, where they lost a narrow first-round game to Creighton, 62-58. No matter—as Eric Johnson had predicted, the Cards were back on the map. Cameron Murray eventually became the founder and director of the Prodigy Athletic Institute, a non-profit in California that mentors student athletes and helps them achieve their goals.

But no one's path compares to the journey of Marques Maybin.

✷✷✷✷✷

Maybin became one of the most beloved stars in Cardinal basketball history. He still ranks 13th all-time on the scoring list, with 1,624 points. When he left Louisville in 2001 (the last season of Denny Crum's coaching career) he played professionally in Lebanon and France.

In 2003, he had returned home to Clarksville from playing overseas. His dream was to try out for NBA teams. But everything changed on Aug. 5, 2003. Maybin was riding his motorcycle when he collided with the back of a pickup truck at an intersection. He was six weeks shy of his 25th birthday.

The accident left him paralyzed from the waist down.

He worked through rehabilitation to get back to some kind of normalcy (sometimes he would work for hours to just try and sit up). After three years he moved back to Louisville to finish his degree. With some nudging—then pushing—from former guard DeJuan Wheat, Maybin was able to finally get back into a gym and watch basketball.

"Everybody has been going through this with me," he told the Associated Press in 2008. "We're all going through this together. I've never felt alone in this whole thing."

But don't think any of it ever becomes easy.

"I battle demons on a day-to-day basis," he said. "But people don't let me slow down at all."

In 2012, both Maybin and Wheat graduated from Louisville as part of the Houston-Bridgeman Fellows Cardinal Degree Completion Program, which helps student-athletes complete their degrees. Dion Edward graduated with them.

Both Maybin and Wheat sat in front of the media and explained the roads they'd taken to graduation. Wheat said his mother cried when he

Cardinals DeJuan Wheat and Marques Maybin each played significant roles in Dream Game upsets of Kentucky. Both also returned to the University to complete their degrees in 2012. *(Photo appears courtesy of University of Louisville Athletics)*

told her. Maybin explained how he'd lost his mother and brother in the past year.

"I've always been so appreciative of the people that helped me get through everything," Maybin said. "Every time I have an issue, I always look at it like I'm still so fortunate to have help through my issues, to have support. We're really talking a glass-half-full thing with me. You've got to keep pedaling, got to keep pushing. I'm just so thankful I chose to go here."

After seeing what Maybin accomplished, how could anyone think life was too difficult?

"What he's accomplished right now is remarkable, because of all he's went through," Wheat said. "One of the strongest people I know."

"I am so proud of him," Coach Denny Crum said of Maybin. "To do what he's done, to accomplish what he has and overcome what he has, you can't be more proud of a guy. You just can't."

Louisville 83

NAME	MIN	FG-FGA	3-3A	FT-FTA	OR-REB	PF	AST	STL	BLK	TO	TP
Williams	36	5-7	3-4	1-3	1-4	2	4	2	0	5	14
N. Johnson	23	3-8	0-1	3-5	0-2	4	0	2	0	0	9
Sanders	30	1-3	0-1	3-4	2-9	2	2	0	0	4	5
Maybin	26	5-9	2-4	7-9	3-3	3	2	1	0	4	19
Murray	36	2-6	0-3	10-11	0-3	0	10	1	0	3	14
E. Johnson	17	3-6	1-3	1-2	4-7	3	0	0	0	1	8
Hopper	17	2-3	0-0	2-2	0-2	2	0	1	1	3	6
Edward	8	4-5	0-0	0-0	2-2	4	0	0	0	0	8
McKinley	5	0-0	0-0	0-0	0-0	0	0	0	0	0	0
Smiley	2	0-1	0-1	0-0	0-0	1	0	0	0	0	0
TEAM					1						
Total	200	25-48	6-17	27-36	12-33	21	18	7	1	20	83

Kentucky 74

NAME	MIN	FG-FGA	3-3A	FT-FTA	OR-REB	PF	AST	STL	BLK	TO	TP
Evans	27	3-7	0-3	2-2	2-4	4	1	2	0	4	8
Padgett	37	6-11	0-3	1-1	1-5	4	2	4	0	2	13
Bradley	23	6-11	0-0	0-3	5-7	2	0	0	0	1	12
Turner	26	5-12	0-1	1-2	3-4	4	4	2	0	6	11
Prince	18	2-4	1-3	0-0	1-1	1	1	0	0	1	5
Smith	27	1-3	0-0	3-4	2-4	4	4	3	1	3	5
Hogan	19	3-11	1-5	4-5	2-3	2	1	1	0	1	11
Magloire	19	4-5	0-0	1-3	2-3	3	1	1	1	0	9
Camara	2	0-0	0-0	0-0	0-0	0	1	0	0	0	0
Allison	2	0-0	0-0	0-0	0-0	2	0	0	0	0	0
TEAM					3						
Total	200	30-64	2-15	12-20	18-34	26	15	13	2	18	74

Chapter 19

Long Distance

UK 76, UofL 46
December 18, 1999 at Rupp Arena

THE GOOD CITIZENS of Toronto, Canada, are no strangers to sports rivalry. Their NHL Maple Leafs and the Montreal Canadians have conducted one of the most intense feuds in athletic history. Toronto's baseball Blue Jays, NBA Raptors, and even CFL Argonauts have had their share of scrapes over the years. But Kentucky versus Louisville? There is a national border and 600 miles of highway between Toronto and either Lexington or Louisville. And while James Naismith, the inventor of basketball, was a Canadian, it's safe to say that Canada had little impact on the UK/UofL rivalry. Enter Jamaal Magloire.

Magloire was born and raised in Toronto, where he lived until he arrived at UK. In sixth grade, Magloire began dedicating his time to basketball. As he began to grow into the frame that would reach 6'10", that decision was rewarded. For his part, Magloire put in time and work, even on the freezing outdoor courts of his native land. "I remember playing basketball in the snow and sleet," admits Magloire. "Resources were limited and all we had was outdoor courts. We just made it work."

Magloire made it work well enough that he chose Kentucky over Purdue out of high school and spent three seasons as a ferocious and rugged low post defensive force. In these three seasons, Magloire climbed to fourth on UK's list of top shot-blockers. He was a bruising rebounder and intimidator who made opponents earn every basket. Magloire had a few scrapes with his own team, as well as his opponents, as he missed five games in his junior season due to violation of team rules. However, few questioned Magloire's will to win, as his defensive intensity had been critical to UK's appearance in consecutive national title games in his first two seasons.

Among the many international players who followed Magloire in making an impact in the UK/UofL rivalry is Gorgui Dieng. Dieng was an integral part of Louisville's 2013 championship squad. His parents first saw him play college basketball against UK *(See chapter 33). (Photo by Tim Sofranko)*

Magloire enjoyed the rivalry with Louisville. "There's nothing like it," he noted. "The magnitude for Kentucky basketball is different than it is for anything else." He noted that the intensity of the game sometimes made it feel like an NCAA Final. He enjoyed the physical intensity of the matchups with Louisville. "I remember on multiple occasions getting into altercations with those guys," said Magloire in a recent interview. "It was something that I embraced, and kind of looked forward to. I always said when it came to nut-cutting time, you would find out who was a soldier and who wasn't."

Magloire was definitely a soldier. Despite scoring just seven points per game as a junior, he had entered his name into the NBA Draft, before he decided to return and play one final season for Tubby Smith's Wildcats. Magloire and junior Saul Smith were the only upperclassmen to play significant minutes for the 1999–2000 Wildcats. They were surrounded by talented sophomores Tayshaun Prince, Desmond Allison, and Jules Camara, as well as freshmen Keith Bogans and Marvin Stone. Magloire recalls fostering these young stars, as the team was forced to move out of Wildcat Lodge during renovations, "We were on our own . . . and I remember taking care of them, making sure they were okay, kind of being the father figure in the household, so to speak."

The ability of this young nucleus to gel would control UK's destiny. The team struggled greatly, losing three of their last four games coming into the Louisville matchup with a 4-4 record and outside of the Top 25.

Louisville, on the other hand, had won its last five games after opening the season with two losses. Junior Marques Maybin and seniors Nate Johnson and Tony Williams led the 5-2 Cards. Unlike Kentucky, whose veterans were a small group but whose youngsters were talented, Denny Crum's Cardinals had limited depth. Freshman Reece Gaines was a significant addition, but otherwise, the newcomers offered little help. For the first time in the history of the rivalry, neither team was in the Top 25 when the annual game occurred.

The Game:

With both teams still building identities, there was no clear favorite in this installment of the Dream Game. Kentucky, having been upset in the past two matchups, was eager to avoid a trifecta. Louisville wished to push its momentum over the struggling Cats. For a half, the two squads played each other evenly, with UK holding a 35-34 advantage at intermission.

However, after intermission, the UK basketball program awoke. Kentucky applied suffocating defense to the Cardinals after the break. For the first nine minutes and ten seconds of the second half, UofL could not convert a single basket. UK's run began at 4-0 and stretched to 17-2 and then to 26-4 in the meantime. UofL shot 3-of-27 in the second half—with the last two makes coming inside the game's final

2:30. Meanwhile, Prince racked up 20 points for Kentucky. Desmond Allison added 16, and Keith Bogans, in his first start at UK, scored a dozen points.

At the center of the frenzied defensive run was the wily old man in the middle—Magloire, the import. Playing with the steady intensity that characterized his game, Jamaal totaled 12 points and 10 rebounds. He also blocked 3 shots—and with the first block, he became UK's career blocked shots leader.

UK rolled, 76-46, thanks to a 41-12 second half. After the game, Magloire was more excited about the victory than his new record. "I didn't know [that I was about to set the record] until right before the game. It doesn't really matter," he said. "I am more happy with the win. . . . This was definitely a big game and a big rivalry."

Tubby Smith was not as inclined to downplay his center's achievement. "That is quite an accomplishment, with all the great players who have come through here over the years," he said in his postgame press conference.

Smith was pleased to have stemmed the tide of UK's recent struggles. "I never got caught up in the dark cloud. We just focused on the job at hand, and that was preparing our kids for this game." Of course, he was even more pleased by the means of victory. Smith admitted, "Today was a tremendous defensive effort by all of our players."

While Smith was pleased with his team's defense, Denny Crum was horrified at his squad's execution. "I've never had a team get just four assists," Crum said. "You can give Kentucky a lot of the credit. Our shot selection wasn't good, and we didn't make the extra pass very often." Noting that UK shot just under 60% for the game, Crum continued, "We didn't guard them at the defensive end, so we got an old-fashioned butt-kicking, and that's the way it's supposed to be. We got what we earned out there."

Postgame:

Nearly a decade and a half later, Jamaal Magloire's name is still written large in the Kentucky record book. His 268 blocked shots remain UK's all-time record. He is among UK's top-15 all-time rebounders and also joined the 1,000-point club late in his senior campaign. The big man has softened his tone on those accomplishments. "I think now, looking back on my career, I'm very happy for all the accolades that I've gotten. I wasn't down-playing the fact that I'm the career leader in shots blocked. I just always learned to put the team and winning first, and if you do that, all the accolades will come."

Magloire demonstrated that geography played no role in the UK/UofL rivalry. Just as the young men from Louisville's inner city or eastern Kentucky's rural hollows bled blue or red, so did the big Canadian.

Magloire scored 13 points and grabbed 9 rebounds per game in his senior season. He was chosen in the first round of the 2000 NBA Draft. He played 13 NBA seasons and even was chosen for the All-Star Game in 2003–04. He finished his career with the hometown Toronto Raptors, and at last information, was employed by the team in player development. A decade and a half after his UK days, Magloire is again mentoring the young talent and teaching them the ropes of basketball.

Other international performers would reach the big stage in Kentucky's intrastate clash. Sophomore Jules Camara of Senegal appreciated Magloire's moment, as he himself added 6 points in 11 minutes of playing time in UK's 1999 blowout. Poland's Lukasz Obrzut was a UK role player who brought some of his best efforts to the UK/UofL matchup in the mid-2000s. Dominician Republic natives Francisco Garcia and Edgar Sosa would go on to shine in future editions of the game for the Cardinals. And Senegal's Gorgui Dieng was a critical part of Louisville's 2013 title run. While it had long since been clear that the borders of the UK/UofL battle didn't end at the Kentucky state line, in future years it became clear that the entire world could play a part in the fight for Kentucky basketball supremacy.

UK went on to a 23-10 season. The Wildcats lost their first SEC Tournament game and then needed double overtime to sneak past St. Bonaventure in the first round of the NCAA Tournament. The second round ended in a 52-50 loss to Syracuse. Magloire had been a rock, and he, Prince, and Bogans gave UK hope for the future, as each was capable of carrying the team on a given night. However, the program had some major questions marks. Sophomore guard Desmond Allison was suspended from the team for violation of a school alcohol policy and never played at UK again. (Tragically, Allison was shot and killed in 2011.) Post players Jules Camara and Marvin Stone had both proven inconsistent, and Saul Smith was often ineffective while logging tons of minutes at point guard.

Louisville finished the year at 19-12. The Cardinals reached the NCAA Tournament, but lost to Gonzaga in their first game. The team's core of Maybin, Johnson, Williams, and Gaines fought doggedly, beating four ranked opponents during the season. However, this team also wasn't destined to be one of the school's more memorable squads. With Johnson and Williams completing their eligibility, the future of Denny Crum's program was very much an open question. It would not remain open for very long.

Kentucky 76

NAME	MIN	FG-FGA	3-3A	FT-FTA	OR-REB	PF	AST	STL	BLK	TO	TP
Prince	36	8-13	3-5	1-2	2-7	2	2	1	5	0	20
Allison	32	6-9	2-3	2-4	1-3	2	4	2	0	2	16
Magloire	30	5-8	0-0	2-2	4-10	1	1	0	3	3	12
Bogans	30	5-6	2-2	0-2	0-2	2	4	2	0	4	12
Smith	29	2-5	0-2	0-0	0-6	3	1	2	0	2	4
Stone	12	2-4	0-0	0-0	1-5	3	1	1	1	3	4
Camara	10	2-3	0-1	2-2	0-1	1	0	0	0	1	6
Blevins	8	0-0	0-0	0-0	0-0	0	0	0	0	0	0
Tackett	7	0-1	0-1	0-0	0-1	0	1	1	0	0	0
Masiello	2	0-0	0-0	0-0	0-0	0	0	0	0	1	0
Knight	2	1-3	0-0	0-0	2-2	0	0	0	0	0	2
TEAM					4						
Total	200	31-52	7-14	7-12	10-41	14	14	9	9	16	76

Louisville 46

NAME	MIN	FG-FGA	3-3A	FT-FTA	OR-REB	PF	AST	STL	BLK	TO	TP
Williams	34	4-12	3-7	1-1	2-7	2	2	0	0	2	12
Johnson	32	4-11	1-2	2-2	2-5	1	0	0	0	3	11
Edward	26	2-4	0-0	0-0	2-4	5	0	0	0	1	4
Gaines	31	3-8	0-3	1-1	1-2	1	0	2	0	4	7
Maybin	31	3-13	1-6	2-2	1-1	0	2	1	0	2	9
Bailey	12	1-3	0-1	0-0	0-0	2	0	1	0	0	2
Hopper	12	0-1	0-0	0-0	0-0	1	0	0	1	1	0
Gervin	11	0-1	0-1	1-2	0-1	1	0	0	0	1	1
Smiley	9	0-2	0-1	0-0	0-0	0	0	0	0	0	0
Turner	2	0-1	0-0	0-0	1-1	1	0	0	0	0	0
Brooks	0+	0-1	0-1	0-0	0-0	0	0	0	0	0	0
TEAM					3						
Total	200	17-57	5-22	7-8	9-24	14	4	4	1	15	46

Chapter 20

The Ice Man

UK 64, UofL 62
January 2, 2001 at Freedom Hall

FANS OF KENTUCKY and Louisville often while away the "dead days" of summer comparing their teams, looking up and down the rosters to fathom an advantage that their squad has over the intra state rival. Of course, those fans dream of matchups deep in the NCAA Tournament or between highly ranked talented squads. While fans of neither school expected that the January 2, 2001, edition of the Dream Game would pit two unranked teams with a combined record of 9-13, the preseason armchair coaches would have been correct in one aspect of the game. If there was one player who would look cool and unflappable in a close game situation, that player, friend and foe were both certain, was UK's Tayshaun Prince. The question was whether Prince would play as cool as he looked.

Prince was a lanky 6'9" wing player from Compton, California. Luring Prince eastward from the west coast rap music capital to the hilly Kentucky bluegrass was Tubby's Smith's first, and perhaps greatest, UK recruiting coup. Despite Prince's McDonald's All-American skill set, his demeanor often suggested a casual, indifferent approach to the game. In fact, time showed that it was purely an illusion—that the wiry Prince was a feisty and tenacious competitor, but that unlike some of his teammates, he did not wear his emotions on his sleeve.

Prince was aware of the perception that he was too quiet, perhaps too laid back to star. He told *The Cats' Pause*, "People want me to be a more vocal leader . . . but I'm the type of person that is more laid back and just likes to go play basketball and lead by example." In his freshman season, Prince scored just under six points per game on a veteran UK team that reached the NCAA Elite Eight. As a sophomore, Prince totaled 13.3 points per game on a mediocre UK squad. As a junior, he was counted on to bear the load for a talented but immature UK team.

That team, featuring Prince and sophomore guard Keith Bogans, as well as freshman guard Gerald Fitch, sophomore post player Marvin Stone, and freshman center Jason Parker, was struggling to finish a close game in the 2000–01 season. UK entered the UofL game with a 5-5 mark, and the five losses were by one point, five points (in overtime), five points, two points, and one point. Simply stated, the Cats were struggling in close games, and Prince had failed to assert himself. He had a crucial turnover late in UK's season-opening loss to St. John's. UK was a team in need of a star, and Prince was in need of an identity.

Denny Crum and Louisville were in need of a miracle. The Cardinals featured sophomore guard Reece Gaines and senior guard Marques Maybin, but the pickings were slim thereafter. Lexington native Erik Brown was a solid forward, and freshmen Luke Whitehead and Ellis Myles fought gamely in the post, but were often too inexperienced to help. Not only was Louisville 4-8 before the UK matchup, but unlike UK's problems, the Cardinals couldn't stay in games. Of the losses, the margins included a 22-point loss to Maryland, a 29-point beating at Alabama, and a 23-point home defeat to Dayton.

About the best thing to be said for this installment of the Dream Game was that, to steal the slogan of the Kentucky lottery, somebody had to win.

The Game:

Louisville opened the game looking like they had adopted a motto from hometown hero Muhammad Ali and were out to shock the world. The

Cards made their first six shots from the floor, including three-point bombs from Gaines and Maybin, and leaped to a 14-4 advantage over the stunned Wildcats.

But the unshakable Prince drained a three-pointer, and after a three-point play from UK's Jason Parker, the game began a trend of swinging back and forth. Kentucky took the lead with just under 9:00 left in the first half, courtesy of a Saul Smith trey. The two teams passed the lead back and forth, and UK had a slim 29-27 halftime advantage.

In the second half, the Wildcats were primed to break the game open. When Keith Bogans nailed a three, UK had stretched its lead to a dozen points, at 41-29. Louisville answered with a lengthy run, keyed by Gaines and freshman forward Luke Whitehead, who combined for 13 points between them to trim Kentucky's lead to 50-48 with 7:47 to play.

Again, the pattern continued. Kentucky, led by Bogans on the outside and Parker and Marvin Stone on the interior, jumped to a ten-point lead with 4:00 to play. In the next three minutes, Louisville returned serve, with Gaines draining two threes, hitting another shot, and tying the game at 62 with a pair of free throws with 59 seconds to play.

In light of UK's shaky play in close games, the Cardinals sensed an opportunity. On the ensuing possession, UK looked tentative, holding the ball deep into the shot clock, looking for someone to step up.

Tayshaun Prince reluctantly took on the task. He handled the ball at the top of the key as the shot clock wound down. He dribbled, looking to drive, to create . . . something. And then, Prince was bailed out. Luke Whitehead, playing a solid game as a freshman reserve, was overly anxious, and delivered a hand check to Prince. Was it a foul? Referee Bob Donato thought so and blew his whistle. Prince agreed, telling the Lexington *Herald-Leader*, "It was too obvious. . . . He had two hands on me."

With 26.5 seconds to play, Prince headed to the foul line.

Always the coolest customer on the floor, Prince calmly drained both free throws, giving UK a 64-62 advantage. Louisville sought to answer and wasted little time going for the victory. Lexingtonian Erik Brown fired up a three-point attempt with four seconds to play, which missed badly, but the ball was batted out of bounds back to Louisville, with time for one final shot. Freshman Ellis Myles, with the five-second count running down, sailed his pass over Reece Gaines's head and out of bounds. UofL never got another shot. Kentucky inbounded the ball to Prince, who held it as the clock ticked to zero and UK escaped Freedom Hall with a victory.

Prince had a typically solid game—13 points, 8 rebounds, and 6 assists. When added to 16 points for Bogans, and 11 each for Parker and Stone, it was just enough for an escape. For Louisville, all was not lost. Reece Gaines had been almost Houdini-like in defeat, raining in 27 points, including 5-of-8 three-point shooting, and being impossible to stop. Denny Crum was encouraged, telling the *Herald-Leader*, "We haven't played this hard all season."

But the last word had gone to the cool and collected Prince, who at last had lived to his image.

Postgame:

The Louisville game marked a turning point for UK—not only did they win a close game, but also Prince emerged as the team's dependable late-game option. UK finished the regular season at 19-9 after their 5-5 start. One of the keys was Prince, who struck again with key plays—like a basket in the closing seconds to knock off No. 8 Florida on February 6.

UK shared the SEC title and won the conference tournament. They rolled through two NCAA games before dropping an 80-76 heartbreaker to Southern California, in a game that would have brought about an Elite Eight matchup with Duke had UK won. Still, 24-10 was a welcome regrouping from a rough December for UK.

Louisville stumbled to a 12-19 season. Gaines and Maybin were superb, and Erik Brown added 10.2 points per game, but the lack of interior experience gashed the Cardinals all year long. The team shot just 41% for the season and was outrebounded by almost three boards per game.

Given the team's struggles, change may have been inevitable. Still, some were shocked on March 2, the day before senior day, when Coach Denny Crum announced that the difficult season would be his last as head coach of the Cardinals. Louisville beat Memphis in Crum's final regular season game, marking his 675th career victory. Four days later,

UofL lost to UAB in the Conference USA Tournament, and the Crum era, with its three decades of dominance, was over. The coach who had done so much to create the rivalry would step aside to a successor. And that would prove to be quite a story as well.

*****

Meanwhile, Tayshuan Prince's career was just beginning. After one more superb year in Lexington, Tayshaun took his game to the NBA, where he starred for a Detroit Pistons squad that captured an NBA title. Prince's superb perimeter defense, solid team play, and cool nerve were responsible for earning him a spot on the US 2008 Olympic team, where he won a gold medal. Today, Prince's NBA career continues with the Memphis Grizzlies.

No longer a youngster, Tayshaun is prized because of his veteran know-how and his ability to make big plays—an ability that many first saw when he canned two free throws to beat Louisville. A dozen years on, Tayshaun is still the coolest guy in the arena.

Kentucky 64

NAME	MIN	FG-FGA	3-3A	FT-FTA	OR-REB	PF	AST	STL	BLK	TO	TP
Prince	40	5-13	1-5	2-2	2-8	0	6	2	1	1	13
Parker	21	5-7	0-0	1-1	0-3	3	1	0	0	0	11
Bogans	36	6-15	3-6	1-1	3-5	2	2	0	0	2	16
Smith	37	2-5	2-5	0-1	0-1	2	4	1	0	0	6
Fitch	23	2-4	0-1	2-2	2-2	2	1	1	0	2	6
Stone	25	5-7	0-0	1-2	2-6	3	0	0	1	2	11
Blevins	7	0-1	0-1	0-0	0-0	0	2	0	0	0	0
Daniels	5	0-0	0-0	0-0	0-0	0	0	0	1	0	0
Estill	5	0-0	0-0	1-2	0-1	1	0	0	1	0	1
Hawkins	1	0-0	0-0	0-0	0-0	0	0	0	0	0	0
TEAM					1						
Total	200	25-52	6-18	8-11	9-27	13	16	4	4	7	64

Louisville 62

NAME	MIN	FG-FGA	3-3A	FT-FTA	OR-REB	PF	AST	STL	BLK	TO	TP
Myles	23	4-5	0-0	0-1	2-3	3	1	0	0	3	8
Brown	29	3-13	1-6	0-0	1-3	2	2	4	0	0	7
Lasege	8	0-2	0-0	0-0	0-0	3	0	0	1	0	0
Maybin	38	3-5	1-2	2-2	1-3	1	2	0	0	2	9
Gaines	32	10-14	5-8	2-2	2-8	3	4	0	1	1	27
N'Sima	30	1-3	0-0	0-2	3-7	2	1	0	3	0	2
Whitehead	21	3-7	0-0	0-0	0-3	1	2	0	0	1	6
Brooks	10	1-1	1-1	0-0	1-2	1	0	0	0	3	3
Turner	7	0-1	0-0	0-0	1-1	0	0	0	0	1	0
Naydenov	1	0-1	0-1	0-0	0-0	0	0	0	0	0	0
Northern	1	0-1	0-1	0-0	0-0	0	0	0	0	0	0
TEAM					2						
Total	200	25-53	8-19	4-7	11-32	16	12	4	5	11	62

Chapter 21

A Tale of Two Coaches

No. 6 UK 82, UofL 62
December 29, 2001 at Rupp Arena

MOST YEARS, THE Dream Game is about the players. With names like Walker, Mashburn, Chapman, Gordon, and Ellison, the battle usually centers around the hardwood protagonists who shoot, rebound, and defend.

But 2001–02 was not most years. Reece Gaines and Tayshaun Prince were almost afterthoughts. This game boiled down to Tubby versus Rick.

In a very real sense, Dream Game 21 began on March 21, 2001. Nineteen days after Denny Crum announced his retirement from the head coaching position at the University of Louisville, Tom Jurich announced that his successor was none other than Rick Pitino.

After three-and-a-half difficult seasons with the Boston Celtics, the man who rebuilt Kentucky basketball had found himself on the unemployment line. But not for long. In January 2001, Jurich and Crum had discussed a renewal of Crum's contract. The intended renewal was for two years, but Crum was not interested in recruiting new players without being able to tell them that he would coach them for four seasons. Accordingly, Crum's three decades of Cardinal coaching came to an abrupt end after a rough 12-19 campaign.

It took little time for Jurich to settle on Pitino. For his part, the new coach tried to downplay the rivalry. "For 364 days each year, we'll pull for each other," Pitino quipped. "But on that one day each year, we'll get it on."

The Kentucky diehards planned to get it on 365 days per year. Pitino later recalled that he telephoned longtime Wildcat equipment manager Bill Keightley to discuss the move. "ARE YOU OUT OF YOUR DAMN MIND?" the venerable Keightley asked.

Former Kentucky guard Sean Woods recalled Pitino's move in a recent interview, "[E]verybody else was pissed off about it, and rightfully so." Speaking hypothetically, Woods continued, "That's just like Mike Krzyzewski leaving Duke and going to Carolina, or Dean Smith leaving . . . from North Carolina and going to Duke, or Roy Williams going to Duke. But in today's society, things happen like that."

Pitino inherited not only a blast of ire from the Kentucky faithful, but a fairly mediocre Cardinal squad. The 12-19 team lost only two players, with Marques Maybin being the only notable loss and solid veterans like Reece Gaines and Ellis Myles bringing experience to the table. They would be augmented by a recruiting class that Hoop Scoop ranked as the second best in the nation. That class, led by Louisville Moore guard Carlos Hurt (who had committed to then-Coach Crum) and Louisville Ballard forward Brandon Bender, was expected to play a pivotal role in Pitino's rebuilding task. Less heralded freshmen like Larry O'Bannon and Otis George would actually play greater roles than the so-called freshman stars, but help was on the way for Louisville.

A remarkable phenomenon broke loose in Lexington, as well. While Tubby Smith had endeared himself to many of the Wildcat faithful with his 1998 NCAA title run, there were still many detractors who stubbornly insisted that Smith had won only with Pitino's players. Entering his fifth season, Smith was still celebrated only reluctantly by certain subgroups of the Big Blue Nation. However, now the entire Kentucky fan base was comparing True Blue Tubby with Traitor Rick.

Smith admitted, in *The Cats' Pause* preseason yearbook, "I'm not going to say we'll approach it like any other game, because the last coach who said that about playing Louisville [Sutton] is not here. Obviously, it's a big game. . . . It will be interesting, but I think it's more fan-oriented. The rivalry has always been there and it will always be there."

Smith returned a talented but underachieving UK team. Senior Tayshaun Prince and junior Keith Bogans led the squad, but the team was so deep and talented that junior post player Marquis Estill was persuaded to give up his scholarship so that Smith could add another recruit.

Sophomores Gerald Fitch and Cliff Hawkins also started, with Estill, junior Jules Camara, and freshman Chuck Hayes dividing time in the low post. The team got a bit thinner two days before the Louisville game, when junior Marvin Stone was dismissed from the team after failing to return from Christmas break.

But when 7-2 Kentucky, ranked sixth in the nation, hosted unranked 9-1 Louisville on December 29, the two figures at the forefront were Smith and Pitino. It was Homecoming Day for either the greatest coach in the Commonwealth or the sneakiest traitor. Louisville fans sported "Got Pitino?" T-shirts and UK fans responded with a variety of signs and banners, one of which said, "We didn't like you either, Joanne," in reference to Pitino's wife.

It was, to borrow Pitino's own phrase, the day to get it on.

The Game:

The game's first surprise came a few minutes before tipoff, when Pitino ducked through the home team entrance in an effort to . . . well, do what? Send a message to the Kentucky faithful? Delay the loud booing that would follow? Who knows. The booing rained down during introductions. Pitino, for his part, professed indifference. "I didn't pay any attention to it," he said after the game. "I am the Louisville coach. They are supposed to boo me."

As is typical in a game with so much hype, both teams came out shooting poorly. UK made only 1 of its first 7 shots, and UofL was 2-for-7. However, Kentucky began making small runs and pulled ahead of Louisville. Kentucky led by five midway through the first half and stretched the lead to 26-18 with 3:30 to go. Pitino's Cardinals hung in the game with their tenacious defensive pressure, and after Erik Brown converted a steal into a dunk seconds before halftime, UK's lead was trimmed to 36-32.

In the second half, Kentucky's star players stepped up their games. After UofL trimmed the lead to one, at 38-37, Prince and Bogans took over. In the next few minutes, the duo led UK on a 14-2 run, with Bogans scoring five points and Prince adding eight in the run, culminating with a two-handed slam that forced Pitino into calling a timeout.

Louisville never threatened again. The Cardinals trailed 63-50 when UK added 10 more unanswered points, the last basket coming when Cliff Hawkins nearly broke a Cardinal ankle or two with a vicious cross-over dribble leading to an open layup.

Rupp Arena, holding its fourth-largest crowd ever, had been very vocal in the second half. But Hawkins's basket cut the crowd loose. "TUB-BY! TUB-BY! TUB-BY!" chants roared through the arena. Vindication was the order of the day as Kentucky rolled, 82-62. In the game where everyone argued over one coach, the other became the star.

✶✶✶✶✶

Orlando Smith was the sixth of 17 children born to a pair of Maryland sharecroppers. Kentucky won an NCAA title the year that Smith was born, but it was not until after his playing career had extended to High Point College in North Carolina that African American players first took the court for Kentucky.

Smith became a coach and spent a dozen years as an assistant—with the last two coming on Rick Pitino's first two Kentucky squads. He had been successful in head coaching stops at Tulsa and Georgia before being hired in the spring of 1997 to succeed Pitino at Kentucky.

While Smith recalls rooting for Texas Western over Kentucky's all-white 1966 team in the NCAA championship, he has repeatedly emphasized that he has long since buried any discomfort over Kentucky's past. In November 1997, he told the *Chicago Tribune*, "I know there have been a lot of people who thought he [Rupp] was racist. But I think the times can dictate how people act—where you're brought up, how you're brought up. . . . I'm never going to judge anybody. . . . That was a long time ago. . . . You learn from the past and you go on."

For African Americans, Smith's hiring was a contentious point. *Herald-Leader* columnist Merlene Davis wrote an editorial, urging Smith to turn down the Kentucky job due to fears of vilification from racist Kentucky "fans." However, for others, like Winston Bennett, Smith's hiring was a touchstone event.

"It meant a lot," says Bennett, "It went against the old adage of the black cloud of prejudice that hung over the program. To me, it was a memento of progression. . . . It's like Obama being president, who would have thought?"

The 1998 title had won over many of Tubby's critics, but even the few remaining stragglers in the fringes of the Big Blue Nation were onboard after Dream Game XXI. In the final calculation, blue and red mattered much more than black and white. Tubby Smith's skin color was infinitely less important than the color of jerseys worn by Rick Pitino's squad.

Postgame:

Pitino was gracious in defeat, saying, "Right now, we are young and inexperienced and Kentucky is a much better basketball team than us." He went on to praise his successor, "Tubby is one of the premier coaches in the business. . . . [N]o one is going to out-coach Tubby."

Smith professed relief on his part. "We got through the game," he acknowledged. But even the businesslike Smith could not deny the power of hearing Rupp Arena chant his name. "It was great," he admitted. "It certainly makes you feel good to be wanted."

Kentucky's players had much more to say. "I think Louisville didn't show us much respect," explained Cliff Hawkins. "I think they thought they would come in here and Coach Pitino would lead them to the promised land and that is not going to happen."

Tayshaun Prince acknowledged the significance of the crowd's chant. "I felt good for Coach Smith," he said. "He needs to be appreciated like that. He should be appreciated like that every time we step out on the court."

Smith's triumph over Louisville was one of few positive moments in his 2001–02 season. That squad, dubbed "Team Turmoil," finished the season awash in player suspensions, transfers or dismissals, and lousy team chemistry. UK went 22-10, and despite an All-America campaign from Tayshaun Prince, ended their season with a Sweet 16 loss to Maryland. Not only had Marvin Stone transferred, but Jason Parker, Rashaad Carruth, Adam Chiles, and Cory Sears also left the team after the season. Tubby Smith had his own rebuilding job in progress.

As for Pitino, his young squad fought their way to a 19-13 finish. Junior guard Reece Gaines averaged 21 points per game in a phenomenal campaign. Sophomore forwards Luke Whitehead, Ellis Myles, and Lexingtonian Erik Brown also helped salvage the Cardinal season, which ended in the second round of the NIT. Highly touted freshmen Carlos Hurt and Brandon Bender did not work out as planned—Bender was dismissed in January and promptly entered his name into the NBA Draft, where his three-point-per-game UofL scoring average did not earn him NBA selection. Hurt suffered a back injury and missed much of the year. After the season, he was dismissed from the team by Pitino for violation of team rules.

Pitino had lost his first UK/UofL game while coaching at Kentucky, as well. Wildcat fans probably recalled that he had then won four in a row over Louisville, and six of his next seven contests in the rivalry. He would be back—aided by some new faces, and one face that was very familiar to Kentucky fans, but turned up in a surprisingly new place.

Kentucky 82

NAME	MIN	FG-FGA	3-3A	FT-FTA	OR-REB	PF	AST	STL	BLK	TO	TP
Prince	31	8-16	1-2	1-3	4-9	2	3	0	1	1	18
Camara	18	1-3	0-0	0-0	0-2	0	2	1	2	2	2
Hawkins	30	1-7	0-3	6-8	1-5	2	5	2	0	6	8
Fitch	27	3-9	1-6	3-3	1-5	2	0	0	0	0	10
Bogans	28	7-12	2-6	1-1	1-7	1	2	1	0	2	17
Estill	17	5-5	0-0	0-0	2-5	1	0	0	1	0	10
Daniels	14	1-5	0-2	1-2	2-2	1	1	0	1	0	3
Carruth	13	3-5	2-3	0-0	0-0	3	0	0	0	0	8
Hayes	9	2-4	0-0	1-2	2-3	1	0	1	0	1	5
Chiles	8	0-2	0-2	0-0	1-1	2	4	0	0	2	0
Carrier	2	0-1	0-1	0-0	0-0	0	0	0	0	0	0
Heissenbuttel	2	0-1	0-0	1-2	0-1	0	0	0	0	0	1
Sears	1	0-0	0-0	0-0	0-0	1	0	0	0	0	0
TEAM					3-6						
Total	200	31-70	6-25	14-21	17-46	16	17	5	5	14	82

Louisville 62

NAME	MIN	FG-FGA	3-3A	FT-FTA	OR-REB	PF	AST	STL	BLK	TO	TP
Myles	23	1-5	0-0	0-2	2-5	1	0	1	0	3	2
N'Sima	26	4-6	0-0	0-0	3-7	0	0	0	5	1	8
Hurt	23	4-11	1-5	1-1	0-2	4	2	0	0	6	10
Gaines	29	4-10	1-4	1-4	0-2	5	2	0	1	0	10
Brown	32	4-10	0-1	1-2	4-9	3	2	0	0	2	9
Northern	18	3-10	2-9	2-2	1-3	2	1	0	0	1	10
O'Bannon	15	0-4	0-0	2-2	1-3	2	0	0	0	0	2
Whitehead	14	2-9	0-0	0-0	1-2	4	0	1	0	1	4
Bender	12	2-3	0-0	0-0	1-4	0	0	3	1	0	4
Naydenov	5	1-1	0-0	0-0	0-0	2	0	1	0	0	2
George	3	0-0	0-0	1-2	0-1	0	0	0	0	0	1
TEAM					2-3						
Total	200	25-69	4-19	8-15	15-41	23	7	6	7	14	62

Chapter 22

Stone's Redemption

UofL 81, No. 14 UK 63
December 28, 2002 at Freedom Hall

Pre-Game:

While there were many intriguing storylines to the 2002 UK/UofL matchup, there is only one name, one person, who can truly tell the tale of that basketball game.

It's the player who had suited up for both squads. He knew more than anyone how much both teams wanted to beat each other.

His name was Marvin Stone.

In 1999, Stone, a 6'10" center with offensive skills, led Grissom High School in Huntsville, Alabama, to its second-ever state championship. Stone was a sensation, the best athlete the city had ever produced, and he was named a *Parade* and McDonald's All-America player that year. A slew of college offers rolled in and, citing the strength of the program and Coach Tubby Smith, Stone signed with the Kentucky Wildcats.

It did not go well. Fans saw the big man with soft hands and nimble feet and expected a collegiate version of his high school self. Instead, Stone was largely ineffective. In just more than two seasons at Kentucky, Stone averaged 5.3 points and 4.2 rebounds.

Down the road at the University of Louisville, a seismic shift was underway, one that would shake the very foundations of college basketball. In 2001, former Kentucky coach Rick Pitino admitted failure in his return trip to the NBA. After sporting a losing record with the Boston Celtics, Pitino plotted to come back to college basketball. He had a choice of three primo jobs: UNLV, Michigan, or Louisville. Each was a basketball power, but Pitino chose to come back to the Bluegrass.

In a rivalry so heated, Pitino opted to coach the other side. In 2001, he became the head man at Louisville. Meanwhile, Marvin Stone decided he was ready to leave Kentucky. He wanted a more up-tempo style where he could showcase his skills for the NBA.

Rick Pitino has now coached in more Dream Games than any other coach. After resurrecting the Kentucky program and subsequently returning to Louisville, there is no more divisive figure in the rivalry between the schools. *(Photo by Tim Sofranko)*

Pitino welcomed him with open arms. By December 28, 2002, Pitino and Stone were ready to take on UK. The Cardinals were welcoming talent. Along with Stone, Pitino had Reece Gaines, a team captain and a holdover from the Denny Crum regime.

Gaines, a talented 6'6", 205-pound guard from Madison, Wisconsin, had come to Louisville as one of Crum's last great recruits. By the time Pitino took over, Gaines was a great fit for the coach's run-and-gun style. With Gaines, Ellis Myles, Francisco Garcia, Erik Brown, and Stone, the Cardinals had their best team since the DeJuan Wheat era. Louisville was unranked, but playing well at 6-1, with its only loss coming by two points to Purdue. But the Cards had a tough test when Kentucky came to town.

"There was a big, big build-up to that game," Gaines said. "We all thought we could hang with them and beat them. We didn't hate Kentucky—we had friends on their team. I was friends with Keith Bogans. But we did want to beat them bad. It was bigger than any regular game."

That season, Kentucky had built maybe its finest team under Tubby Smith, though no one really knew it yet. Kentucky came to Louisville's Freedom Hall ranked 18th in the land, 6-2, with losses to Virginia and No. 21 Michigan State. But just prior to the Louisville game, UK had faced sixth-ranked Indiana in Freedom Hall and dispatched the Hoosiers 70-64.

Kentucky had Bogans, who like Gaines was one of the better guards in the country, along with massive Madison County native Marquis Estill at center, forwards Chuck Hayes and Erik Daniels, point guard Cliff Hawkins, and guard Gerald Fitch.

When the Cats came in to Freedom Hall to face the Cards, the house was rocking.

"I've never heard Freedom Hall that loud," Gaines said.

The day would belong to Gaines, and to Rick Pitino. And maybe more than any of them, to Marvin Stone.

The Game:

Kentucky came out to start the game just as they had finished against Indiana in the previous game. They were tenacious. The plan? Attack the inside.

That meant using Estill, Hayes, and Daniels to pound the paint—or in other words, to pound Marvin Stone and Ellis Myles. Pitino and Stone knew UK would try just that. For a half, it worked.

Kentucky jumped out to a 20-9 lead with 10:12 to go, spurred by an outrageous 15-1 rebounding advantage. Myles, the Cards' leading rebounder, was nowhere to be found. Kentucky looked to be in control.

"We could have punished them," UK center Marquis Estill said afterward. "But we didn't take control."

Instead, Louisville came back. Curiously, Kentucky's offense did not go through the post like everyone thought it would. That was due in part to the Cards' smothering defense. Every time Estill touched the ball, two Cardinal defenders quickly swarmed him, causing him to defer. Estill got off just two shots in the entire game.

Louisville came out cold, making just one of their first eight three-point shots. But they found their stride near the end of the half, canning three in the last three minutes. Little-used guard Bryant Northern, who had hit just 2-of-13 threes coming into the game, hit another pair before the end of the half, cutting the lead to 33-30.

Louisville fans had to feel pretty good about their position. They had been largely outplayed in the paint. They had been out rebounded. They had shot poorly. Yet they were only down by three. Still, Pitino was not pleased. At the half, he issued a warning.

"We were getting killed on the glass," the coach told the *Lexington Herald-Leader*, referring to UK's 24-14 first-half rebounding edge. "If they killed us in the second half, we would have practiced [that night]. We had two options."

The second half was a different story completely. Myles showed up to claim 12 of his 14 rebounds. Estill was double-teamed seemingly everywhere on the court. Louisville began to make shots, force turnovers, and Kentucky—which had long abandoned its plan to pound the inside—started forcing outside shots. It quickly developed into a rout.

Brown hit a three to give Louisville its first lead since 5-4. Then Gaines got involved.

"I ended up getting a steal off the press [off UK guard Fitch], and I saw Francisco heading to the rim," Gaines said. "I was able to get it to him for the layup. Then the crowd got really loud."

While many Cards were having good games, no Kentucky player could guard Marvin Stone. He hit jumpers and took the ball inside for layups. He was putting on a show for his old coach and teammates.

Two key Cardinal runs put the game out of reach for Kentucky. To start the second half, it was a 25-9 burst. Then, after a small UK rally that cut the lead to 60-53 with 9:07 to play, UofL responded with another 11-0 run to seal the game. It gave Louisville its biggest win in the series since 1988. The Cards held Kentucky to 37.1% shooting, and out-rebounded UK 21-12 in the second half en route to an 81-63 victory.

It was Pitino's first win over his former school.

"This is a very big win for our program," Pitino said afterward. "We are going to embrace this for the next year. We want to be a Top-25 program. This is a big builder for our program. Our respect level for Kentucky is off the charts."

Marvin Stone earned the ultimate redemption. He led all scorers with 16 points and grabbed 7 rebounds in what would be one of his greatest collegiate performances. He completely outplayed every UK player.

Gaines contributed 10 points and 4 assists. He was one of seven Cardinals to score at least 9 points. An announced crowd of 20,061 packed Freedom Hall to see the game.

"We were up by 20 for a large part of it," Gaines said. "It felt so good. By the time you're a senior, you get the feeling how much it means to the fans to win it."

Reece Gaines was a Cardinal fan favorite who spanned the transition from Crum to Pitino. He is pictured in his current role as an assistant coach at Bellarmine University in Louisville. *(Photo by Martha Work, appears courtesy of Bellarmine University)*

Postgame:

As they had in 1998, Kentucky would again use the Louisville loss as a springboard to greatness. Although they started 6-3, UK would finish 32-4 overall and a perfect 16-0 in the SEC. It was the first time a team had run the table in the conference since Pitino's squad pulled the trick in 1996. The 2003 Wildcats won the SEC Tourney and finished the regular season No. 1 in the country. They made a run all the way to the NCAA Regional Final before facing another great guard from Conference USA—Dwyane Wade, who led Marquette to a shocking 83-69 victory over UK to claim a spot in the Final Four.

Louisville went on to have a season that is still fondly remembered by its fans. In his lone season at Louisville, Stone averaged 10.3 points, 7.1 rebounds, and 1.5 blocked shots. He later played several seasons overseas until 2008. In 2005, he failed medical tests with multiple German squads due to unspecified cardiac problems, and he was also diagnosed with hypertension. Sadly, Stone suffered a heart attack and died during halftime of a playoff game in Saudi Arabia in 2008. But he will always have a place in the lore of the UK/UofL rivalry.

Gaines became known as one of the more clutch Cards during his career, as he hit shots to win or clinch games against Marquette, Princeton, Tennessee, and Cincinnati. Louisville reeled off 17 straight wins as part of an 18-1 start, and they finished the year 25-7. The Cards made it to the second round of the NCAA Tournament (an improvement on the previous season's NIT appearance) before bowing to Butler, 79-71.

"When you build a program back up, with a great coach who left this unbelievable tradition in Denny Crum, your only chance of rebuilding it without it taking a number of years is hard work and dedication—and the likes of this young man," Pitino said of Gaines at a postseason awards ceremony. "He got the rebuilding process going."

In 2012, Dwayne Wade said on Twitter that Gaines was the best college player he ever faced. Gaines finished as the fourth all-time leading scorer in Cards history. He was drafted No. 15 overall in the first round by the Orlando Magic in 2003. He played three seasons in the NBA before playing another six overseas. In 2012, he was hired as an assistant coach at NCAA Division II Bellarmine University in Louisville (whose head coach is former Louisville assistant Scotty Davenport).

Now that he's back in Kentucky coaching, fans constantly come up and ask Gaines about his senior season. The Kentucky game is one memory that will always stand out.

"I got to go out on top," he said. "Yeah I had friends at Kentucky. Me and Keith [Bogans] talked all the time. But we didn't talk for a long time after that game."

Louisville 81

NAME	MIN	FG-FGA	3-3A	FT-FTA	OR-REB	PF	AST	STL	BLK	TO	TP
Myles	28	3-7	0-0	5-6	6-14	3	5	0	0	4	11
Garcia	28	5-11	2-6	0-0	1-4	4	1	2	1	2	12
Stone	30	4-7	0-0	8-12	2-7	3	1	0	2	3	16
Gaines	29	2-5	2-4	4-4	0-1	4	4	2	1	2	10
Brown	27	2-5	1-2	4-4	0-0	1	1	1	0	0	9
Dean	21	4-10	2-6	0-0	0-3	2	1	0	0	0	10
Whitehead	15	1-2	0-0	2-2	0-1	3	1	0	0	1	4
Northern	11	3-4	3-3	0-0	0-3	2	2	0	0	0	9
Dartez	7	0-1	0-0	0-0	0-2	0	0	0	0	0	0
O'Bannon	4	0-0	0-0	0-0	0-0	0	0	0	0	0	0
TEAM					3					1	
Total	200	24-52	10-21	23-28	9-38	22	16	5	4	13	81

Kentucky 63

NAME	MIN	FG-FGA	3-3A	FT-FTA	OR-REB	PF	AST	STL	BLK	TO	TP
Daniels	24	4-8	0-0	1-1	4-7	3	2	1	1	1	9
Hayes	31	37	1-2	4-4	3-5	1	2	0	0	2	11
Estill	23	2-2	0-0	2-2	2-6	5	0	1	2	2	6
Fitch	23	2-10	1-4	0-0	2-6	3	1	0	0	4	5
Bogans	34	5-15	1-9	3-6	0-1	2	4	2	0	2	14
Barbour	21	2-6	0-1	1-1	1-1	0	0	0	0	1	5
Camara	19	4-9	0-0	0-1	1-4	2	1	0	0	2	8
Hawkins	16	0-1	0-0	2-2	0-1	4	5	0	0	0	2
Azubuike	6	1-3	0-1	1-2	1-1	0	0	0	0	0	3
Stockton	3	0-1	0-1	0-1	0-0	0	0	0	0	0	0
TEAM					1-4						
Total	200	23-62	3-18	14-20	15-36	20	15	4	3	14	63

Chapter 23

Playing Through
the Pain

No. 20 UofL 65, No. 2 UK 56
December 27, 2003 at Rupp Arena

DECEMBER 2003 WAS the best of times for Francisco Garcia, the basket-ball player. The 6'7" sophomore wing player tied a career high by scoring 24 points in a win over Seton Hall. He added 21 more points in upsetting No. 1 Florida in Freedom Hall. He was the National Player of the Week, and entering the annual matchup with Kentucky, then No. 2 in the AP rankings and No. 1 in the CNN/SI poll, he believed that there was more to be done.

December 2003 was the worst of times for Francisco Garcia, the person. On December 8, 2003, a young man named Hector Lopez was shot and killed in an apartment building in the Bronx. The apartment was the residence for his family, a group that had moved to the United States only six years earlier from the Dominican Republic. Hector Lopez was Francisco Garcia's brother.

The two had been inseparable—while Garcia was serious and focused, Lopez was funny and outgoing. From the opposing personalities came a great closeness. The two spoke daily on the telephone. Dick Weiss wrote in the *New York Post*, "Lopez was his brother's biggest fan and could rattle off his stats from memory. Garcia looked out for Lopez and made sure he was in the stands . . . at Freedom Hall [in March 2003], when the Cardinals won the Conference USA tournament."

Garcia learned of the murder of his brother the day after it occurred, the day before the Seton Hall game. In a move that still amazes those who witnessed it, Garcia decided to honor his brother in the most appropriate way he could—by playing his heart out. Garcia's best friend, UofL guard Taquan Dean, told the *New York Post*, "I told him, 'You've got to keep going because that's what Hector would want.'"

Garcia kept going. He put up 24 points in a win over Seton Hall, but was too emotionally exhausted to speak with media after the game. Pitino marveled at Garcia's focus. "I don't think there are too many young men that could play tonight," he told the media after the Seton Hall game. "We admire his strength, and he is a special young man," Pitino said.

Garcia flew to New York for the funeral and returned to start in the upset of Florida. Garcia had been a budding star for Pitino but, suddenly, his game took on a new intensity and grit as Garcia played through his pain.

As for his team, Louisville began the season by losing to Iowa, but had since won six consecutive games, rising to No. 20 in the AP rankings. Aside from Garcia, who was emerging as his team's primary scoring threat as a sophomore, Louisville was led by senior forward Luke Whitehead, smooth junior forward Larry O'Bannon, and the streaky sophomore point guard, Taquan Dean.

Meanwhile, Kentucky had won its first seven games, leaping into the top two in the country. Wins over Michigan State, UCLA, and Indiana highlighted the Cats' early successes. Kentucky was a veteran squad, led by a trio of seniors—shooting guard Gerald Fitch, quirky forward Erik Daniels, and point guard Cliff Hawkins. Tough junior forward Chuck Hayes and sophomore scorer Kelenna Azubuike rounded out the UK attack. The team lacked a single dominant player, but was as talented and well-rounded as any squad in the country.

With two red-hot squads meeting in Rupp Arena for the annual rivalry, anything seemed possible. In fact, the game divided into two very different halves, and the man who turned it around was Francisco Garcia.

The Game:

Kentucky had won 27 consecutive games in Rupp Arena. UK began the game shooting the ball efficiently, jumping out to a 24-10 lead. With the post presences of Hayes and Daniels, Kentucky's offensive effectiveness centered on three-point shooting and, early in the game, the shots were going down, particularly for streaky guard Cliff Hawkins, who drained four treys.

Louisville, however, could not get untracked. Pitino made a gamble, switching to a 2-3 zone and daring Kentucky to beat the Cards from long range. As the Cats suddenly went cold, Louisville trimmed its halftime deficit to 31-26. Still, Garcia had zero points and the Cardinals had their own offensive struggles.

Kentucky opened the second half with a modest run, extending their lead from five points to nine. But then Louisville's defense, constantly switching from aggressive low post traps to the gambling zone, forced Kentucky into bad shot after bad shot. And finally, the shots began to drop for the Cardinals.

The run culminated in a dunk by reserve forward Otis George, who had a strong game, and then a trey for Garcia, moving UofL into a 46-43 lead with 8:00 to play. Kentucky moved back ahead by three, but then went ice cold again. Louisville clung to a 52-51 lead when Taquan Dean nailed a three-point shot. The lead extended to 57-51 for Louisville before Gerald Fitch was fouled while draining a trey for Kentucky. The four-point play trimmed the lead to 57-55.

Louisville had its answer. Garcia, playing with the fervor he had shown for much of the last month, got a sliver of opening, and drained a three-point shot with 1:15 to play, ultimately sealing the victory. "Francisco's [shot] was just a dagger to the heart," Tubby Smith told the Lexington *Herald-Leader*.

UK drew no closer than four points, and Louisville claimed a 65-56 win as more than a few boos met the final result in Rupp Arena. "We were not playing our game, we were playing their game," Smith admitted after the game. Indeed, Kentucky shot just 34% and Azubuike and Hawkins, with 12 points each, were the only Cats in double figures.

Pitino was even more emphatic. "Our defense was a 12 on a 10-point scale," he noted in the press conference. Offensively, it had been a struggle, but a winning struggle. Otis George finished with 13 points and 8 rebounds. Whitehead and O'Bannon added 11 points each, while Garcia had just his 10 second-half points, and Dean scored only 5.

When asked about the big shots from Dean and then from Garcia, Pitino called the duo "the glue at the end." In horse racing country, it may have seemed unusual, but the glue carried the day.

Postgame:

Despite a fine season from Garcia, who scored 16.4 points per game while leading the team in assists, Louisville could not keep up the pace from their 7-1 start. The Cardinals were still a bit young and were thin on the backboard, leading to a 9-7 record in Conference USA. The Cardinals reached the NCAA Tournament, but as a No. 10 seed, lost their first NCAA game to Xavier, finishing the year at 20-10.

Pitino added freshman post player Juan Palacios and welcomed Ellis Myles back to the squad from his injury redshirt season. The other component parts, excluding Luke Whitehead, all returned and gave UofL a chance at a special season in the near future.

Kentucky's future was now, with its senior-dominated squad. The Wildcats lost only three more games in the regular season, rolling to an SEC Championship, an SEC Tournament championship, and a No. 1 seed in the NCAA Tournament.

But Tubby's best team since the 1998 title ran into a stifling Alabama-Birmingham squad in its second NCAA game. UAB fought, pressured, and hustled its way to a 76-75 lead. Kentucky had a final shot to win, but Gerald Fitch's open jumper rolled off, and the promising season was over in the NCAA second round.

While Smith could not replace the experienced veterans he lost, he did set about bringing in a top-ranked recruiting class, with stars like Rajon Rondo and Randolph Morris. Kentucky would also have a transfer available in 2004–05—Western Kentucky University star Patrick Sparks, who had a reputation as a player who was not afraid to take a big shot.

✳✳✳✳✳

For Francisco Garcia, the 2003–04 season retained its dual dream/nightmare quality. The following season, he continued to impact the rebirth of UofL basketball in a profound way. Garcia became the poster child—the guy who completed UofL's transition back from pretty good team to national power. Future Cardinal Edgar Sosa recalled watching Garcia and being drawn to UofL by his game.

Garcia remains active in the NBA, now with the Houston Rockets after spending seven-and-a-half seasons with the Sacramento Kings. He averaged more than 10 points per game in Houston's 2013 postseason play. He also played for UK Coach John Calipari on the Dominican Republic national team. The tragedy of the death of Hector Lopez provided another odd connection between Garcia and his old rival—Kentucky center Jamaal Magloire similarly lost his younger brother to a shooting in their hometown of Toronto.

While Garcia's pain may have faded somewhat since December 2003, his memory has not. In 2006, he reflected on his lost brother in an interview with the *Sacramento Bee*. At that time, he hoped to establish a foundation in Hector Lopez's memory to help at-risk youth avoid his brother's fate. "I look at life differently now," Garcia admitted. "I have to be there for everybody."

Louisville 65

NAME	MIN	FG-FGA	3-3A	FT-FTA	OR-REB	PF	AST	STL	BLK	TO	TP
Whitehead	34	4-13	0-0	3-4	3-6	2	2	2	1	3	11
Garcia	32	4-9	2-5	0-0	0-7	4	5	1	3	2	10
Dartez	19	3-4	0-0	0-0	1-3	1	0	2	0	5	6
Dean	32	2-11	1-6	0-0	1-5	3	2	0	0	4	5
Daniels	4	0-1	0-1	0-0	0	0	0	0	0	0	0
O'Bannon	26	1-4	1-1	8-8	1-3	0	0	0	0	0	11
George	25	5-7	0-1	3-3	4-8	2	0	0	0	1	13
Mohammed	16	3-4	0-0	1-1	0-3	2	0	2	0	0	7
Jenkins	10	1-1	0-0	0-0	0-1	1	0	0	0	1	2
Diakate	2	0-0	0-0	0-0	0-0	1	0	0	0	0	0
TEAM					2-2						
Total	200	23-54	4-14	15-16	12-38	16	9	7	4	16	65

Kentucky 56

NAME	MIN	FG-FGA	3-3A	FT-FTA	OR-REB	PF	AST	STL	BLK	TO	TP
Daniels	32	4-11	0-1	1-2	5-8	4	1	1	0	3	9
Hayes	39	2-8	0-0	0-0	4-9	2	3	0	4	1	4
Hawkins	27	4-11	4-6	0-0	0-2	4	3	3	0	5	12
Fitch	32	3-12	2-10	1-1	0-0	1	3	1	0	3	9
Azubuike	33	4-10	2-5	2-3	0-1	1	0	3	0	1	12
Stockton	18	2-5	1-3	3-3	0-0	1	1	1	0	1	8
Barbour	10	1-2	0-0	0-0	2-3	1	1	0	1	1	2
Obrzut	9	0-0	0-0	0-0	1-1	1	0	0	0	0	0
TEAM					0-4						
Total	200	20-59	9-25	7-9	12-28	15	12	9	5	16	56

Chapter 24

Sparks Ignites Comeback

No. 9 UK 60, No. 13 UofL 58
December 18, 2004 at Freedom Hall

Pre-Game:

When Kentucky faced Louisville in 2004, it could be said that it was a must-win for both teams.

Louisville had, without question, its finest squad since Rick Pitino had taken over as coach. Led by junior guard Francisco Garcia, point guard Taquan Dean, and forward Juan Palacios, the Cardinals were a formidable team on the national scene for the first time in years. Coincidentally, Kentucky had recently acquired the No. 1 recruiting class in college basketball.

Led by freshman point guard Rajon Rondo, as well as transfer shooting guard Patrick Sparks, Kentucky was back in the top five of the national polls. Throw in senior leader Chuck Hayes, and Kentucky had its most talented team since 2003. Still, there were questions. Pitino had bested Kentucky coach Tubby Smith before, so history suggested he could accomplish the feat again. Additionally, the Wildcats had to discover how to respond to the Cardinals' relentless pressure.

Kentucky had to do it all with a freshman point guard, no less.

Of course, the most interesting stories revolved around the Kentucky kids. On the Louisville side there was homegrown star Larry O'Bannon. A product of Male High School, O'Bannon had grown into a typical Pitino player—a hard-working, sweet-shooting backup guard. Many national services would call him the nation's best sixth man by the end of the year.

On the Kentucky side, there was Rondo, a product of Eastern High. Rondo chose to play at Kentucky rather than play for Louisville. Similarly, there was the shooting guard, Sparks. A transfer from Western Kentucky University, Sparks had led the Hilltoppers to two of their three consecutive NCAA tournament appearances. But before his junior year could begin, head coach Dennis Felton left Western to become the head coach at Georgia. Sparks had a decision to make:

Should he stay at Western? Should he follow Felton to Georgia? And then, other colleges came calling for his services. Stanford, Kentucky, and Louisville all inquired about Sparks's intentions.

Coming out of Muhlenberg North High School, Sparks led the state in scoring at more than 31 points per game. But only WKU offered a scholarship. Kentucky's Tubby Smith offered him a chance to walk on, but Sparks balked.

Now, many college coaches were rethinking their original decisions. Pitino was one of the first to offer a scholarship. He wanted Sparks to commit and become a Cardinal. But then Tubby Smith called—and Kentucky would offer a scholarship as well. Having coached at Kentucky before, Pitino knew the pull of the state school all too well. Upon learning that Smith had called—and that Sparks was interested—Pitino rescinded his scholarship offer. It didn't matter. Sparks wanted to be a Wildcat.

After sitting out the season as a transfer, it all came down to this.

*****

For these athletes, winning the Kentucky/Louisville game meant everything. But it was also big for the coaches. Pitino wanted to show the nation that his team, 6-1 and No. 13 in the country, could beat a quality opponent. Tubby Smith just wanted to beat Louisville. Also at 6-1, the Wildcats were No. 9 in the nation, their only loss coming at top-10 North Carolina. But everyone knows this game is different.

"There will be people at Kentucky that will have a nervous breakdown if they lose to us," Pitino told CBS Sports before a UK/UofL game.

The former UK coach knew best. This game can create heroes. By the end of the evening, a hero in blue would emerge.

The Game:

The game did not look good for Kentucky early on. But for Louisville fans, it could not get any better. The Cardinals utilized their pressure defense and considerable size inside to force turnovers from the young Kentucky guards. Louisville's quickness and athleticism proved too much for Kentucky to handle. In what would become the symbol for Louisville all season long, their shooting and rebounding carried them throughout the half as they built a seemingly insurmountable 32-16 halftime lead.

It was the least amount of points scored in a half by Kentucky since the Cats suffered a 3-for-33 shooting nightmare against Georgetown in the 1984 Final Four.

It seemed as if the Cardinals could not miss. Garcia, O'Bannon, and Dean led the attack from the outside. In the paint, foreword Ellis Myles and Palacios out rebounded the world. Louisville was winning in every facet of the game. Tubby Smith lit into his team.

"We all kind of lost a little of our religion," Smith told the *Lexington Herald-Leader*.

If what analysts say is true, and you can tell the most about a game from the first five minutes of the second half, things did not look good for the University of Kentucky. Louisville was able to keep its lead at 16 points. And while Louisville seemingly could not miss a shot, Kentucky was not hitting anything. It looked to be a Cardinal beatdown, and Kentucky fans were already grumbling about Tubby Smith's inability to beat Pitino in a big game. But Louisville was tiring, and the Cards lost a key contributor when Palacios suffered an eye injury with 17:00 to play.

With under 8:00 remaining, Kentucky still trailed by 10. Then the Wildcats ditched their plan to pound the ball inside and played small ball, unleashing their guards to run and shoot. Joe Crawford and Kelenna Azubuike started hitting shots, and the up-tempo style worked. But Sparks became the catalyst, hitting three three-pointers and getting an old-fashioned three-point play to bring UK within four, 54-50.

"It was such an exciting game," Sparks said. "I'm not sure what was going through my head, other than what I could do to get us back in the game. I mean, some shots finally had to go down."

Other heroes emerged. Ravi Moss, a walk-on from Hopkinsville, Kentucky, who hadn't seen any action in two games, canned a three. Azubuike hit two free throws, and just like that, Kentucky had its first lead since 5-4 with 1:27 to play.

Somewhere in Central City, Kentucky (where Sparks was raised), thousands of fans gathered around televisions to watch what would become a legendary performance. His own father Steve, a basketball coach of course, was on a trip in London, Kentucky, and could only hear the game through Sparks's mother's cell phone, which she held high from inside Freedom Hall.

"It's one of those wonderful stories, to be honest," Steve Sparks told ESPN.com. "It's truly a Cinderella story."

Undeterred, Louisville came back, too. Over the last 72 seconds, the two teams traded the lead three times, capped off by O'Bannon's two free throws that gave UofL a 58-57 lead with 15.2 seconds to go.

Kentucky came right back, but Sparks lost his dribble in a double-team near the baseline. He was forced to call timeout with 4.8 seconds remaining. During the timeout, Coach Tubby Smith called for a play where Sparks would inbound to Azubuike, who would then find Sparks back in the corner.

It worked—sort of.

Sparks inbounded, and Azubuike was quickly trapped. Thinking quickly, Azubuike passed back to Sparks, who pump-faked (and traveled, but it was not called) just as Ellis Myles came flying out to defend.

Sparks leaned into Myles, who came crashing on to the UK guard, causing the referee to call the defensive foul. Sparks was awarded three free throws and, with Kentucky down one point, the deadeye shooter had a chance to win the game.

"That place is loud, but I just try to concentrate on making the shots," Sparks said.

All three went in, giving Kentucky an improbable comeback lead. All that was left was to defend an inbounds play, which resulted in an errant shot at the buzzer. Kentucky had come back to win.

Postgame:

Both teams moved on from the game and had extraordinary seasons. Louisville eventually won a classic NCAA Regional Final against West Virginia and made the Final Four for the first time in nearly 20 years. Pitino crafted a great team and it rewarded him with a return to the national semifinals. Kentucky was not so fortunate. While the Wildcats also had a great season, their luck ran out in the Regional Final against Michigan State.

But the legend of Patrick Sparks continued to grow. Facing elimination, down three points to the Spartans, Sparks took a circus three-point shot that bounced and rolled around the rim before falling in to tie the game as time expired, sending the game into overtime.

The duel went into a second overtime before the Spartans prevailed. Still, Sparks's heroics would be remembered for all time in Big Blue country.

"I don't know that I've ever seen someone hit two bigger shots during the course of a season than what Sparks did against Michigan State and Louisville," said commentator Dick Vitale.

And at least for one of those games, Sparks can say that his shots led to a victory.

Kentucky 60

NAME	MIN	FG-FGA	3-3A	FT-FTA	OR-REB	PF	AST	STL	BLK	TO	TP
Azubuike	31	3-12	2-6	4-4	0-1	2	0	0	1	0	12
Hayes	36	2-10	0-0	2-2	3-9	3	4	2	1	0	6
Morris	17	1-1	0-0	0-2	2-3	0	2	1	1	1	2
Rondo	27	2-7	0-2	0-0	1-4	0	3	1	1	1	4
Sparks	32	8-15	5-8	4-4	1-5	2	3	1	0	2	25
Carrier	13	0-1	0-1	0-0	0-0	2	0	0	0	1	0
Crawford	12	2-6	1-4	0-0	1-1	0	0	0	0	0	5
Perry	9	1-2	0-1	0-0	0-0	0	0	1	0	2	2
Alleyne	9	0-0	0-0	0-0	0-2	1	0	0	0	0	0
Moss	7	1-2	1-2	0-0	2-3	0	0	0	0	0	3
Bradley	5	0-0	0-0	0-0	0-0	1	0	0	0	1	0
Obrzut	1	0-0	0-0	0-0	0-0	0	0	0	0	0	0
Thomas	1	0-1	0-0	1-2	1-1	0	0	0	0	0	1
TEAM					1-1						
Total	200	20-57	9-24	11-14	12-30	11	12	6	4	8	60

Louisville 58

NAME	MIN	FG-FGA	3-3A	FT-FTA	OR-REB	PF	AST	STL	BLK	TO	TP
Myles	30	4-5	0-0	0-0	4-10	4	2	1	0	3	8
Palacios	20	5-9	0-2	1-1	0-2	0	0	0	1	0	11
Garcia	40	3-12	2-7	0-0	3-6	2	5	0	3	4	8
Dean	34	3-10	3-8	0-0	0-7	2	2	1	0	3	9
O'Bannon	38	4-9	2-5	6-6	0-4	1	1	0	2	1	16
George	21	1-1	0-0	4-4	1-6	3	1	0	1	1	6
Jenkins	17	0-0	0-0	0-0	0-0	1	1	0	0	2	0
TEAM					0-0						
Total	200	20-46	7-22	11-11	8-35	13	12	2	7	14	58

Chapter 25

Rondo's Revenge

No. 23 UK 73, No. 4 UofL 61
December 17, 2005 at Rupp Arena

Pre-Game:

Doug Bibby has been a legend in the Louisville prep basketball scene for years. The championship coach has guided numerous all-state players, including current NBA point guard Rajon Rondo. In the early 2000s, both were at Eastern High School. Bibby was the tough-minded coach; Rondo was a stubborn but ridiculously talented guard.

Did the two have their arguments? Of course. Rondo wanted to do things his way. Bibby had to show the player who was in charge. Ultimately, the two joined forces and became a power in the State's seventh region. By his junior season, Rondo was an all-state force. Many national college basketball powerhouses came recruiting.

That is, except one. The University of Louisville and Coach Rick Pitino were fishing for a bigger prize. The city of New York had produced amazing guards in the past: Bob Cousy, Kenny Anderson, and Stephon Marbury, among others. It just so happened that the next great NYC guard wanted to play for Pitino. The player was Sebastian Telfair.

Telfair was thought to be a can't-miss prospect. He had Allen Iverson's quickness and a smooth jumper. The only problem? He was so good he was thinking of going straight to the NBA, which at the time had no age restriction on players jumping directly to the league. Unafraid, Pitino went after Telfair, and in a sense, ignored Rondo.

"We took Sebastian Telfair instead," Pitino told ESPN. "We should have waited. I always loved Rondo. He was at my camp every year, but a point guard had never gone directly to the NBA so I didn't see that coming with Telfair. And then not only did we lose [Rondo], we lost him to a bitter rival."

In 2004, Rondo left Eastern High and Bibby and prepped his senior year at Oak Hill Academy in Virginia with Coach Steve Smith. Telfair made headlines when he committed to Louisville, supposedly choosing the Cards over the NBA. Rondo saw the writing on the wall. He decided to look elsewhere for college.

But as former UK star—and Pitino player—Derek Anderson tells it, Pitino may have never had a shot with Rondo anyway. Anderson's son was good friends with Rondo, and Anderson had taken the star player under his wing.

"I told Rajon he didn't want to play for Coach Pitino," Anderson said. "[Pitino] yells too much for Rajon. He wouldn't have responded to that. I told him I thought Coach [Tubby] Smith at Kentucky might be better."

In 2004, Rajon committed to be a Wildcat. It was an established program where his family could come watch him play. And he would get to face Louisville once a season. But he would not be playing against Telfair. Telfair reneged on his Cardinal commitment and declared for the NBA Draft. The Cards lost both players.

"I never held anything against [Louisville]," Rondo said. "Kentucky was just the place that was best for me."

✳✳✳✳✳

Leading up to the December 17, 2005, matchup with UofL, Kentucky and its sophomore point guard Rondo were in a state of confusion. The Wildcats were 6-3, ranked No. 23, and coming off a 26-point loss at

Indiana (the worst loss for UK in the past 16 years). It seemed like Rondo and Tubby Smith weren't communicating. The point guard did not know what his coach wanted. Fans criticized Smith for not unleashing Rondo's driving ability during games.

Bibby, Rondo's former coach at Eastern High, said as much leading up to the annual Dream Game. His opinion carried weight. He and the point guard talked in the week before the matchup; then Rondo and Tubby Smith did the same. No one knew if it would help.

Louisville, however, was sky-high. Ranked No. 4 in the country, the team boasted an undefeated record (6-0) coming into the game. The Cards had senior point guard Taquan Dean (who had helped the squad to the Final Four the previous year), a talented transfer in center David Padgett, and a force in scoring small forward Juan Palacios. Many thought they could dominate the boards against Kentucky.

What the Cardinals had no answer for was Rajon Rondo.

"Coach Smith was pretty mad leading up to that game," Rondo said. "You could tell this game meant a lot."

The Game:

Things did not start off well for Louisville. Within the first 90 seconds the center Padgett had two fouls, taking away the Cards' major advantage.

To Rondo, it must have looked as though the seas had parted. Kentucky jumped to an 8-0 lead on the strength of two Rondo drives and an assist to center Lukasz Obrzut. While Louisville shot poorly (1-14 from the field to start), Dean led a surge and they closed to within 15-11. Then Rondo hit overdrive. He hit two free throws, a layup, and a three-pointer before finding Shagari Alleyne for a dunk. Like that, it was 25-13 with 7:00 to go.

"Rajon got us going early with his attacking the rim, pushing the ball, and finding people open," Tubby Smith told the *Lexington Herald-Leader*. "He was taking what they gave him. Under control. Being very poised."

By halftime it was 39-24.

"We did what young teams do," Pitino told the Associated Press. "We panicked and we shot quickly and we took bad shots, and then it mushrooms and goes the other way. We did as bad a job as we did all year in running our offense."

Eventually Louisville found itself in a 23-point hole. But behind Dean, who finished with 14 points and 6 assists, and Padgett, who returned to score all 12 of his points in the second frame, the Cards crawled back to 66-53.

Rondo then took over again, driving and drawing fouls. He hit six consecutive free throws to stretch the lead back to 19. By the end, he led all scorers with 25 points, including 10-of-15 from the free throw line. He chipped in 7 assists, 2 steals, and 3 rebounds.

As a team, UK took advantage of the Cards' lack of height. Obrzut had a career-high 9 rebounds, as well as 2 blocks. Unheralded forward Sheray Thomas had 11 points and 6 rebounds of his own, while Kentucky

CBS broadcasters Vern Lundquist and Billy Packer flank Kentucky coach Tubby Smith and guard Rajon Rondo. The 2005–06 season was rather stormy for Smith and Rondo, but they were triumphant in the Dream Game, 73-61. *(Photo by Jamie Vaught)*

outrebounded the Cards 36-35. The Cardinals shot just 21-of-60 from the field, for 35%.

By the end, the Cards lost to UK, 73-61.

A crowd of 24,432 packed Rupp Arena—then the second-largest crowd to ever see a game in the arena's 30-year history.

"I was just happy," Rondo said. "I could go home and brag."

Postgame:

The win was one of the high points of the UK season. The Wildcats finished 22-13, 9-7 in the SEC, and in general, most fans expected more from the team. The Wildcats lost by 27 points at unranked Kansas, by 6 to Vandy at home, and by 4 to Alabama at home. They had another three-game losing streak a month later, to Florida, Tennessee, and at Vandy. Kentucky regrouped to defeat UAB in the first round of the NCAA Tournament before taking No. 1 seed (and second-ranked overall) Connecticut to the brink but eventually losing, 87-83.

Louisville finished a disappointing 21-13, but found its way to the Final Four of the NIT. The Cards lost in the NIT Semifinal to South Carolina at Madison Square Garden. But Louisville fans needn't have worried. With a core of young players, including Terrence Williams and Andre McGee, the Cards would be back soon.

As for Rondo, and the aforementioned Telfair, their paths would cross again. Telfair never became a consistent NBA starter. But Rondo declared for the NBA Draft after his sophomore season at UK. He was drafted No. 21 in the first round by the Phoenix Suns and then was traded to Boston, where he took over as a starter in his second season. There he won a championship and become an NBA All-Star, once and for all leaving Telfair in the rearview mirror.

"I don't regret my decision at all," Rondo said. "I love UK."

Kentucky 73

NAME	MIN	FG-FGA	3-3A	FT-FTA	OR-REB	PF	AST	STL	BLK	TO	TP
Thomas	29	3-6	1-1	4-4	3-6	3	1	0	1	0	11
Obrzut	30	2-3	0-0	0-1	4-9	3	0	0	2	0	4
Rondo	35	7-12	1-3	10-15	0-3	2	7	2	0	3	25
Sparks	20	2-3	0-0	2-2	0-2	3	0	0	0	2	6
Crawford	31	3-8	0-0	3-4	2-7	2	0	1	1	1	9
Moss	18	1-4	1-3	2-2	0-3	2	0	0	0	0	5
Bradley	17	3-6	1-4	1-2	0-0	3	2	0	0	2	8
Perry	8	0-1	0-1	0-0	1-1	1	1	0	0	1	0
Sims	8	0-2	0-1	1-4	0-3	0	1	0	0	1	1
Alleyne	4	2-3	0-0	0-0	0-1	0	0	0	2	1	4
TEAM					1-1						
Total	200	23-48	4-13	23-34	11-36	19	12	3	6	12	73

Louisville 61

NAME	MIN	FG-FGA	3-3A	FT-FTA	OR-REB	PF	AST	STL	BLK	TO	TP
Williams	22	1-7	0-3	3-3	0-1	1	1	0	0	0	5
Palacios	26	6-9	2-5	1-2	2-7	4	0	0	2	1	15
Padgett	20	5-8	0-0	2-4	1-3	3	1	0	0	1	12
Dean	34	5-16	2-10	2-2	2-5	4	6	0	0	4	14
Jenkins	34	2-6	2-2	0-0	3-4	4	2	0	0	0	6
McGee	19	1-5	1-4	2-5	0-1	3	2	1	0	4	5
Johnson	16	1-7	0-1	0-0	4-5	2	0	0	1	0	2
Millard	14	0-0	0-0	0-0	1-2	1	1	0	1	1	0
Gianiny	10	0-0	0-0	2-2	0-1	2	1	1	0	0	2
Huffman	4	0-2	0-0	0-0	1-1	2	0	0	0	1	0
Farley	1	0-0	0-0	0-0	0-1	0	0	0	0	0	0
TEAM					2-4						
Total	200	21-60	7-25	12-18	16-35	26	14	2	4	12	61

Chapter 26

Meeks Inherits Leading Role

UK 61, UofL 49
December 16, 2006 at Freedom Hall

Pre-Game:

By the time Jodie Meeks was a high school senior in 2006, he had basketball scholarship offers from most of the schools in the south and
nearly all of the schools in the Southeastern Conference. The 6'4", 200-
pound shooting guard had just led a loaded Norcross High team to its
first state championship, and he was on top of the world. The *Atlanta
Journal-Constitution* named him Player of the Year. But he took it all in
stride—even when the University of Kentucky came calling, though he
was clearly impressed with the school and its tradition.

"Growing up I was pretty well grounded from my parents," Meeks
told *The Sporting News*. "I think it all plays a factor on the basketball
court. Being patient in life and being patient on the basketball court are
the same thing."

When Tubby Smith offered him a scholarship to Kentucky, Meeks
was wowed by the tradition, facilities, and coaching staff. He committed.

He wanted to be a Wildcat. No one knew the rollercoaster ride his college career would be.

*****

In 2006, Kentucky was competitive, but fans seemed frustrated because the team had not been to a Final Four since 1998. Meanwhile, Louisville had been to the national semifinals as recently as 2005, but they were still trying to regain a bit of that magic. With freshmen center Derrick Caracter, backcourt mates Jerry Smith and Edgar Sosa, as well as Terrence Williams, Juan Palacios, and transfer David Padgett, the Cards had a solid core.

Kentucky had just bid farewell to all-conference point guard Rajon Rondo. But with a returning cast of guards Ramel Bradley and Joe Crawford, along with formidable center Randolph Morris, Kentucky looked to be able to hold their own with anyone. Of course, that's not how the early season played out. Coming into the Louisville game, UK was unranked at 6-3, with losses to No. 5 UCLA, No. 11 Memphis, and No. 7 North Carolina.

Louisville was also unranked, marking the first time since 2001 that the two teams played each other and neither was in the top-25 at the time. The Cards were 5-3, with losses to Dayton, UMass, and No. 14 Arizona. Fans on both sides wanted to see improvement from their respective teams.

A win over the archrival would go far in helping that cause.

On December 16, Kentucky traveled to Freedom Hall for the annual showdown. Neither side really knew what to expect. Louisville was more athletic, but they were young and inconsistent. Kentucky had experience, but could they score and rebound with a deeper, more talented team? Both sides knew that the Kentucky offense ran through the big man, Randolph Morris. What would happen if he were to get into foul trouble? And how would he fare defensively against the two-headed monster of Padgett and Caracter?

Depth, so far, for Kentucky appeared to be a detriment. Bobby Perry, Shagari Alleyne, Lukasz Obrzut, Sheray Thomas, and Michael Porter—they weren't exactly household names. And Jodie Meeks had scored eight points total in the previous three games.

As always, the questions were answered on the court.

The Game:

Four minutes into the game, Kentucky's Randolph Morris had two fouls. Louisville's strategy had worked—UK's leading scorer and rebounder was out. He had exactly no points and no rebounds, and he'd tried to guard Padgett, but all that got him was a pair of quick whistles. The two times he did touch the ball on offense resulted in quick Cardinal double-teams that forced the big man to pass.

"We're like, 'Wow,'" UK guard Ramel Bradley told The Associated Press. "We planned on having him right now. We had a lot of plays we were going to run to get it to this guy."

Louisville scored the first six points of the game and led 7-4 when Morris went to the bench. The game looked to be very favorable for the boys in red.

"Six minutes into the game, we were beaten already," UK assistant coach David Hobbs said.

Then Kentucky's bench players took lead roles. Kentucky's starters scored just six first-half points, but the Cards couldn't capitalize, due in part to ice-cold shooting of their own.

"It's a matter of being ready when the opportunity presents itself," Tubby Smith said.

Even with everything seemingly going Louisville's way, 9:00 into the game they led by a score of just 9-6.

"It should have been easy. We should have been up 25-6," Card forward Terrence Williams said.

Instead, Meeks and others picked up the slack for UK. Down 16-6, Meeks hit a three to start the UK comeback. He scored nine first-half points, while the center Obrzut made three shots of his own—one less than he'd made in the rest of the season combined. When Obrzut made a 15-footer at the 6:00 mark, UK had its first lead.

At the half the Wildcats led Louisville 27-24.

For Kentucky, the second half did not start well. Morris, freshly inserted back into the game after sitting out 16 minutes of the first half, played 34 seconds (and missed one shot) before earning his third personal foul. Back to the bench he went.

But once again, the reserves stepped up, and UofL could not capitalize. The Cardinals were held to their second-lowest point total of the Pitino era and the lowest shooting percentage (27%) of the season.

Early in the second half, with the game tied at 29, Ramel Bradley showed his experience, reeling off 7 straight points (of his 15 total) to give Kentucky its biggest lead with 16:38 to play. But Louisville showed its toughness. Led by a double-double from Padgett (16 points and 10 rebounds) the Cardinals fought back to take a 41-40 lead midway through the second half.

Then both teams went cold once again. From 10:43 until 4:00, Meeks was the only player who could find the bottom of the basket. He hit two threes, three more free throws, and gave his team an eight-point lead with 6:36 to go.

Louisville scored its first basket in seven minutes when Andre McGee hit a putback to make it 49-45 with 4:00 to play. But another Kentucky reserve—Sheray Thomas—swished a jumper to stretch the lead back to six.

"I believe guys are on the team for a reason," Tubby Smith said of his bench. "Because they can help us win basketball games. And they stepped up and produced."

By the end, Kentucky had won it ugly, 61-49. The teams missed 84 combined shots, turned the ball over 25 times, and committed 42 fouls. Meeks led all scorers with a career-high 18 points, while Morris and Crawford combined for just 7 points—24 below their average. They weren't the only players to disappoint.

The much-ballyhooed Caracter matched Morris for ineffectiveness: 8 minutes, 0 points, and 5 fouls. Sosa and Jerry Smith combined for only 8 points.

"We've got to learn how to make easy shots," Pitino said.

Postgame:

Kentucky went on to another sub-par season, by Wildcats fans' standards. The Cats finished 22-12 and bowed out in the second round of the NCAAs for the second consecutive year, this time to second-ranked Kansas.

Louisville finished 24-10 and, like most Pitino teams, found themselves playing their best basketball by the end of the year. They took out Stanford by 20 points in the first round of the NCAA Tournament (in Rupp Arena) before facing one of the hottest teams in the country, ninth-ranked Texas A&M. Coached by Billy Gillispie and led by hotshot point guard Acie Law IV, the Aggies were also playing their best. It was a knock-down fight, but Gillispie and the Aggies prevailed 72-69 and advanced to the Sweet Sixteen.

Still, Louisville could build on its performance. One team seemed to be on the rise, while another seemed to be falling. What no one knew is that the leader of the Wildcats was already looking to jump ship.

Spurred by a combination of the pressure to win, pressure to hire new assistants, a nepotism law not allowing him to hire his son, and a desire to just move on, Tubby Smith left Kentucky after the 2006–07 season. He was immediately hired as the new coach at Minnesota, and Kentucky searched for a new leader. The first choice was Florida head man Billy Donovan, who declined. Various other names were discussed.

In the end, Kentucky offered the job to the hotshot coach from Texas. Billy Gillispie, the man who had just beaten Pitino and the Cards in Rupp Arena in the NCAA's second round, was coming to Lexington.

*****

Tumultuous—that would be the word to describe the relationship between Jodie Meeks and his new head coach. After an injury-plagued sophomore season, a season where Kentucky lost to Gardner-Webb, UAB, Houston, and San Diego, Meeks came back to lead the way in 2008–09. While the team was still a bit of a disaster (they lost to the Virginia Military Institute), Meeks became the story, averaging nearly 24 points a game and earning second team All-America honors.

And in a game at Tennessee, Meeks broke Dan Issel's single-game scoring record at UK, dropping 54 points (and 10 three-pointers) in a win over the Vols.

But none of that seemed to be enough for Gillispie. The coach didn't get along with the players, the media, or the former UK stars. After the season, he was gone, replaced by Calipari, who offered Meeks a shot at redemption—a senior year with a possible championship. But Meeks decided he was finished with college. He declared for the NBA Draft and was selected in the second round by the Milwaukee Bucks.

The second round is a dangerous place to be, because contracts are not guaranteed. But Meeks made the team roster and earned a spot in the league as a shooter, eventually playing with the Bucks, Sixers, and Lakers.

Most would agree that Meeks's coming-out party actually occurred in December 2006 in Freedom Hall.

Kentucky 61

NAME	MIN	FG-FGA	3-3A	FT-FTA	OR-REB	PF	AST	STL	BLK	TO	TP
Perry	12	0-6	0-2	0-0	0-2	3	1	1	0	2	0
Morris	16	0-1	0-0	2-2	1-3	4	0	1	0	0	2
Bradley	31	4-10	1-4	6-7	1-6	1	2	0	1	3	15
Jasper	20	3-3	0-0	0-0	0-3	2	0	1	0	2	6
Crawford	31	2-9	0-3	1-4	1-4	0	5	2	1	1	5
Obrzut	26	3-5	0-0	0-0	2-5	4	0	0	1	0	6
Meeks	21	5-10	4-7	4-5	0-3	2	2	1	0	1	18
Thomas	18	1-1	0-0	1-2	2-5	3	1	0	1	1	3
Porter	15	1-2	1-2	1-2	1-5	1	1	0	0	2	4
Stevenson	10	1-1	0-0	0-0	0-0	1	1	0	0	1	2
TEAM					1-4						
Total	200	20-48	6-18	15-22	9-40	21	13	6	4	13	61

Louisville 49

NAME	MIN	FG-FGA	3-3A	FT-FTA	OR-REB	PF	AST	STL	BLK	TO	TP
Williams	28	3-11	1-5	0-1	4-6	3	2	2	0	2	7
Palacios	36	4-12	0-4	2-4	2-6	2	0	2	0	1	10
Padgett	32	4-4	0-0	8-10	3-10	4	2	0	3	1	16
Jenkins	26	1-5	0-3	1-1	1-4	1	2	2	0	1	3
McGee	20	1-8	0-4	0-1	4-4	2	1	1	0	2	2
Smith	18	1-7	1-4	0-0	2-7	1	0	0	0	1	3
Sosa	14	2-7	0-1	1-1	1-1	2	0	1	0	1	5
Scott	8	0-1	0-1	0-0	0-0	0	1	0	0	0	0
Caracter	8	0-3	0-0	0-0	1-2	5	0	0	0	3	0
Gianiny	7	1-3	1-2	0-0	0-1	1	0	0	0	0	3
Clark	3	0-2	0-0	0-0	1-2	0	0	0	0	0	0
Farley	0+	0-0	0-0	0-0	0-0	0	0	0	0	0	0
TEAM					1-1						
Total	200	17-63	3-24	12-18	20-44	21	8	8	3	12	49

Chapter 27

The Glue Guy

UofL 89, UK 75
January 5, 2008 at Rupp Arena

Pre-Game:

If only Louisville had beaten Texas A&M. The Cardinals would have advanced to the Sweet Sixteen, again outlasting Kentucky in March Madness. And, had the most diehard Wildcat backers been blessed with foresight, they would have stood and applauded. Because in the aftermath of Texas A&M's win over Louisville in Rupp Arena, a series of dominoes were set in motion that nearly destroyed UK basketball.

When Tubby Smith headed to Minnesota, most sources agree that Kentucky intended to replace him with Billy Donovan. While Donovan had won consecutive national titles at Florida, he also doubtlessly knew that Noah, Horford, Green, et al., were bound for the NBA. Given his prior assistant coaching days under Pitino at Kentucky, Donovan knew the potential for building a dynasty at Kentucky. But after careful contemplation and many believe, a little helpful advice from mentor Pitino, Donovan elected to stay put.

By this point, it was early April, and UK athletic director Mitch Barnhart was scrambling. Other candidates were mentioned—Texas's

Rick Barnes, among others, was a popular rumor at the time. But ultimately, Barnhart could not wipe away the memory of the popular young coach who had just defeated UofL in Rupp Arena. And he hired Billy Clyde Gillispie.

Gillispie was believed to be the Dr. Pepper-swigging basketball junkie who was just crazy enough to satisfy some of the more rabid UK backers. This was a coach who didn't have a family, who worked 18-hour days, and who liked to eat peanut butter crackers. It sounded like a match made in heaven. It would take two seasons for sufficient details to emerge for most fans to conclude that Gillispie was a manipulative, dictatorial coach who drove his team to near mutiny and that his drink of choice was apparently stronger than Dr. Pepper.

As 2007–2008 approached, Gillispie returned senior guards Ramel Bradley and Joe Crawford. He added talented freshman Patrick Patterson to a nucleus that also included Jodie Meeks and Derrick Jasper. Talented freshman guard Alex Legion was one of several defectors from the program, as he did not last until Christmas before clashing with Gillispie and transferring.

Pitino's Cardinals were an experienced, well-rounded group. Senior center David Padgett, wing players Earl Clark and Terrence Williams, and guard Jerry Smith each averaged double-figure scoring for the season. Enigmatic sophomore forward Derrick Character and fellow sophomore Edgar Sosa added depth to the squad. Despite the abundance of depth on Pitino's team, Terrence Williams remained the heart and soul of the Cardinals.

Williams had been a star in football as well as basketball at Seattle's Rainier Beach High School. However, he was apparently destined to end up in America's heartland. His recruiting finalists guaranteed that Williams would make Kentucky fans' blood boil—he chose between Kansas, Indiana, and Louisville. Despite his high-profile suitors, Williams was an under-the-radar recruit—Rivals.com ranked him as the 111th best player in the class of 2005, placing him below five other Louisville commitments.

But at the Kentucky Derby Classic in Louisville, Williams showed his skills, winning the slam dunk competition and scoring 32 points in the All-Star Game. Once he arrived at Louisville, the silky-smooth forward continued to evolve into a consummate team threat—Williams could score, pass, rebound, defend, or probably sell popcorn if needed. Teammate Edgar Sosa recalls, "He's a stat-sheet stuffer. He's one of those players who you look up and . . . maybe Terrence didn't play great today, but he had [for example] 8 rebounds, 12 points, 2 steals, 2 blocks. That's just what he did every game."

Unfortunately, in Terrence's junior season, much was required of him.

The Cardinals, who had begun the season as No. 6 in the nation, were 9-4 when the two teams met for the annual Dream Game in Rupp Arena. Home losses to Dayton and Cincinnati showed that the squad, despite its well-rounded depth, was still a work in progress. Meanwhile, Kentucky was 6-6 with losses to Gardner Webb, UAB, and Houston, exposing Kentucky's lack of talent. Jodie Meeks and Derrick Jasper were injured for much of the season, and while Ramel Bradley, Joe Crawford, and Patrick Patterson fought gamely, their battle was uphill. For the second year in a row, and only the fourth time in the history of the rivalry, neither team was in the AP top-25.

The Game:

While the Cardinals had won only three times in Rupp Arena since the renewal of the rivalry, they brought an aggressive game plan into the UK game. Particularly ear-marked was the precocious freshman Patterson, whom Louisville pressured every time he neared the ball. With Kentucky struggling, Louisville jumped to a 16-5 lead in the first eight minutes, as Williams and Andre McGee each nailed three-point shots.

From there, however, Kentucky's defense tightened, and UofL shot just 4-for-15 for the remainder of the half. While Patterson was slowed by Louisville's defensive pressure (and, by shooting 3-of-14, had perhaps his worst collegiate game), Bradley and Crawford each scored 8 points in the first half, and at the halftime buzzer, UK held a surprising 31-30 lead.

For Terrence Williams, his early three-pointer constituted his only first-half points. Though he had four rebounds and two blocked shots, if UofL was to overcome Gillispie's pesky Cats, Terrence had to score.

The second half looked like a different game. Louisville went on a 9-0 run in the first two minutes of the second half, with Williams contributing an old-fashioned three-point play to the run. The Cardinals never trailed again, and in fact, spent much of the second half conducting an offensive clinic. The Cardinals shot 56% in the half and were an astounding 28-of-37 at the free throw line. With 59 points, the Cards almost doubled the 30 they managed in the first half.

Williams was at the center of the onslaught. Terrence had 12 points and 3 assists in the second half. What was more, when he wasn't scoring, dishing, or rebounding, Williams was cementing the Cardinals into a team. Around 8:00 before the final buzzer, with Louisville's lead swelling to 20, UK's Ramel Bradley made a flying tackle on Louisville's David Padgett when Padgett attempted a layup. An extended shoving match broke out between the teams, and Williams found himself in the middle of the fray, drawing a technical foul for explaining just how unwelcome Bradley's hard foul had been.

Bradley had 19 second-half points for Kentucky, and his gritty effort kept UK from getting embarrassed. But the day belonged to the Cardinals, whose 89-75 win was their biggest margin of victory in the rivalry since the dark days of Eddie Sutton's final UK season.

Postgame:

Williams was direct in his assessment following the game. "We watched the *Gladiator* movie two nights ago and it was my movie," he recalled. "Rupp Arena was the Coliseum. We were trying to survive and we did. The main message was we had to stick together. If we stick together, we will survive. That's what we did. We survived."

Rick Pitino, after three straight Dream Game losses, was pleased with the victory and assessed the situation as a bit more than survival. "Our guys played a good, smart basketball game," he noted in the postgame press conference.

There was plenty of credit to go around for UofL. Oft-injured center Juan Palacios and wing player Jerry Smith each scored 17 points. But the man who provided the glue was Williams—scorer, passer, and when needed, enforcer. When asked about his rush to David Padgett's aid,

Williams said simply, "He's my center and I was just protecting him like a brother."

Williams was the consummate teammate for Louisville in 2007–2008. His all-around game was so strong that he managed two triple-doubles during the season, matching the total Cardinal all-time output of that statistic on his own in one season. Despite his strong run, Williams stuck around for his senior campaign the following season. He was the 11th selection in the 2009 NBA Draft by the New Jersey Nets. Terrence has played for four NBA teams and has logged some minutes in China as well. Williams had a bit of legal trouble stemming from a domestic altercation in 2013, and at the time of writing, was still weighing his options in professional basketball. Wherever he plays, the man they call "T-Wil" is virtually guaranteed to be an instant favorite of his teammates.

✳✳✳✳✳

Rick Pitino's task of melding Louisville into his own band of brothers was lightened by the victory over Kentucky. UofL at one point reached as high as a No. 12 national ranking and a 24-6 record. A regular season-ending loss to Georgetown and a Big East Tournament loss to Pitt dulled the shine a bit entering the NCAA Tournament. But the Cards rattled off three NCAA victories, reaching an Elite Eight matchup with top seed North Carolina. UNC led by a dozen at the half before UofL rallied to tie the game at 59 midway through the second half. However, from there UNC pulled away, winning the game and Final Four berth, 83-73.

Kentucky would've gladly settled for an Elite Eight loss. Billy Gillispie's reduced roster leaned heavily on seniors Bradley and Crawford, particularly after Patterson sustained a season-ending leg injury. The 18-13 Cats were a scrappy group, but a first round NCAA Tournament loss to Marquette was as much as they could muster. Gillispie's fire and brimstone tactics drove this UK team farther than many thought possible in December. When a healthy Jodie Meeks was added to the mix the following season, conditions were right for a classic Dream Game matchup.

Louisville 89

NAME	MIN	FG-FGA	3-3A	FT-FTA	OR-REB	PF	AST	STL	BLK	TO	TP
Williams	40	4-11	1-4	6-7	1-6	1	3	0	3	5	15
Palacios	34	5-9	1-4	6-7	2-6	5	4	1	0	1	17
Caracter	19	2-5	0-0	2-4	2-5	5	0	3	1	2	6
McGee	21	3-6	1-3	4-6	0-1	2	4	1	0	1	11
Smith	23	4-7	1-4	8-9	0-4	4	2	1	1	2	17
Sosa	23	3-6	2-3	2-2	1-3	0	1	0	0	1	10
Knowles	17	1-4	0-2	0-0	1-2	1	0	2	0	0	2
Padgett	15	2-3	0-0	5-11	0-5	4	1	0	2	2	9
Chichester	4	1-1	0-0	0-0	0-0	1	0	0	0	0	2
Farley	4	0-0	0-0	0-0	0-0	2	0	0	0	0	0
TEAM					1-3						
Total	200	25-52	6-20	33-46	8-35	25	15	8	7	14	89

Kentucky 75

NAME	MIN	FG-FGA	3-3A	FT-FTA	OR-REB	PF	AST	STL	BLK	TO	TP
Harris	14	3-3	1-1	1-2	1-4	3	0	0	0	0	8
Coury	6	0-1	0-0	0-0	0-0	4	1	0	0	0	0
Patterson	32	3-14	0-2	0-0	2-7	5	0	1	2	6	6
Bradley	40	8-12	3-6	8-9	1-2	4	5	1	0	4	27
Meeks	31	1-8	1-5	4-4	0-1	2	2	3	0	1	7
Crawford	35	5-13	0-5	9-12	2-8	3	3	0	0	7	19
Jasper	31	2-4	2-3	0-0	0-7	3	0	0	0	2	6
Stevenson	8	1-1	0-0	0-0	1-1	4	0	1	0	1	2
Stewart	3	0-0	0-0	0-0	1-2	3	0	0	0	0	0
TEAM					1-2						
Total	200	23-56	7-22	22-27	9-34	31	11	6	2	22	75

Chapter 28

The Comeback Kid

No. 18 UofL 74, UK 71
January 4, 2009 at Freedom Hall

Pre-Game:

"I remember that like it was yesterday," says Edgar Sosa, even though the day in question is now four-and-a-half years ago. Sosa, the talented junior point guard of the Louisville Cardinals, had played his way into the basketball dog house just before UofL's annual showdown with Kentucky. But the struggles that had come before had not prepared him for what happened next in his basketball studies under Rick Pitino.

"I just remember him bringing me up to his office," Sosa says. "He said, 'The team is struggling right now because you're not playing well.' He was just telling me, 'I don't know how to coach you anymore. I don't want . . . people looking at me when your four years are up and you leave Louisville and you're not in the NBA, I don't want people to say that it's because of me. So I think if you're not happy here, you should transfer.'"

"I remember telling him, 'I can't play my game. I can't be the player that you see every day in practice . . . because I'm on a short leash. Anything I do, there's a sub coming in for me during the next dead ball.'"

Pitino agreed. Sosa recalls, "He said, 'You're right. I do have you on a short leash. I do sub you out and yell at you for things that I don't do for the other players.'"

Sosa was nonplussed. He recalls telling Pitino, "If you agree with me, you should at least let me play my game."

Apparently, the message was delivered. Sosa had not started all season. Later, in practice, Pitino told the team about his conversation with Sosa. Sosa recalled shedding tears. He also recalled that Pitino named him as one of the first-teamers that day. Edgar would play his game after all.

Sosa, a highly touted point guard from New York City's Rice High School, admits that he essentially recruited himself to UofL. Sosa notes, "My brother . . . played Division II. When I was younger, we used to stay up late, watching college basketball games. The team I gravitated to most was Louisville, because Francisco Garcia was there. . . . I just fell in love with the school, I fell in love with the system, and with Coach Pitino."

Edgar had been a freshman phenom, averaging 11.4 points per game and running the UofL attack with intensity. In the year's final game, he scored 31 against Billy Gillispie's Texas A&M squad in Rupp Arena, but missed two crucial free throws in the loss. The following year was a definite slump—he scored only 7.6 points per game and had fewer assists and steals. As a junior, he was averaging only 5 points per game, and he had only 6 points and 2 assists total in UofL's three losses. The Cardinals badly needed Edgar to play his game.

It had been a difficult 2008–09 season not only for Sosa, but also for the rest of his teammates. UofL had begun the season as the No. 3 team in the nation, but after losses to unranked Western Kentucky, Tubby Smith's Minnesota squad, and UNLV, the Cardinals were 8-3 and had fallen to No. 18 in the nation. Guards Jerry Smith and Andre McGee joined Sosa in the backcourt, and forwards Terrence Williams and Earl Clark were UofL's top two scorers. Center Samardo Samuels added a legitimate post presence. Preston Knowles and Terrence Jennings added depth, but despite their talent, UofL was struggling as a team.

Kentucky had its own problems. The Wildcats, keyed by junior guard Jodie Meeks, sophomore post player Patrick Patterson, and a group of component parts, had lost a shocking home opener to VMI before getting thumped by North Carolina by 19 points in their second game.

Since then, UK had gone 11-1 and was showing signs of the type of improvement that had made the previous season interesting. Meeks had already scored 30 points in four different games, including a 46-point matchup in Freedom Hall against Appalachian State. Back in Freedom Hall again, UK needed big games from its stars to compete.

The Game:

This game, the final game in the series to be played in venerable Freedom Hall, lived up to its billing. Louisville took an early advantage. Sosa played aggressively, and just over four minutes into the game, he had five quick points and keyed the Cardinals to a 13-4 advantage. Kentucky answered with a healthy dose of Meeks and Patterson and closed the gap to a single point.

UofL again answered with a run, and when Sosa drained two free throws with 2:21 to go in the half, the Cardinal advantage was again nine points. Kentucky scored the last six points of the half, though, and UofL's halftime advantage was just 38-35. At the intermission break, Sosa and Earl Clark led the Cardinals with 9 points each, but Meeks had 14 and Patterson added 8 points for UK.

In the second half, the Cardinals again seemed to open the game up. After Kentucky took a brief lead at 43-42 less than three minutes into the half, UofL went on a 12-0 run to open up a 54-43 advantage, with the final points coming on a three-point play by Sosa. "We were rolling," says Sosa. "I thought the game was in the bag."

Kentucky made another run, but when Sosa drained two free throws with 50 seconds to play, UofL led 71-64, and the game appeared over. But nobody told UK.

Jerry Smith fouled Meeks, who was in the act of shooting a three-pointer, and the accurate scorer drained all three free throws to cut the margin to 71-67 with 38 ticks on the clock. With Kentucky pressing, Patterson came up with a deflected pass and shoveled the ball to Meeks, who laid the ball in, cutting the gap to 71-69 with 28 seconds remaining. After a second consecutive turnover from Earl Clark, Meeks was fouled and swished both shots, tying the game only 28 seconds after UK trailed by seven points.

Louisville did not call a timeout. Sosa took the inbounds pass and motioned everyone away for the final possession. Sosa says, "I remember, [UofL's] Will Scott had a big man on him, and Coach P was trying to get Will Scott to pick-and-roll . . . and I thought, 'If Will does the pick-and-roll, they're either going to trap me or they're going to switch and I'll have a bigger player on me.' So I just waved Will off. I had every intention of going to the basket . . . and [UK's Michael] Porter just kept backing up and backing up. I didn't even know where I was at, at that moment in time. I just know I stopped and I pulled up. It felt like I left it up short, so I kept my follow through up. . . . But it went in."

Sosa was a 20% three-point shooter on the season, but his NBA-length trey swished cleanly through the hoop, giving UofL a 74-71 advantage with just 2.3 seconds left. Porter's heave just across half court banged off the backboard, leaving Sosa as the hero of the day. Sosa recalls, "That [shot] is special, just because it's Kentucky and it's a rivalry, but also because of everything that I was going through." Edgar the Inconsistent had become Edgar the Survivor.

Postgame:

Louisville never looked back after the day that Edgar played his game. In the ultra-competitive Big East, UofL lost only twice and headed into the NCAA Tournament with a 7-1 mark against top-25 opponents. In fact, UofL was ranked No. 1 in the nation for the first time in school history in the pre-tournament AP poll. The Cards had the top seed in the tournament and cruised through their first three tournament games, beating Arizona by 39 in the Sweet 16. But in the Elite 8, Tom Izzo's Michigan State Spartans upset the Cardinals, 64-52, and Pitino's best UofL team yet was denied the Final Four.

Sosa did play four seasons for Pitino, much to the relief of both, as he totaled 1,363 career points as a Cardinal. After a season in Italy, Sosa was playing for the Dominican Republic national team in 2011—under UK coach John Calipari, making him one of few players to play for both coaches. "Both [Pitino and Calipari] are great teachers of the game," says Sosa. "Coach Cal's system is just built for guards to go."

During that time, the Dominican team trained in Lexington. Sosa enjoyed the experience, relating, "I didn't know DeMarcus Cousins or [Eric] Bledsoe or John Wall . . . but I was able to meet those guys outside of Louisville/Kentucky, and those guys are great guys, and we're cool. When you're suited up in your UofL uniform and they've got their UK [uniform], you've got to go to war. But otherwise, those guys are cool dudes."

Sadly, just as NBA insiders were gaining interest in Sosa, he drove to the basket in a Dominican game and broke his leg in a horrific injury that was not dissimilar to the one that Kevin Ware suffered in the 2012 NCAA Tournament. "It was really the worst time of my life," recalls Sosa. After intense rehabilitation (and the setback of breaking the *other* foot), Sosa is back to 100%, he says. He is still playing for the Dominican squad, along with UofL's Francisco Garcia and UK's Eloy Vargas (and future UK commit Karl Towns). In 2013, the team earned a spot in the 2014 FIBA World Basketball Cup, where they will compete with the best teams in the world, including the US Olympic Team. Sosa still hopes to make the NBA and plans to play overseas if that dream is deferred.

✳✳✳✳✳

Kentucky continued on an uptick after almost beating UofL. The team won its first five SEC games and was 16-4 and back in the nation's top-25 when it played Ole Miss in late January. Billy Gillispie had a minor outburst at ESPN reporter Janine Edwards at the end of the first half, and suddenly, any illusions that Billy G. was the solution at Kentucky dissolved rapidly.

Kentucky lost that game and went 6-9 for the rest of the season. UK's season ended in an NIT loss at Notre Dame. Jodie Meeks had one of the best scoring seasons in UK's history and Patterson was a solid NBA-level talent, but Gillispie's poor recruiting and player development were almost as offensive as his behavior. Slowly, as the Cats disintegrated, stories of Gillispie's mistreatment of players came to light. He continued to have problems with the media and generally seemed ill-prepared to coach in the spotlight of Lexington.

On March 27, 2009, UK athletic director Mitch Barnhart fired Gillispie. He had gone 40-27 at Kentucky and had won zero NCAA Tournament games. An arrest for drunk driving shortly after the firing gave credence to some of the circulating rumors about Gillispie's personal life.

On April 1, Barnhart wasn't fooling as he announced his new Kentucky basketball head coach. An enormously charismatic and successful coach took the job. His last two collegiate employers, through no fault of his own, had ended up in NCAA hot water. He was such a successful recruiter that whispers followed him everywhere. And he had once been aligned with Pitino, taking the head coaching job at Pitino's alma mater, University of Massachusetts, either with the blessing of, or despite a denunciation from Pitino, depending on whom is believed.

John Calipari became the new coach of the Wildcats. Barnhart had fired his shot heard around the Commonwealth, if not the world.

Louisville 74

NAME	MIN	FG-FGA	3-3A	FT-FTA	OR-REB	PF	AST	STL	BLK	TO	TP
Williams	36	7-12	3-5	2-2	1-8	2	1	5	0	3	19
Clark	36	2-11	0-4	6-8	3-8	5	3	1	3	7	10
Samuels	11	2-3	0-0	0-0	1-1	4	1	0	0	1	4
Sosa	26	4-7	2-4	8-9	0-1	1	2	2	0	2	18
Smith	29	3-3	3-3	2-2	0-0	1	2	0	2	1	11
Knowles	10	1-2	1-1	0-0	1-1	2	0	1	0	0	3
Kuric	4	1-1	1-1	0-0	0-0	0	0	1	0	0	3
Scott	2	1-1	1-1	1-2	0-0	0	0	0	0	0	4
Swopshire	4	0-1	0-0	0-0	0-0	0	0	0	0	0	0
Goode	22	0-2	0-0	0-0	0-1	4	2	1	2	0	0
Jennings	6	0-2	0-0	0-0	1-1	1	0	0	1	1	0
McGee	14	1-2	0-1	0-0	0-1	1	3	0	0	0	2
TEAM					0-0						
Total	200	22-47	11-20	19-23	7-22	21	14	11	8	15	74

Kentucky 71

NAME	MIN	FG-FGA	3-3A	FT-FTA	OR-REB	PF	AST	STL	BLK	TO	TP
Stevenson	31	3-5	1-1	0-1	3-6	4	2	0	3	4	7
Patterson	40	8-13	0-0	6-7	6-15	1	4	1	0	3	22
Galloway	4	1-1	0-0	0-0	0-0	0	0	1	0	1	2
Porter	33	2-5	2-4	2-2	0-0	4	1	1	0	0	8
Meeks	40	8-19	3-9	9-9	1-3	3	0	2	0	6	28
Miller	13	0-1	0-0	0-0	0-0	0	1	0	0	0	0
Stewart	3	0-0	0-0	2-2	0-1	1	0	0	0	0	2
Harris	23	0-3	0-1	0-0	0-3	3	1	0	0	1	0
Liggins	8	1-1	0-0	0-1	0-0	1	2	1	1	3	2
Harrellson	5	0-1	0-1	0-0	1-1	0	0	0	0	3	0
TEAM					3-3	1					
Total	200	23-49	6-16	19-22	14-32	18	11	6	4	21	71

Chapter 29

Someone (Relatively) Old, Someone New

No. 3 UK 71, UofL 62
January 2, 2010 at Rupp Arena

DESPITE HIS PROTESTS, following John Calipari's April 1, 2009 hiring, Kentucky fans wasted little time appointing him the Grand Poobah of Kentucky basketball. Why not?

Despite the public statements of both men, the majority of college basketball believed then and now that it was a barely concealed secret that Calipari and Rick Pitino hated each others' guts. Calipari certainly gave his critics plenty to envy. He could coach, he could sell a program, and he could sweet talk the alumni and media, often at the same time. But most of all, he could recruit.

Calipari wasted no time in hitting the recruiting ground running. Two consensus top-five players in the class, point guard John Wall and center DeMarcus Cousins, each decided to join the Wildcats. Guard Eric Bledsoe and Gillispie holdover Daniel Orton were two more All-America talents, and guard Darnell Dodson was another skilled addition. A few talented returnees like junior forward Patrick Patterson and sophomore wing player Darius Miller were expected to contribute as well.

Calipari's Wildcats were young and talented, and until they caught on to his Dribble Drive offense, the early season had a wild, seat-of-the-pants quality to it. Wall was a hero in his first game, draining a jumper in the final second to hold off Miami of Ohio. UK needed overtime to dispatch unranked Stanford in the Cancun Challenge. But the Cats also beat ranked North Carolina and Connecticut squads, and on December 21, by beating Drexel, UK became the first NCAA school to win 2,000 basketball games. UK was 14-0 leading into the annual matchup with Louisville and was ranked No. 3 in the nation.

Meanwhile, Rick Pitino had problems that extended beyond his new rival. A few days after the 2009 season concluded, Pitino publicly announced that he had been the target of an extortion attempt. Karen Sypher, the wife of a former UofL equipment manager, was subsequently charged and convicted of extortion and lying to federal agents. However, within the context of Sypher's prosecution and conviction, Pitino's own reputation came under fire. Pitino subsequently admitted that he had sex with Sypher in 2003 and that he paid for her to have an abortion. In August 2009, Pitino made a public apology and UofL president James Ramsey indicated that he would retain his coaching position.

In the context of the off-court distractions, the problems presented on-court seemed a bit less taxing than usual. Sophomore center Samardo Samuels and senior guard Edgar Sosa led Louisville's team. Senior guards Reginald Delk (nephew of UK legend Tony Delk) and Jerry Smith rounded out the Cardinal lineup with sophomore forward Jared Swopshire. Louisville lacked UK's athleticism, but had a wealth of experience and brought a rugged determination into the annual Dream Game. The 10-3 Cardinals were unranked and an underdog, but they planned to bring the fight to the Cats. Calipari's one-and-dones were certain of a physical test from a wily group of Cardinals.

The Game:

The game was every bit as rugged as expected. Seconds into the game, Eric Bledsoe was called for a pushing foul on Reginald Delk. Something in the exchange perturbed Calipari, who rarely engages in conversations with officials or opponents. Coach Cal went into a miniature eruption on his sideline, apparently at Delk.

Seconds later, Cousins and Swopshire went to the floor after a loose ball. What happened next depended mostly on who did the telling. Kentucky fans would note that as the two players rolled on the floor, Swopshire's knee flew into Cousins's face. UofL partisans would counter by noting that as Cousins rolled over Swopshire, he threw his right elbow into Swopshire's face. Officials reviewed the play and gave both players technical fouls, adding another on Reginald Delk for his own part in the melee, which followed the kneeing/elbowing.

Calipari had been saying since taking the Kentucky job that opponents saw UK as their Super Bowl. In this instance, the teams played as if it were the Super Bowl. The two teams combined to pick up 51 fouls on the day. While no one fouled out of the game, six players finished with four fouls each.

Amidst the physical play, Cousins and Patterson starred early. Patterson drained a three and had multiple easy baskets for his 12 first-half points. The veteran junior from West Virginia who had survived Billy Gillispie brought much-needed calm and maturity to the UK squad. On the other hand, Cousins may have been one of the most talented and unrefined players in the nation. His skills were undeniable, even if Louisville fans believed he should've been watching from the locker room after his tussle with Swopshire. Cousins totaled 8 points, 12 rebounds, and 3 assists in the first stanza. Louisville shot only 17%, but due to good foul shooting, trailed only 27-19 at the half.

In the second half, UofL mounted a run, even briefly taking a 42-41 lead midway through the half. For much of the day, UofL had contained John Wall. The 6'4" point guard who hailed from ACC country in North Carolina had been Kentucky's difference maker throughout the season. Wall was cat-quick off the dribble, explosive near the basket, and capable of draining clutch shots whenever needed.

Against Lousville, Wall had struggled, but with the game on the line, he showed the stuff that made him an overnight Kentucky sensation. First he drove to the basket for a layup. Next, he canned a jumper, and after stealing the ball and getting fouled, Wall drained a pair of free throws. Louisville never got closer than four points for the rest of the day.

Kentucky won 71-62, ending UofL's two-game winning streak in the series. Cousins had 18 points and 18 rebounds, and Wall heated up late to finish with 17 points. Relative graybeard Patterson added a quiet 17 points, but his steadying influence in the game was apparent. Sosa and Swopshire had each put up double-figure scoring totals in the second half, but Louisville shot only 32% for the game.

After the game, most of the talk was about the physical play. "It was heated," admitted Calipari. "This start was physical, but neither team was going to give an inch."

Pitino concurred. "That's rivalry games. . . . That's what rivalry games are all about," he said.

Postgame:

Calipari's Kittens established that experience was not a prerequisite for success in the modern collegiate game. UK was 32-2 entering the NCAA Tournament. Wall was heroic whenever needed, and Cousins developed from an oversized kid to an All-America center. In the SEC Tournament, Cousins laid in a Wall miss at the buzzer to send the game to overtime, and then was tackled by the ebullient Wall in celebration. UK eventually won. The Cats were No. 2 in the nation and cruised to an Elite Eight matchup with West Virginia. UK's outside shooting suddenly went cold, and the Mountaineers ended Kentucky's season with a 73-66 setback.

Louisville struggled throughout the season, reaching the NCAA Tournament with a 19-13 mark. The team earned a No. 9 seed in the NCAA Tournament, but lost their first round matchup with California. Pitino reloaded with a quiet recruiting class, which was short on notoriety but long on talent. Russ Smith and Gorgui Dieng were hardly household names—but they would be.

This was the first shot across the bow in the new philosophical rivalry of college basketball. Calipari recruited teams of Kentucky thoroughbreds—thoroughbreds who knew they would probably not stay in college long enough to claim an old Kentucky home. Pitino countered with an aggregate of solid parts—the athletic equivalent of a group of blue-collar workers who knew they would punch the collegiate clock for three or four years. While the winner of that battle remains uncertain, the annual skirmishes made a phenomenal addition to the rivalry.

$$\ast\ast\ast\ast\ast$$

Kentucky's unlikely trio of stars—one "old" and two new—were all fan favorites, and it was with some combination of awe and sadness that the UK fan base bid all three adieu after the season, when freshmen Wall and Cousins and junior Patterson all entered the NBA Draft. Wall became UK's first top selection in NBA Draft history when the Washington Wizards selected him. The Sacramento Kings chose Cousins four picks later. The Houston Rockets took Patterson 14th, although he has subsequently been traded to Sacramento, teaming up with Big Cuz again.

UK's Eric Bledsoe and Daniel Orton were also first round choices, meaning that one-sixth of the NBA Draft's first round picks were spent on UK Wildcats. All of the above players are still plying their trades in the NBA.

Many across college basketball expressed doubt that in a single season Kentucky's fan base and their blue-chip stars could build a meaningful relationship. Calipari's first team (and his freshman-star-studded group two years later) has mostly laid that idea to rest. The love affair extends both ways.

After UK's recent Alumni Game, Wall was asked about the Louisville rivalry, and he all but bled Kentucky blue despite playing in only one UK/UofL matchup.

"That's not even a rivalry anymore. [Louisville's] right up the street, and it's bigger than basketball," Wall said. "That's something that everybody lives for, and I think if we went 0-30, that's the biggest game that everybody cares about."

Sounds like one year was enough to get the idea.

Kentucky 71

NAME	MIN	FG-FGA	3-3A	FT-FTA	OR-REB	PF	AST	STL	BLK	TO	TP
Cousins	26	7-14	0-0	4-8	4-18	3	3	1	2	2	18
Patterson	38	7-10	1-1	2-5	2-4	1	1	1	0	1	17
Miller	8	0-1	0-0	0-0	1-2	3	0	0	0	1	0
Wall	36	5-10	0-3	7-12	0-1	3	4	2	0	5	17
Bledsoe	30	3-8	0-3	6-6	2-2	2	4	2	0	4	12
Harris	23	1-3	1-3	0-0	0-2	4	1	0	0	3	3
Dodson	13	0-5	0-4	2-2	0-4	1	1	1	0	1	2
Stevenson	10	1-1	0-0	0-0	1-2	0	0	0	1	0	2
Orton	8	0-0	0-0	0-1	0-0	4	0	1	2	1	0
Liggins	8	0-0	0-0	0-0	1-1	0	1	1	0	0	0
TEAM					1-2						
Total	200	24-52	2-14	21-34	12-38	21	15	9	5	18	71

Louisville 62

NAME	MIN	FG-FGA	3-3A	FT-FTA	OR-REB	PF	AST	STL	BLK	TO	TP
Samuels	25	3-9	0-0	3-5	6-9	4	2	1	1	3	9
Swopshire	30	4-13	2-4	0-2	1-4	4	0	0	1	3	10
Smith	25	4-7	2-4	1-2	2-6	3	0	4	0	2	11
Sosa	34	3-11	0-4	5-6	1-2	2	2	0	0	6	11
Delk	28	2-3	1-2	4-4	0-4	4	1	1	0	0	9
Knowles	17	1-8	0-2	05-5	0-1	3	0	2	0	0	7
Jennings	15	2-3	0-0	1-2	2-4	3	0	0	3	1	5
Buckles	10	0-2	0-0	0-0	0-3	4	0	0	0	2	0
Kuric	10	0-2	0-0	0-0	0-3	2	0	0	0	0	0
Siva	6	0-1	0-1	0-0	0-0	1	0	1	0	1	0
Van Treese	0+	0-0	0-0	0-0	0-0	0	0	0	0	0	0
TEAM					3-3						
Total	200	19-59	5-17	19-26	15-39	30	5	9	5	19	62

Chapter 30

Harrellson Tweets, Then Dominates

No. 11 UK 78, No. 22 UofL 63
December 31, 2010 at the Yum! Center

Pre-Game

His career, it could be said, began—and could have ended—with a tweet.

Along the way there was a pair of jorts, a rather infamous stay in a bathroom stall, and a lot of running. Oh, the running.

But wait, we're getting ahead of ourselves. Let's start at the beginning.

Josh Harrellson, a junior college transfer from St. Charles, Missouri, just outside of St. Louis, was taking a campus tour of the University of Kentucky in 2008 when the photo was taken. It showed him wearing jean shorts, or "jorts." When the popular website Kentucky Sports Radio posted it, it went, as they say, viral.

Harrellson loved the idea of playing for the Wildcats and loved Kentucky. He committed, and by that time he was already known as Jorts. The nickname would stick with him through his entire career. It was a career of ups and downs.

Under Coach Billy Gillispie, Harrellson was once punished for ineffective play by being forced to spend a halftime in a bathroom stall.

"I wasn't really fond of Gillispie, playing for him," Harrellson told Kentucky Sports Radio in 2013. "I didn't despise anybody more than him."

The feeling from UK fans toward Gillispie was the same. After that season, he was gone, replaced by John Calipari. Immediately, fans wondered who the new coach would keep on the team. Would Harrellson make the cut?

The 6'10", 270-pound big man could shoot, which was intriguing. But could he fit in Calipari's offense? Because of his skills and his addition to the team's chemistry (teammates loved Jorts's sense of humor), Calipari kept Harrellson on the team, which was somewhat of a surprise. Instead, forward Matt Pilgrim was sent packing, and Harrellson got a great seat to watch John Wall and Demarcus Cousins lead UK back to the national spotlight. He never played much that season, but he was on the team.

In his senior season, everything changed. He was slated to back up future NBA pick Enes Kanter, who was an incoming freshman center from Turkey. But the NCAA decided Kanter had accepted too much money from playing as a professional and ruled him ineligible.

Suddenly, Jorts was the main man. He would be the starting center for the Kentucky Wildcats. In the annual preseason Blue/White scrimmage, Harrellson played the best he ever had, grabbing 26 rebounds, but Calipari was less than impressed afterward and said so, essentially calling the scrimmage a glorified pickup game. It was a challenge to Harrellson.

Jorts responded . . . by tweeting.

"Just amazing to me I can't get a good job or way to go . . . It is just amazing to me but I look past it and keep trucking!"

"I will always call it the dumbest/smartest thing I ever did," Harrellson has said on multiple occasions.

The next day, his Twitter privileges were revoked by an irate Calipari. He was almost kicked off the team, but Calipari thought about it and instead just punished him—he made Jorts run the steps at the practice facility every morning. It transformed the player into the best shape he'd ever been in and, coupled with practicing against Kanter every day, Harrellson became very, very good.

It was just what his Kentucky team needed.

✳✳✳✳✳

Preston Knowles played at Clark County High School in Winchester, Kentucky, a stone's throw from Lexington, where he averaged 21 points per game, earned all-state basketball honors, and helped the school win its first regional title in 17 years. He became a top sleeper recruit in the state, but UK didn't come calling—Louisville did, along with Virginia Commonwealth, Kansas State, LSU, and Miami (Ohio).

Knowles chose to be a Card.

"I needed a change in my life, and I knew Coach Pitino would help guide me in the right direction," Knowles told the UofL official athletics website. "[Coach Pitino will] help you succeed as a person as well as an athlete, and he will never let you settle for anything in life."

Whereas Josh Harrellson admitted to not knowing much about the Kentucky/Louisville rivalry, for players like Knowles who hailed from the state, the Kentucky/Louisville rivalry meant more. On December 31, 2010, Kentucky, ranked No. 11, sat at 10-2, with losses to a surprisingly good Connecticut squad and at North Carolina, by just two points. The Cats visited No. 22 Louisville, who was 11-1 with wins over ranked Butler and UNLV. The only blemish was a surprising home loss to Drexel, where the Cards scored just 46 points.

It was the first season for Louisville's sparkling new Yum! Center arena, which held nearly 23,000 fans and set the standard for how basketball venues could be transformed.

A national television audience tuned in to watch Knowles and the Cards in their new home as they hosted the intrastate rivals. Most thought the teams were very evenly matched. Louisville had a slew of shooters: Knowles, Kyle Kuric, Mike Marra, Chris Smith, Russ Smith, and Elisha Justice. Could Terrence Jennings and Gorgui Dieng protect the paint? As usual, UK was young, boasting all-everything point guard Brandon Knight from Florida, along with fellow freshmen Terrence Jones and Doron Lamb. But without Enes Kanter, the Cats hadn't been stellar in the paint. Jones had showed some explosion so far, leading the team in scoring and rebounding, so Pitino geared his attack to stopping the power forward from Oregon.

That essentially left Josh Harrellson open to make plays. No one counted on him to do that.

The Game:

The Cards jumped out to an early lead, and by the 14:00 mark, Doron Lamb was out of the game—sent to the bench with two fouls. It looked like trouble for Kentucky. Down 12-6, Harrellson rebounded a miss, got the putback, and drew the foul. Junior Deandre Liggins got a steal and a layup before blocking a shot to set a defensive spark.

Then junior Darius Miller got involved. Miller was the star who led Mason County to a state title. Mason County also just happened to be the rival of Clark County, which produced Preston Knowles. Miller backed down Kuric, then hit a turnaround jumper. The basket gave UK its first lead at 15-14 and Miller his first points ever scored against Louisville.

Then Kentucky went on an execution spree. As Louisville doubled Jones, they failed to rotate to defend Harrellson, who kept hitting wide-open dunks and layups. He also pounded the Cards on the boards with putbacks and defensive rebounds. Another Miller layup, a Doron Lamb three, and a drive and score by Knight swelled the lead to 26-16 with 6:00 to go.

By the half, UK led 35-24. Knowles had just six points and Louisville was being outrebounded.

"I wouldn't say [Harrellson] caught us by surprise, because [Coach Pitino] told us he was a good player," Chris Smith said. "But maybe we did underestimate him a little bit. He went out there and did his job."

Harrellson said Kentucky spent the entire week leading up to the game preparing for working on what to do when Jones was double-teamed. It worked in the second half as well.

Within the first five minutes of the second period, Harrellson hit a 16-footer and a three-pointer (his first of the year). The lead was 44-26, Kentucky. With under 12:00 to play, Harrellson hit a turnaround jumper, and with 7:00 to go, Jones found Jorts all alone inside for the dunk. It was 63-51, Cats.

"I got more confidence," Harrellson told Kentucky Sports Radio. "I started playing better. I started doing things that my teammates knew I could do because they see me do it in practice, but just things I wasn't doing in a game because I wasn't comfortable doing it yet."

But Knowles did not let the Cards go quietly.

The guard scored 13 points in just five minutes to bring his team back to within nine. But they just didn't have the muscle inside to hold Jones and Harrellson. Nor did they have enough quickness to keep up with Brandon Knight, who hit four threes and led all scorers with 25 points. Time and again the guard pulled up and connected or drove to the hole for a score.

Brandon Knight scored 25 points in his only Dream Game appearance and formed an outside-inside punch with Josh Harrellson in leading UK to a surprising Final Four appearance. *(Photo by Tim Sofranko)*

Knowles finished with 22 points—16 in the second half—to make it a game effort. Chris Smith added 15 for Louisville, which was outrebounded 36-25.

Harrellson finished with an amazing 23 points, 14 rebounds, and 2 assists. Jones finished with 12 points, 8 rebounds, and 5 assists—many of them to Harrellson.

It became a rude opening for the Yum! Center's first rivalry game.

When Harrellson came out of the game, his coach gave him a bear hug.

"He looked at me like, 'Did you really do that?'" Harrellson said. Calipari then gave the player the recognition he'd wanted for two months.

"Good job, kid," the coach said.

Postgame:

Harrellson was named Player of the Game against Louisville. But Kentucky had a lot to overcome as the season progressed. The Cats seemingly could not find a way to win any SEC games on the road. Then, with just a few games remaining in the season, they pulled it together. Knight and Harrellson led the way.

Kentucky went on to beat ranked Vandy, Florida (twice), West Virginia, No. 1 Ohio State, and No. 7 North Carolina en route to the Final Four. Along the way Harrellson notched 17 points and 10 rebounds against All-America center Jared Sullinger of Ohio State. Knight hit the game-winner in the 62-60 win. UK finished the season 29-9.

For Louisville, Preston Knowles went on to become one of the most clutch players in college basketball. He performed at a level few could have ever imagined, hitting game-winners against Providence and Syracuse, among others.

Louisville bowed out to Connecticut by three points in the Big East tourney, as UConn was in the middle of one of the most legendary runs in postseason tourney history. Unfortunately, Louisville was upset 62-61 in the NCAA first round on a last-second three by Morehead State. The Cards finished 25-10.

Connecticut took the Big East tournament by winning five games in five days, before winning the national championship game. The Huskies then took out Kentucky 56-55 in the National Semifinals before defeating Butler for the title.

*****

"We got lucky with him," Pitino said of Knowles. "Give me 12 guys like Preston Knowles, and we'll go to the Final Four every year. His work ethic, his passion—he brings it every day. He's a tough kid. We got really lucky." Knowles went on to play in the NBA Developmental League and overseas, including the Israeli league in 2013.

Kentucky's Brandon Knight and Deandre Liggins declared early for the NBA Draft and were selected, Knight in the first round, Liggins in the second. But a third member of that team—a senior—was also drafted in the second round.

Josh Harrellson. That's right—the New York Knicks made Jorts an NBA player. For a season he played with the Knicks, then the Miami Heat. He also played overseas in Puerto Rico and was named best newcomer in China. By fall 2013, Jorts was back in the NBA with the Detroit Pistons.

"It definitely feels good [to win] at Louisville," Harrellson told Kentucky Sports Radio in 2013. "A lot of people doubted me my whole career. I'm sure I'll have a lot more doubters in the future. But it's good to prove people wrong."

Kentucky 78

NAME	MIN	FG-FGA	3-3A	FT-FTA	OR-REB	PF	AST	STL	BLK	TO	TP
Jones	33	5-11	0-2	2-2	3-8	2	5	1	3	1	12
Harrellson	37	10-12	1-1	2-3	6-14	3	2	1	1	1	23
Miller	29	3-6	0-1	1-1	1-3	4	0	0	1	2	7
Knight	36	7-13	4-6	7-8	1-3	2	4	0	0	5	25
Liggins	39	1-7	0-4	0-0	0-4	2	2	4	2	4	2
Lamb	23	3-6	1-2	2-2	2-3	2	1	0	0	0	9
Vargas	2	0-2	0-0	0-0	0-0	0	0	0	0	0	0
Hood	1	0-0	0-0	0-0	0-0	0	0	0	0	0	0
TEAM					0-1						
Total	200	29-57	6-16	14-16	13-36	15	14	6	7	13	78

Louisville 63

NAME	MIN	FG-FGA	3-3A	FT-FTA	OR-REB	PF	AST	STL	BLK	TO	TP
C. Smith	33	6-8	1-1	2-5	4-6	3	4	0	0	3	15
Kuric	37	3-7	1-4	0-0	1-3	4	2	2	0	2	7
Dieng	12	2-4	0-0	0-0	0-4	1	0	0	0	1	4
Knowles	37	8-16	6-10	0-0	0-2	2	3	4	0	3	22
Siva	33	2-9	0-3	2-3	0-2	4	4	2	0	3	6
Jennings	28	4-6	0-0	1-3	2-4	1	1	1	2	1	9
Marra	11	0-3	0-2	0-0	0-1	1	0	0	1	0	0
R. Smith	5	0-1	0-0	0-0	0-0	1	0	0	0	0	0
Justice	3	0-0	0-0	0-0	0-1	0	0	0	0	0	0
Van Treese	1	0-0	0-0	0-0	0-0	0	0	0	0	0	0
Henderson	0+	0-0	0-0	0-0	0-0	1	0	0	0	0	0
TEAM					2-2						
Total	200	25-54	8-20	5-11	9-25	18	14	9	3	13	63

Chapter 31

MKG, Davis Win Round One

No. 3 UK 69, No. 4 UofL 62
December 31, 2011 at Rupp Arena

Pre-Game:

In the 2011–2012 season, there were two epic basketball games between Kentucky and Louisville. One would culminate in the two meeting in the Final Four, and the winner would win a spot in the national championship game. But before that, before all the hoopla and buildup, UK and UofL met in the regular season, in Rupp Arena, on New Year's Eve, 2011.

The storylines were already set: Kentucky, 12-1, ranked No. 3, had lost one game that season on a buzzer-beater at Indiana. Louisville, No. 4, was still finding itself, but at 11-1, they had only lost to Georgetown. Led by junior point guard Peyton Siva, sophomore shooter Russ Smith, senior captain Kyle Kuric, and sophomore center Gorgui Dieng, the Cards were young but formidable. Add in forward Chane Behanan, who was recruited by both Kentucky and Louisville, and the Cards had the foundation for one of their most purely talented teams of the Pitino era.

Kentucky was favored, but fans on both sides expected a fight, and that's exactly what they saw. Louisville's pressure defense forced a low-scoring, tough basketball game. But the story of this game revolved around two young UK superstars—one from New Jersey, the other from Chicago. Louisville wanted to force a physical game, but the bad news for the Cards was that Kentucky had two players ready for a street fight.

*****

Michael Kidd-Gilchrist grew up in Somerdale, New Jersey, and tragedy followed him from an early age.

Before he was three years old, his father was shot and killed, so his mother Cindy Richardson raised him. His best friend, his uncle Darrin Kidd, moved the young player and his mother into his own house to help raise him. He attended powerhouse St. Patrick's High School and was ranked one of the best players in the country in 2010, but on the day Kidd-Gilchrist committed to play college basketball at Kentucky, Darrin suffered a heart attack and died. For 18 minutes, Kidd-Gilchrist tried to give him CPR, but it was to no avail.

It was in honor of Darrin that he added "Kidd" to his last name.

Michael Kidd-Gilchrist bested the Cardinals with 24 points and 19 rebounds on New Year's Eve, 2011. His toughness and intensity were central to UK's 2012 title run. *(Photo by Tim Sofranko)*

"He put the ball in my hands," Kidd-Gilchrist said of his uncle in an interview with CoachCal.com. "He introduced me to the game. I didn't really have a dad. That was him."

By the time he got to UK, he was one of the toughest freshmen—and possibly one of the toughest players of any age—in the nation.

"I've never seen him go anything but absolutely all out," Calipari told his website. "What will happen is he'll either take over practices or guys will try to step up with him and then it becomes a team on fire, an absolute team on fire. So what I'm asking him to do is every day I want him to raise that level that we practice with and raise the level that we play with."

*****

Anthony Davis did not seem to have basketball superstardom in his future. Growing up in Chicago, Davis attended Perspectives Charter School, which was better known for its academics than its basketball reputation. The school didn't even have a gym.

Davis started his career as a 6'0" shooting guard, and by the end of his sophomore season he was 6'4". As a junior he grew to 6'8", and even though he was a dominant talent on the inside, he was forced to bring the

Kentucky's Anthony Davis contests a shot. In his two matchups with UofL, Davis totaled 36 points, 24 rebounds, and 11 blocked shots. *(Photo by Tim Sofranko)*

ball up the court for his team. By his senior year he was a nearly 7'-tall center with guard skills. Virtually unnoticed in Chicago, he burst onto the AAU scene and quickly became a star. Although his high school team went just 8-15 his senior season, the 6'10", 250-pound Davis was being recruited by the likes of Syracuse, Georgetown, Kansas, and Kentucky. Scout.com rated him the No. 1 player in America.

He decided to be a Wildcat.

Davis starred in the Nike Global Challenge (23 points, 9 rebounds) and was named a McDonald's and *Parade* All-America selection.

On those teams, he was joined by another future Wildcat—a tough-minded, 6'7", 230-pound kid from New Jersey.

*****

After everything Kidd-Gilchrist had been through, it seemed even more meaningful when his mother was hospitalized with an illness the week before the Kentucky/Louisville game, but was able to recover. By December 31, 2011, she was in Rupp Arena for the game, along with Ashley Judd and Jay-Z, who joined 24,387 others and about a dozen NBA scouts, who also came along to watch.

It was the highest combined ranking in the series' history.

Could Louisville hang with the depth and athleticism of Kentucky?

The state—as well as a national television audience—was about to find out.

The Game:

Louisville scored first for a 2-0 lead. Then everything changed.

Darius Miller, a senior from Maysville, Kentucky, knew all too well what the UK and UofL rivalry means. He answered with a three-pointer to give Kentucky the lead.

Then it became Kidd-Gilchrist's game, a fistfight on the court. There was bad shooting, with loose rebounds to be corralled and bodies flying in all directions. It was not an atmosphere for the meek. Over the next 14 minutes, the New Jersey freshman was the only one to make a field goal. Louisville freshman Chane Behanan was the first to crack. Behanan, originally from Cincinnati by way of Bowling Green, Kentucky, was recruited by both schools, but chose Louisville.

With 16:16 to play in the first half, Behanan was called for a charging foul and, in response, threw the basketball back at UK forward Terrence Jones. Behanan was issued a technical foul, which gave him two fouls and took him out of the game until the second half. It effectively helped open the lane for Kidd-Gilchrist.

But Kentucky's Davis also suffered two fouls, sending him early to the bench at the 12:29 mark. Neither team shot the ball well, and the fouls piled up as Kentucky built a 31-16 lead. The Cards then came back, led by Russ and Chris Smith, who by themselves led a 13-0 run.

By halftime, Kentucky led just 36-33 and Kidd-Gilchrist had scored 16. The teams retired to the lockers to regroup.

"It was crazy out there," Kidd-Gilchrist said.

In the second half, Russ Smith put the Louisville team on his back. Down 40-36, Smith drilled a three and Kidd-Gilchrist fouled him. Smith connected on the free throw and the game was tied.

"We never feel like we are out of it," Russ Smith said. "Any basketball player would know the game is not over until the 40 minutes is up, so we play hard. If we were down a few points less, it could have gotten interesting."

Louisville had the ball and a chance to retake the lead with the game tied at 40. Peyton Siva pulled up from 18 feet—but his shot drew only air.

The second half changed again on the tweet of a whistle. Cardinal center Gorgui Dieng, who had been effective in the first half, was called for three fouls in about two minutes. With 16 minutes to go, he was out of the game.

Enter Michael Kidd-Gilchrist and Anthony Davis.

Davis made four free throws, while Kidd-Gilchrist hit a free throw and a layup to make it 47-40, UK. Davis then blocked a shot, got a putback, and slammed home an alley-oop from Doron Lamb for a 56-48 lead with under 7:00 to play.

At the 3:41 mark, Kidd-Gilchrist got an old-fashioned three-point play for an 11-point lead. It effectively ended the game, part of a Herculean 24-point, 19-rebound effort from the New Jersey freshman.

Louisville sophomore Russ Smith matched him with a 30-point effort, hitting 10-of-20 from the field with three three-pointers.

Davis added 18 points—all in the second half—with 10 rebounds and 6 blocks.

Kentucky won a hard-fought game, 69-62. There were 52 total fouls called and 70 free throw attempts.

"This is what I live for right here. Why? Because I've always been that way," Kidd-Gilchrist said. "I'm built for this."

Calipari agreed.

"He wasn't bothered as much as some of the others by the physical play," Calipari said. "He almost relished it."

Davis was impressed with the ferocity of the fans. "The crowd was crazy because of the rivalry," Davis said. "It was fun."

And Pitino was proud of his squad. "I've never coached a team that is willing to give the effort that this team gives," Pitino said. "Unfortunately there are no moral victories. We struggled shooting the basketball tonight."

Louisville held the Cats to just 17-of-57 from the field—29.8%. Louisville shot 32.2% but was outrebounded 57-31.

The Associated Press reported that according to ESPN researcher Jason McCallum, UK was only the fourth team in the last decade to win a game in which it shot less than 30% and had 20 or more turnovers.

"This team is special," Kidd-Gilchrist said. "We know what we have here. We're hungry. If you're a leader, you care about your teammates more than yourself.

"So I'm going to play my heart out. That's what I'm going to give. My heart."

Postgame:

During the Louisville game, Kidd-Gilchrist and Davis became leaders on a national stage. UK solidified the belief that it was a championship-caliber team—in winning ugly, the Cats were still impressive. And for the third time, Pitino had yet to beat Calipari at UK.

But Louisville proved its toughness. The team showed it could beat anyone—if the players could hit a few more shots.

The stage was set. Three months later, the teams would meet again in what would be the biggest game the series had ever seen.

$$*****$$

Kentucky finished 38-2 on the year, winning its eighth national championship. Along the way, UK defeated Louisville a second time in a strikingly similar type of game, this time in the Final Four. The Cardinals would finish 30-10, finding their stride at the end of the season. They won the Big East Tournament in Cinderella fashion, winning four games in four days, before upsetting Michigan State and Florida on the way to the national semifinals.

In a way, the Cards' March run had just set the table for the next season.

$$*****$$

All five of Kentucky's underclassmen starters, along with senior sixth man Darius Miller, declared and were selected in the 2012 NBA Draft. Anthony Davis was the No. 1 pick to the then-New Orleans Hornets (later changed to Pelicans). Davis was an All-America star, Kentucky's first Player of the Year, and won an Olympic gold medal that summer in London. Kidd-Gilchrist was chosen No. 2 overall in the draft, going to the Charlotte Bobcats. In 2013 he was named to the NBA All-Rookie Second Team.

Together, along with Russ Smith, they gave three of the biggest performances in the history of the UK/UofL rivalry.

Kentucky 69

NAME	MIN	FG-FGA	3-3A	FT-FTA	OR-REB	PF	AST	STL	BLK	TO	TP
Kidd-Gilchrist	39	7-16	2-4	8-13	6-19	3	1	0	0	0	24
Davis	27	3-4	0-0	12-13	2-10	3	0	3	6	2	18
Miller	32	2-8	1-3	2-2	3-4	4	1	0	0	8	7
Lamb	24	1-7	0-3	8-9	0-0	4	2	0	0	4	10
Teague	29	1-8	0-3	2-2	0-3	5	5	0	1	4	4
Jones	30	1-9	0-1	0-4	3-11	1	0	3	0	1	2
Wiltjer	15	2-5	0-2	0-0	0-2	2	0	0	0	1	4
Beckham	2	0-0	0-0	0-0	0-0	0	1	0	0	0	0
Vargas	2	0-0	0-0	0-0	0-0	0	0	0	0	0	0
TEAM					6-8						
Total	200	17-57	3-16	32-43	20-57	23	10	6	7	21	69

Louisville 62

NAME	MIN	FG-FGA	3-3A	FT-FTA	OR-REB	PF	AST	STL	BLK	TO	TP
Kuric	38	1-4	0-2	0-0	0-2	4	1	1	0	1	2
Behanan	15	1-3	0-0	2-2	2-5	5	1	0	0	1	4
Dieng	33	2-5	0-0	1-2	0-5	4	0	1	6	3	5
Siva	29	2-13	0-4	4-6	0-2	4	4	1	1	3	8
C. Smith	21	2-10	1-3	2-2	2-3	3	0	3	0	0	7
R. Smith	27	10-20	3-8	7-10	2-5	3	0	3	0	3	30
Swopshire	17	1-2	0-1	2-3	0-2	2	0	3	1	0	4
Buckles	15	1-4	0-0	0-0	2-3	4	0	0	0	2	2
Ware	4	0-1	0-0	0-2	0-0	0	0	0	0	1	0
Justice	1	0-0	0-0	0-0	0-1	0	0	0	0	0	0
TEAM					2-3						
Total	200	20-62	4-18	18-27	10-31	29	6	12	8	14	62

Chapter 32

Round Two:
The Final Four

No. 1 UK 69, No. 17 UofL 61
NCAA National Semifinal

MARCH 31, 2012, at Superdome, New Orleans, La.
   (Please review Introduction for details on this game.)

Kentucky 69

NAME	MIN	FG-FGA	3-3A	FT-FTA	OR-REB	PF	AST	STL	BLK	TO	TP
Jones	33	3-8	0-0	0-3	2-7	2	0	2	2	0	6
Kidd-Gilchrist	23	4-6	0-0	1-4	0-4	3	1	0	0	4	9
Davis	39	7-8	0-0	4-6	2-14	2	2	1	5	3	18
Lamb	35	4-9	0-2	2-3	0-1	1	1	0	0	4	10
Teague	33	4-8	0-0	0-0	0-2	4	5	1	0	2	8
Miller	29	4-7	1-4	4-4	0-3	2	0	2	0	1	13
Wiltjer	8	2-3	1-1	0-0	1-1	0	0	1	0	0	5
Vargas	0+	0-0	0-0	0-0	0-0	0	0	0	0	0	0
TEAM					1-1						
Total	200	28-49	2-7	11-20	6-33	14	9	7	7	14	69

Louisville 61

NAME	MIN	FG-FGA	3-3A	FT-FTA	OR-REB	PF	AST	STL	BLK	TO	TP
Kuric	28	3-8	1-2	0-1	4-5	3	0	1	0	0	7
Behanan	34	4-6	0-2	2-2	2-9	1	0	0	0	2	10
Dieng	40	3-10	0-0	1-1	8-12	2	2	2	4	3	7
Siva	31	4-11	1-2	2-2	0-3	2	3	0	0	3	11
C. Smith	23	3-11	1-2	1-2	0-1	1	1	0	0	1	8
R. Smith	26	4-15	0-1	1-2	1-3	2	1	2	0	3	9
Blackshear	14	3-5	1-2	2-3	1-4	4	0	0	0	0	9
Swopshire	4	0-0	0-0	0-0	0-0	1	0	0	0	0	0
Justice	0+	0-0	0-0	0-0	0-0	0	0	0	0	0	0
TEAM					3-3						
Total	200	24-69	4-11	9-13	19-40	16	7	5	4	12	61

Chapter 33

Sweet Victory
at the Yum!

No. 3 UofL 80, UK 77
December 29, 2012, at the Yum! Center

Pre-Game:

It had all come down to this. One shot. One try. One game.

The whispers from the Cardinal faithful could be heard even weeks before. Could they do it? Could the Cardinals beat a John Calipari-led Kentucky team?

In what had proven to become the biggest and nastiest college basketball rivalry in the country, Calipari's Kentucky team had defeated UofL four times in three years. With another talented crop of freshmen slated to play for UK in 2013, fans on both sides of the rivalry knew Rick Pitino, and Louisville would have no better chance to defeat the Wildcats than in the waning days of 2012. UK, coming off its eighth national championship, had defeated Pitino's squad twice the previous season. But the five starters (and the sixth man) from that team left for the pros, and a new batch of freshmen came in to take their place.

It was not the same. Kentucky came in with a record of 8-3, unranked, and with no true quality wins. Louisville, on the other hand, may have featured its best team of the Pitino era. Ranked No. 3, the Cardinals were deep and talented, with shooters, scorers, and rebounders. They also played the best defense of anyone in the country. They had lost only one game so far that season, coming into the game against the Wildcats.

For senior captain Peyton Siva, the Cardinal point guard, each loss to UK had been especially tough. He had been vilified in many games by fans and coaches for his decision-making, and against Kentucky he had not performed well enough to win. But by the end of 2012, Siva had developed into one of the best point guards in the country.

Louisville forward Chane Behanan had ties to the Bluegrass State, playing his senior year of high school in Bowling Green. After being recruited by both UK and UofL, Behanan chose Louisville—and he desperately wanted to beat Kentucky. Neither he nor Siva knew what that was like. They wanted to win for their fans, surely, but also for their coach. The rivalry between Pitino and Calipari was well known, and the Louisville players knew what a victory over the Wildcats would mean for the entire program.

But to a man, each player and coach remained complimentary and polite in the week leading up to the game. They said the game meant more to the fans than it did to the players and coaches. While that may have been true for the freshmen at Kentucky (they hadn't yet experienced the full craziness of the rivalry), for the seniors at Louisville, they wanted to beat Kentucky. The game was bigger than other games, whether anyone admitted it or not.

"It's just a game," Gorgui Dieng, Louisville's Senegalese center, told The *Courier-Journal* a few days before the game. "We're going to have a game plan, like we did with Memphis."

"I don't get into the bitterness of it," Pitino told the newspaper. "I don't denigrate Kentucky in any way."

Of course, they hadn't played their annual game yet.

The Game:

At the start, it couldn't have gone any worse for Louisville. The vaunted defense Louisville was known for was nowhere to be seen. Kentucky was out and running. Point guard Ryan Harrow was in control, hitting threes and dropping in teardrop jumpers. With 10:43 to go in the first half, Kentucky controlled the game, building a lead of six points.

Nearly 23,000 fans crammed into the Yum! Center, and the vast majority were wearing Cardinal red. They had little to cheer about. In fact, worry settled into the new arena by the river.

Turns out it was unfounded. Over the next 10 minutes, the Cards showed why they were a favorite to make it back to the Final Four. Using an explosive inside-outside attack, Louisville went on an 8-0 run to come back and lead at halftime, 36-28. Two of Kentucky's primary scorers hadn't played well at all (freshmen Archie Goodwin and Alex Poythress), and without their scoring punch, a comeback looked difficult.

For the Cardinals, a desperately wanted win over their archrivals was just 20 minutes away. It proved to be tougher to get than they thought.

The Cardinals came out with the same intensity they took into the intermission. The shots were falling and the Cards were running their patented fast break off rebounds. By the 15:00 mark of the second half, Louisville had surged to a 49-34 lead when Siva crossed over his man, went to the rim, and scored a layup while drawing a foul from talented UK big man Nerlens Noel.

Top-ranked center Nerlens Noel was another blue-chip recruit in Calipari's extensive array. Noel set UK's single-game blocked shots record later in the season, but was 0-1 in the Dream Game. *(Photo by Tim Sofranko)*

Now the Yum! Center crowd smelled blood in the water. For UK fans, the unthinkable was occurring: the Big Blue were getting blown out. In a previous game that year against Duke, the Wildcats found themselves in a similar situation. UK fought back and lost a close one. Could they do the same?

The answer was yes. Goodwin came alive in the second half to score 17 of his 22 points. Sophomore Kyle Wiltjer drained two huge threes to cut a 17-point lead to 11, and eventually, the Cats found themselves down only two with 5:00 to go.

Both fan bases were on their feet. Once again, it seemed the game had lived up to its hype. If Louisville was going to beat UK and Calipari for the first time, the Cats were going to make it as difficult as possible.

With 33 seconds to go, Louisville led by four points, but Kentucky had the ball. The game was on the line, and when the Cats needed it most, they had to rely on their new crop of freshmen to come through. Archie Goodwin took a handoff and drove to the hoop, right into a Cardinal trap.

As he fought for control and looked for an open teammate to pass to, Calipari saw it all occurring not far from the UK bench.

We need a timeout, Calipari thought. *I should call timeout.*

Too late. Goodwin turned the ball over to Behanan, who drove the length of the floor for the game-clinching dunk. Behanan then blew a kiss to the crowd.

Calipari turned to Assistant Coach John Robic. "What was I thinking?" he asked. Later he would blame himself for not helping his player.

As the seconds ticked away, Goodwin nailed a final three. It didn't matter. Louisville won, 80-77, and for the first time, Louisville fans could enjoy a win over a Calipari-coached UK team.

Postgame:

Every fan knows that a rivalry must be competitive to be relevant. For three years, Kentucky had beaten UofL. But all at once, Louisville made the rivalry relevant again. Pitino had beaten Calipari, and afterward, the Louisville coach looked as happy as he'd been in a long while.

"I thought this was the first year that we had as much talent as them," Pitino said. "Quite frankly, I thought we had more talent than them because our talent is experienced."

Both coaches complimented the other teams. Both felt their own squads could play better. For Kentucky, it was obvious they could shoot better from the free throw line: 11-for-23 (0-for-4 from center Willie Cauley-Stein).

But for Louisville, it was about finally getting a win over Big Blue.

"For me, it's another game—another big non-conference game," Peyton Siva said afterward in the locker room.

Then he relented: "It feels good to finally beat them."

Chane Behanan agreed. "I enjoyed myself tonight," he said, smiling.

Chane Behanan, shown here scrapping for a rebound, was recruited by both Kentucky and Louisville. His 20 points and 7 rebounds were critical in UofL's 2012 victory. *(Photo by Tim Sofranko)*

Russ Smith, the Cards' shooting guard who led the way with 21 points, said it best. "I'm more happy for our fans," he said. "I guess *revenge* is the best word to describe it."

*****

Louisville completed that revenge in April. On April 8, 2013, the Cardinals won the school's third NCAA Tournament title with a hard-fought 82-76 win over Michigan. Transfer Luke Hancock seemed to channel the ghosts of Louisville heroes of the past by shooting daggers through the Final Four, first in a semifinal win over Wichita State, and then in the title game. Hancock had 20 and 22 points respectively in the two games, and helped the usual suspects fight their way to victory.

Peyton Siva was particularly ebullient, because Pitino had promised the team that he would get a tattoo if they won the title. Indeed, shortly after the Tournament, the man who had brought UK back from the dead had a Louisville logo branded on his skin.

Siva completed his career as a champion and hopes to catch on in the NBA. Dieng was selected with the 21st pick in the NBA Draft by the Utah Jazz. Smith chose to wait another year for the NBA, instead returning along with Hancock and Behanan, among others, to try to help the Cards and Pitino mark one more rivalry notch on their belts—and perhaps bring home another title.

✸✸✸✸✸

Kentucky fans were miserable, not only because of the success of Louisville, but also because UK had an awful season. UK limped home with a 21-12 record and a first-round NIT loss at Robert Morris University. Nerlens Noel blew out his knee in a February game at Florida. He did not play again at Kentucky and "slipped" to the fifth pick in the NBA Draft.

Much of Kentucky's problems stemmed from horrible team chemistry. Whispers centered much of the issues around starting guards Ryan Harrow and Archie Goodwin. Goodwin made an ill-advised jump into the NBA Draft, but surprised experts when he was selected near the end of the Draft's first round by the Phoenix Suns. Harrow decided he would transfer to Georgia State to be closer to his ill father. Kyle Wiltjer elected to transfer to Gonzaga.

For his part, Calipari has sworn to avoid the chemistry demons that plagued the 2012–13 team. He promptly signed another epic recruiting class—with forward Julius Randle as the centerpiece. The team's likely starting backcourt in 2013–14 consists of brothers Aaron and Andrew Harrison, which should certainly help UK avoid chemistry issues.

Preseason expectations seem to indicate that 2012–13 was the aberration, and that Cal's Cats will again be back amongst the programs at the top of college basketball.

Louisville 80

NAME	MIN	FG-FGA	3-3A	FT-FTA	OR-REB	PF	AST	STL	BLK	TO	TP
Blackshear	31	2-7	1-2	0-2	1-7	1	0	0	0	0	5
Behanan	35	8-13	0-0	4-6	2-7	3	3	3	1	1	20
Price	2	0-0	0-0	0-0	0-0	1	0	0	0	0	0
Smith	30	9-20	0-1	3-6	1-7	4	3	3	0	3	21
Siva	31	6-11	2-4	5-5	1-2	5	1	1	0	3	19
Harrell	23	1-3	0-0	5-6	2-4	1	0	0	1	0	7
Dieng	20	3-4	0-0	0-0	3-7	4	1	0	2	1	6
Ware	14	1-4	0-0	0-0	0-0	2	1	2	0	0	2
Hancock	14	0-0	0-0	0-0	0-1	0	2	0	0	1	0
TEAM					1-1						
Total	200	30-62	3-7	17-25	11-36	21	11	9	4	9	80

Kentucky 77

NAME	MIN	FG-FGA	3-3A	FT-FTA	OR-REB	PF	AST	STL	BLK	TO	TP
Noel	31	4-5	0-0	0-1	3-8	4	0	2	2	2	8
Cauley-Stein	23	3-4	0-0	0-4	4-8	4	2	0	3	0	6
Goodwin	36	8-15	3-5	3-4	0-5	3	2	1	0	5	22
Harrow	39	6-15	1-1	4-6	3-5	4	3	2	0	0	17
Mays	35	1-8	1-6	0-0	1-3	3	2	0	0	2	3
Wiltjer	19	4-7	4-7	2-2	0-3	1	1	0	0	3	14
Poythress	15	2-4	1-2	2-6	1-5	2	0	0	0	2	7
Polson	2	0-0	0-0	0-0	0-1	0	0	0	0	0	0
TEAM					0-1					1	
Total	200	28-58	10-21	11-23	12-39	22	10	5	5	15	77

Afterword

The first preseason poll is out. It's from *The Sporting News*.

Kentucky is No. 1. Louisville is No. 3.

Even after Kentucky's disappointing NIT appearance in 2013, Coach John Calipari reloaded with another top-ranked recruiting class.

Louisville won a national championship in 2013 but lost its point guard to graduation and its center to the NBA. But the Cards kept leading scorer Russ Smith and added a strong recruiting class of their own.

If the rankings hold, the teams will rank the highest they've ever been when they meet this season. Both could vie for a national title. Maybe they could meet in the championship game.

Who will win?

"Is that even a question?" said former UK star Brandon Knight, laughing. "Kentucky."

Tony Williams, the former Cardinals guard and Louisville native, disagreed.

"It's the Cardinals' time now," he said.

One thing is certain. The rivalry is better than it's ever been.

"Both teams are going to contend for national championships," Denny Crum said. "What these two coaches have built is pretty remarkable."

It's like nothing the rivalry has ever seen.

And in Richardsville, Kentucky (as in a thousand other towns in and around Kentucky), where a UK and UofL fan are married to one another, there could be more uncomfortable games to watch. Both Brent and Lauren Young have seen their teams win championships in the past two seasons. By early fall, the trash talk is heating back up.

Could 2014 be the rubber match?

When asked about the possibility of the New Dream Game—a UK/UofL national title matchup—Lauren and Brent find common ground:

The hypothetical national title matchup would mean two televisions in two different rooms, if not different houses or even different towns. The idea of a future UK/UofL title game has Lauren in mid-season form in September. "If that happens, it'll be ON!"

Brent smiles. "It will be on," he agrees.

Sources

Books

Clark, Ryan. *Game of My Life: Kentucky, Memorable Stories of Wildcat Basketball.* Champaign, IL: Sports Publishing, 2007.

Clark, Ryan and Joe Cox. *100 Things Wildcats Fans Should Know and Do Before They Die.* Chicago: Triumph Books, 2012.

Doyel, Greg. *Kentucky Wildcats: Where Have You Gone?* Champaign, IL: Sports Publishing, 2005.

Einhorn, Eddie and Ron Rapoport. *How March Became Madness: How the NCAA Tournament Became the Greatest Sporting Event in America.* Chicago: Triumph Books, 2006.

Fitzpatrick, Frank. *And the Walls Came Tumbling Down: The Basketball Game That Changed American Sports.* New York: Simon and Schuster, 1999.

Harrison, Lowell H. and James C. Klotter. *A New History of Kentucky.* Lexington, KY: The University Press of Kentucky, 1997.

Ledford, Cawood with Billy Reed. *Hello Everybody, This is Cawood Ledford.* Lexington, KY: Host Communications, 1992.

Pitino, Rick with Pat Forde. *Rebound Rules: The Art of Success.* New York: HarperCollins, 2008.

Pitino, Rick with Dick Weiss. *Full-Court Pressure: A Year in Kentucky Basketball.* New York: Hyperion Books, 1993.

Reed, Billy. *Born to Coach, How Denny Crum Built the University of Louisville Into a Basketball Powerhouse.* Lousiville, KY: The *Courier-Journal* and *The Lousiville Times*, 1986.

Rice, Russell. *Kentucky Basketball's Big Blue Machine.* Huntsville, AL: Strode Publishers, 1976.

Terhune, Jim. *Tales from the 1980 Louisville Cardinals.* Champaign, IL: Sports Publishing, 2004.

Trease, Denny. *Tales From the Kentucky Hardwood—A Collection of the Greatest Basketball Stories Ever Told!* Champaign, IL: Sports Publishing, 2002.

Wallace, Tom. *The University of Kentucky Basketball Encyclopedia.* Champaign, IL: Sports Publishing, 2012.

Newspapers

Lexington Herald-Leader
Louisville *Courier-Journal*
Various others as named in the text

Websites

Jon Scott's UK basketball history site. http://www.bigbluehistory.net/bb/wildcats.html
University of Kentucky official athletics site. http://www.ukathletics.com/
University of Louisville official athletics site. http://www.gocards.com/

Other Sources

Numerous interviews over the past several years, but mostly in 2013. Other articles and websites as listed

Acknowledgments

First thanks go to our families, without whom this book could not have been written. The work took us away from time with them, but they allowed us to follow our fun dream. This is especially true for Julie Cox, who Joe will vouch for as a great wife, but who we both will vouch for as a superb first reader/editor/and general cleaner-up of messes.

Thanks to all those players who helped out and were eager to speak to us—some of you even did so from other countries. Big thanks to Judy Cowgill at the University of Louisville, who not only helped us interview Coach Crum, but was an incredible source for tracking down past Cardinals. Like Luke Hancock, Judy drilled every big shot just when we needed it. Additionally, JoEllen Wilhoite deserves thanks for a John Wall-like assist in connecting us with Coach Hall.

Our gratitude goes out to Tim Sofranko and Jamie Vaught for sharing their wonderful photographs of Wildcats and Cardinals with us. Tim is a great friend, and Jamie was one of the first people to show us that writing about these athletes could be done and could be enjoyable for writer and reader. Both guys are solid All-Tournament team selections in the roster of folks who made this book possible. Additional thanks are due to John Spugnardi and Bellarmine University, and to Sue Patrick and Shannon Gilkey from the Council on Postsecondary Education for photographic help, as well as University of Louisville Athletics. Matt Harper and Michelle Jenkins Lauersdorf each deserve a shout-out as well!

Thanks also to the sports information staffs at both the universities, especially Kenny Klein, John Hayden, and DeWayne Peevy. Those officials at the Yum! Center and Rupp Arena were especially helpful, as were several journalist friends at the *Louisville Courier-Journal* and *Lexington Herald-Leader*, especially Kyle Tucker, C. L. Brown, and Jerry Tipton.

Other media members who lent a hand and must be mentioned include: Adam Lefkoe, Rory Owen Delaney, Matt Jones and Kentucky Sports Radio, Clark Kellogg, Oscar Combs, Tom Leach, and Dick Gabriel.

To Jon Scott and his web-based historical archive, we are especially grateful (www.bigbluehistory.net/bb/wildcats.html) and to Russell Rice and Billy Reed, authors of some of the first works on these schools, their work was invaluable. These authors and their books also provided wonderful insight: Jim Terhune, Dick Weiss, Tom Wallace, Gregg Doyel, Denny Trease, Pat Forde, Frank Fitzpatrick, Eddie Einhorn, and Larry Vaught.

Eternal wishes for an eventful March go out to Brent and Lauren Young, whose divided house is doing just fine.

To those public relations personnel in the NBA and NCAA, as well as the players' agents, we could not have done this without you.

To Denny Crum and Joe B. Hall, there are no better gentlemen in the sport, and our time spent with them was the best. Our eternal thanks.

Finally, to everyone at Skyhorse and Sports Publishing, especially Julie Ganz. You allowed the story to be told, and we are forever grateful.

—RC and JC,
September 2013